W9-BJT-922

AMERICA'S SOLUBLE PROBLEMS

Also by John Mills

EUROPE'S ECONOMIC DILEMMA

GROWTH AND WELFARE: A New Policy for Britain

MONETARISM OR PROSPERITY? (*with Bryan Gould and Shaun Stewart*)

TACKLING BRITAIN'S FALSE ECONOMY

America's Soluble Problems

John Mills

First published in Great Britain 1999 by
MACMILLAN PRESS LTD
Houndmills, Basingstoke, Hampshire RG21 6XS and London
Companies and representatives throughout the world

A catalogue record for this book is available from the British Library.

ISBN 0–333–73237–5 hardcover
ISBN 0–333–73238–3 paperback

First published in the United States of America 1999 by
ST. MARTIN'S PRESS, INC.,
Scholarly and Reference Division,
175 Fifth Avenue, New York, N.Y. 10010

ISBN 0–312–22276–9

Library of Congress Cataloging-in-Publication Data
Mills, John.
America's soluble problems / John Mills.
p.   cm.
Includes bibliographical references and index.
ISBN 0–312–22276–9 (cloth)
1. United States—Economic conditions—1981–   2. United States–
–Economic policy.   3. Monetary policy—United States.   4. Inflation
(Finance)—United States.   I. Title.
HC106.8.M544   1999
338.973—dc21
                                                            98–18670
                                                            CIP

This book is printed on paper suitable for recycling and made from fully managed and
sustained forest sources.

10   9   8   7   6   5   4   3   2   1
08   07   06   05   04   03   02   01   00   99

Printed and bound in Great Britain by
Antony Rowe Ltd, Chippenham, Wiltshire

Contents

Preface   vii

1. **Introduction**   1
   The Case for Economic Growth   7
   Current Problems   11
   History and Ideology   16
   Choices for the Future   21

2. **The Historical Setting**   23
   US Economic History up to World War I   24
   Boom and Depression: from World War I to World War II   30
   Prosperity post-World War II   36
   Gathering Clouds   41

3. **The Monetarist Era**   44
   Monetarist Theory and Practice   48
   The Years when Monetarism Reigned   54
   Clinton and the 1990s   64

4. **Economic Growth**   69
   Competitiveness   71
   Protectionism and Free Trade   75
   Recapturing Home and Export Markets   78
   Returns on Investment   84
   Changing the Exchange Rate   87
   Policy Implications   92

5. **Full Employment**   95
   Comparative Experience   98
   False Trails   102
   Supply-side Mirages   106
   Growth and the Trade Balance   111
   Wider Perspectives   116

6. **Inflation and Living Standards**   121
   Devaluation and the Price Level   125
   Leading Sector Inflation   129
   Shocks to the System   132
   Excessive Demand   136
   Labour Costs   139
   Summary   143

7. **America's Soluble Problems**   147
   Agenda for the Future   151
   Pitfalls and Realism   156
   Reassessing the Past   159
   Choices for the Future   164

Bibliography   169

Index   172

Preface

I have only ever spent one night in gaol. It was in August 1959 in Phoenix, Arizona. I was hitchhiking round the US, unaware that in the state of Arizona this activity counted as vagrancy. The policemen who arrested me, however, were as kind as everyone else I came across on an epic trip which took me 7000 miles from coast to coast in two weeks. Finding that I was reasonably respectable – and therefore not a serious threat as a vagrant, but also with nowhere to stay for the night – they offered me a bed in the county gaol. I have to say that it was not particularly comfortable in the reception area where I was bedded down. Furthermore, I was regularly woken up by the arrival of a succession of drunks – a more serious danger to the quiet enjoyment of life in Arizona than I was – who were arrested and brought into custody during the course of the night. I was relieved, therefore, to be let into the main part of the gaol about 5.00 a.m. to wash and shave. The police then kindly gave me a lift to the outskirts of Phoenix where I hitched my next lift – outside their jurisdiction.

Travelling round the US was a wonderful experience. I kept a diary, and in total about 140 people gave me lifts. Without exception, they were kind, considerate and often hospitable into the bargain. This was the first time I had visited the US extensively, and I returned to Europe with an overwhelmingly positive view of America, which I have never lost during the dozens of times I have been to the US since. Over the past decades, I have visited almost every state in the union. I have many personal friends in America. For some years I was involved in running a business in Atlanta, Georgia, with interests all over the States. Later, I worked with other corporations in Minneapolis, Minnesota and Wichita, Kansas. I have also pursued other involvements in the US. For a long time I have been an elected representative in local government in Britain, specialising in housing, finance and inner-city problems. I have followed up these interests in America, visiting many cities and talking to their senior officials and politicians in the process. I think I can therefore say that I know the United States fairly well.

While my work and other matters have often taken me to the US, I have also travelled widely in many other parts of the world. Part of the reason for my writing this book is to explain clearly to myself, as much as to anyone else, the reason for what at first sight seems a strange paradox. For all the time I have known it, the US has had a much higher standard of living than other countries. It was obviously a great deal more efficient at providing services than most other economies. Its plants were much more productive than elsewhere. Nevertheless, the US was clearly losing ground. Other countries were catching up. Vast ranges of consumer goods, which the US could apparently easily have produced itself, were increasingly being imported from the Far East – a process to which, in a small way, I contributed. Much of the infrastructure in the US, although always impressive, was beginning to look rather shabby and in need of replacement, but the work required was not being carried out. It was also clear that however high the average standard of living in the US might be, there were large numbers of people who were eking out an existence at a long way below this level, some of them in conditions which by any measure were very poor, and getting worse.

Thus, while in many ways the US was doing exceptionally well, it was clear that in some areas the performance of the economy was well below what it might have been. In this regard, it mirrored to a substantial extent the experience of the British economy (where I have lived and worked almost all my life). Like the US, Britain was on the winning side in both the twentieth century's world wars, but relative to other countries, its economic record, especially since World War II, had been very disappointing. Britain, in fact, has done considerably worse than the US. Its growth rate has been lower, and its relative decline longer and steeper. From having the highest standard of living in the world until shortly before the outbreak of World War I, by the end of the twentieth century, OECD figures show Britain overtaken by almost twenty countries. Most of them were much poorer than Britain at the beginning of the century. Britain's military and diplomatic influence in the world is now a pale reflection of what it used to be, and its position to influence events correspondingly circumscribed. I, and others with whom I have collaborated closely, have worked hard at trying to understand what went wrong with the British economy. We have published books, articles and bulletins based on a substantial research effort, gaining some recognition in the process. This present book builds on the experience acquired in a British and European context, where some of the problems afflicting the advanced economies of the world are perhaps more obvious than they are the other side of the Atlantic. Applying the type of analysis developed for dealing with European problems suggests that some of the US's difficulties may be a great deal more deep-seated than they appear to be at first sight, but also more amenable to solution than is often realised.

While preparing this book, therefore, I have drawn on the work of many other people. Some are close associates. I have been very fortunate in having a circle of friends and acquaintances who have shared my interest in economic affairs for a long period, many of whom have made distinguished contributions to economics and politics in their own right. Douglas Jay, Peter Shore and

Bryan Gould were or still are major political figures in Britain. The economist who most influenced the ideas in this book, who sadly died in 1997, was Shaun Stewart – who, incidentally, won the Distinguished Service Cross of the United States at the end of World War II for his combat service. This is the highest American military decoration which can be granted to a non-US citizen. It is awarded rarely, and only in cases of quite exceptional bravery and courage. Other people with whom I have worked closely, and whose ideas are reflected in this book, include Austin Mitchell, Brian Burkitt and Geoffrey Gardiner. In addition, there are the many people whose books and articles I have read, but whom I do not know personally. Rather than adding to the text with footnotes, or providing endnotes to each chapter, there is a bibliography listing the main publications and articles which I have read in preparation for writing this book. The bibliography is inevitably incomplete, however, and I need to thank not only the authors cited but all the others whose writings have influenced my views on the way American economic history has developed.

However important the books listed may be in shaping my approach, I have only relied on any of them to a limited extent for factual and statistical information. It is not that I necessarily distrust second-hand figures, although it is surprising how often they are wrong. I believe you are always more likely to get the fullest and most accurate picture from primary sources. Luckily, an enormous range of publications is available to provide the quantitative as well as qualitative backing that the kinds of arguments found in this book require, and I am particularly grateful both to Eric Essinger of the Brookings Institution, to Michael Hudson of the Institute for the Study of Long Term Economic Trends, and to a number of exceptionally helpful and courteous people at the US Government Printing Office for helping me to find my way round American statistics. The major US sources I have used are the February 1998 *Economic Report of the President*, the 1997 *Statistical Abstract* of the United States, and the *National Income and Product Accounts* of the United States for earlier years. I have also used a range of publications from the International Monetary Fund, the World Trade Organization, the United Nations, the European Commission and the Organization for Economic Co-operation and Development. I also need to acknowledge how much I have drawn on the work of Angus Maddison, not only in his invaluable OECD publication *Monitoring the World Economy 1820–1992*, but also other books by him which are cited in the bibliography. I have, in addition, relied on figures in a publication by Thelma Liesner for *The Economist* called *Economic Statistics 1900–1983*, which provides long and revealing runs of statistics for a number of the world's major economies, going back to the beginning of the twentieth century. Again, references to all the figures cited in the text are not provided individually, but many of them came from these sources.

There are other people who need to be thanked too, especially among my extended family. My wife Barbara has not only tolerated with very little complaint all the time I have spent reading and writing while preparing this book, but has also checked and corrected successive drafts. We share the view that books should read well, whatever their contents. Sentences should be short. Adverbs should be used sparingly. The text should be clear and concise. These worthy objectives are easy to list, but more difficult to achieve consistently, and her help, and that of Charles Starkey and Austin Mitchell, both hard taskmasters in similar vein, have been invaluable. My sister Eleanor and her husband Stephen have allowed me and my wife to use their house near Avignon in France as a retreat from distractions, to allow drafting to be done. My mother has provided another exceptionally pleasant environment for redrafting and revisions at her house near London. My office, and especially my secretary Jan and her colleague Janet, have been very tolerant of my use of all the facilities there, and have been exceptionally helpful. Ruth Weinberg has also played a supportive role in finding missing information, checking facts and suggesting improvements to the text.

I am also very grateful to Macmillan, and especially to Tim Farmiloe, Publishing Director, for publishing another of my books. With its international connections, the quality of its production and the care taken over every book produced, no-one could ask for a better publisher or a more professional organisation with which to work.

This preface needs to end, however, on a note of some trepidation. I am well aware of the enormity of the task which this book tackles, and the size of the canvas which it covers. I am sufficiently familiar with the literature on economics in the States, in both its academic and its more popular form, to know that the ideas this book sets out are not ones which are common currency. The proposals this book contains for dealing with some of the more important problems which the US faces are not ones, therefore, which the average reader is likely to have seen put forward before. I know they go against the grain. I am well aware of the fact that they do not conform to established views. Obviously they involve confronting and attempting to alter the opinions and probably the deeply held convictions of many people, some of them eminent. I ask you, therefore, perhaps more than most authors would, to look at them with an open mind. Please do not pre-judge the issues which are tackled. Let the argument unfold, and see whether, at the end, you find it convincing. There must be some reason why the US has peculiarly serious problems with its balance of payments, why many Americans are still earning the same amount now as they were twenty-five years ago, why the US swung round in much less than a decade in the 1980s from being the world's biggest debtor to being its largest creditor, and why almost every toy bought in America nowadays is made in China. Let this book see whether it can provide you with convincing explanations for these developments, and persuade you that there are solutions to the problems they present to the American people.

1 Introduction

'No great improvements in the lot of mankind are possible, until a great change takes place in the fundamental constitution of their modes of thought.'

John Stuart Mill

A sense of perspective is needed when writing about the economic problems facing the United States, especially if the author is an outsider. The US economy is not faultless, but judged by the standards of an imperfect world it is in most respects outstandingly successful. It provides its citizens, on average, with a higher standard of living than anywhere else in the world. It has done so almost continuously for the whole of the twentieth century. It acts as a magnet to people from poorer countries, and from many richer ones too, not only because of its prosperity, but because America always has been a land of exceptional opportunity. The US is a beautiful and varied country, pulsing with vitality and innovation. The efficiency with which much of its economy works is breathtaking. No-one can arrive in New York, or spend a day in Yellowstone National Park, or visit the Smithsonian Institution in Washington DC, or watch the best of American films, without realising that the achievements of the United States of America stand, in many respects, in a class of their own.

America's problems, therefore, need to be seen in context. The US is not a country which is heading for disaster. It is politically stable. It is acknowledged to be the world's leading military and diplomatic power. Its citizens have a degree of self-confidence and pride in their country which few, if any, can rival. Industrially and economically, the US is still in a strong technological position. The dollar is the pre-eminent world currency, and likely to remain so for the foreseeable future. The US has huge strengths to which to play.

Yet all is not well. There are many respects in which the US economy has performed surprisingly poorly. Despite its richness, the talent of its people and the robustness of its institutions, the US economy appears to have under-achieved in a number of important respects. The growth rate, which averaged 3.9% per annum cumulatively between 1950 and 1973, fell by nearly 40%, to 2.4% between 1973 and 1992. Between the same two periods, the average increase in output per annum per head of the population fell by an even larger percentage, from 2.4% to 1.4%. Other countries, particularly Japan, did

1

much better than this, with Japanese growth averaging 9.2% cumulatively between 1950 and 1973, though it fell to only 3.8% per annum between 1973 and 1992. A sense of perspective is therefore required. Nevertheless, the result has been a much more rapid increase in Japanese living standards than in those in the US. For the world as a whole, the cumulative growth rate was 5.2% for the earlier period and 2.8% for the later one, both significantly higher than the performance of the US economy.

Taking the whole of the period 1950–92, the US economy grew at an average of 3.2% per annum, but the world as a whole grew cumulatively 0.8% per annum faster. This may not seem a very large difference taken a year at a time, but the compound effect over forty-two years with a variation in performance of this size is enormous. Over this period the US share of world output fell from 28% to 20%, as the US gross domestic product (GDP) grew to 3.8 times its 1950 size. Output in the world as a whole, however, grew to 5.2 times its level of forty-two years previously. Partly because of relatively slow growth, American unemployment rates were well above the developed world average for the period between 1950 and 1973, at an average of 4.8%, compared to about 2.0% in most of Western Europe at the same time. The fact that US unemployment is now relatively low compared with the levels in other developed countries is partly due to other economies, particularly those in the European Union, doing significantly worse at present than they did before, rather than the US doing better. In different ways, however, the US is doing worse too.

For the last thirty years the US has had serious problems in paying its way in the world, reflected in trade deficits of increasingly massive proportions, especially since the early 1980s. In consequence, the US has changed from being by far the world's largest debtor to much its biggest creditor. Japan, in particular, has run a large balance of payments surplus on current account with the US for many years, and still does so. The American economy is so strong that financing large trade deficits has not been a major problem, although whether this state of affairs could continue indefinitely if the deficits increase in size is another matter. There are troubling questions, however, as to whether the only problem caused by these deficits is a financial one. Are they a symptom of a deeper malaise to do with the US, or more accurately American companies, losing their ability to compete in the world?

On the domestic front, successive administrations have had apparently insuperable problems in avoiding budget deficits, many of them of huge size, with the consequence that the US government has become increasingly indebted. Many of its liabilities are overseas, involving payments across the foreign exchanges. This, in turn, is partly a reflection of the fact that the US savings ratio – the percentage of the GDP which is saved in total by US citizens, corporations and the public sector – is very low by international standards. So also is the proportion of the GDP which is reinvested every year, although the return on much investment in the US is relatively high, an important compensating factor. The fiscal deficit position now looks substantially better, but the savings ratio is showing little sign of improving, and the balance of payments gap is widening still further – to an alarming extent even for an economy as strong as America's.

While the average standard of living in the US has been slowly growing, it is still at the top of the world league. When the totals are broken down, however, it appears that there have been disturbing changes over the last few decades. In short, the rich have become very much richer, blue-collar living standards have stagnated, and the poor have become significantly poorer. Unemployment in the US is relatively low by world standards, and certainly much lower than in most of Europe, but the quality of jobs, the levels of productivity and security, and the rates of pay for much of US employment at the lower end of the spectrum, leave a great deal to be desired. The consequence of very low pay or no jobs at all has been the development of an economic underclass in the US on a scale which would have seemed inconceivable three or four decades ago.

Demographic changes and evolving social attitudes have produced a series of other potentially serious threats to future US prosperity. The American population is ageing, generating more and more people to be supported by a proportionately smaller working population. The costs of looking after people as they live for longer rises steeply because their need for care and medical attention increases exponentially. At the younger end of the age spectrum, all over much of the Western world, but especially in America, the traditional nuclear family is becoming less and less the norm. As a result, more and more children are being brought up with only one parent to provide an income and all the duties and obligations of parenthood. The help which many then inevitably need presents the state with difficult and expensive choices between welfare payments, on the one hand, and the consequences of workfare and child care and other costs, on the other. Either way, without adequate support, the educational achievements and life-time expectations of the children of one-parent families tend to suffer.

Many of the problems which have caused the distribution of income to become much more skewed than it was have been attributed to the decline in the requirement for blue-collar jobs in the US. In 1958, 27% of the jobs in the US were in the manufacturing sector. By the end of the 1980s, the figure was only 17%, as service provision, as a percentage of GDP, grew proportionally much more rapidly. There is a world-wide tendency for the ratio of output deriving from manufacturing to fall in relation to services, partly for reasons which almost everyone should welcome. Productivity increases are much easier to achieve when producing goods rather than services, and as a result the cost of manufactured goods has fallen dramatically everywhere in comparison to other output. The proportion of the US economy involved in manufacturing, however, is exceptionally low. It is hard to argue that this has nothing to do with both the lack of well-paid blue-collar jobs and the US merchandise balance of payments deficit. It is often contended, however, that these developments are a necessary consequence of the high US standard of living. This shades into the argument that as economies get more prosperous, their growth rates will inevitably slow down, with all that this entails in terms of employment prospects for the labour force and the balance on foreign trade, as the shift to services continues. A major theme of this book is to challenge this assumption, and to question whether the US has not lost out heavily by taking much too insouciant an attitude to the decrease in its industrial base.

The declining role of manufacturing in the US, and its consequent reduced contribution to growth and foreign trade stability, point the way to other significant developments in the US's economic history and trends in American policy during the last few decades. Taken together, are there patterns to be detected which might provide a general explanation for other major problems the US faces? The case which will be presented strongly suggests that there are, and that all the problems outlined above are inter-connected. They are not the product of ineluctable economic or social forces. On the contrary, there are root causes for them all, which are not beyond the wit of policy makers to overcome. They are the result of decisions which could have been different, and which, had alternative policies been implemented, would have produced a considerably more satisfactory outcome than has actually materialised. However well the US economy has performed compared to other countries since the end of World War II, it could have done very much better, particularly during the thirty years since the late 1960s.

Part of the downturn in US economic performance came in the 1970s, mirroring similar difficulties in many other parts of the world as inflation rose and growth fell, in some cases leading to absolute reductions in output. The causes were events in the late 1960s, of which perhaps the most important was the over-straining of the American economy during the Lyndon Johnson era. The Vietnam War and the implementation of the Democrat Great Society programme were both substantially funded by government borrowing from the banking sector rather than taxation. The resulting inflationary pressures, combined with the trade and government deficits, led to the devaluation of the dollar. The world was then left with a rapidly increasing credit base, for which the American trade deficit was substantially responsible, but without the anchor of a stable dollar. This led to the boom and bust of the early 1970s. Commodity prices rose everywhere, capped by a fourfold increase in the price of oil following the Yom Kippur War and the determined action of the Organization of Petroleum Exporting Countries (OPEC) to take advantage of the temporary strength of its members' cartel.

The break-up of the Bretton Woods system for regulating exchange rate changes, combined with the levels of inflation prevalent in the 1970s, swept away the Keynesian certainties which had provided the lodestar by which most economies had been run since the end of World War II. Their place was largely taken by a very different economic doctrine, albeit one with a long pedigree. The monetarist explanations of how economies work held centre-stage for the next two decades, both in America and in most other parts of the world. Much of the history of the 1970s through to the 1990s derives from the impact of this sea change in economic perceptions. A central issue, then, is whether the monetarist view of the world is essentially correct and, if not, whether alternative policy proscriptions might be on offer, with greater prospects of getting the US and other economies to perform better. Getting to grips with this issue and setting out an alternative policy framework is the second major theme of this book.

The abandonment of the Keynesian policies of growth and full employment, reflected in the best side of the Roosevelt New Deal in the 1930s, and the post-war consensus on economic policy in the 1950s and 1960s, came at a high price. It is true that the US economy did not grow quite as fast as the world average from the end of World War II to 1973, and that unemployment during these years was relatively high for a developed country. In almost all other respects, however, US economic performance over this period was noticeably better, at least for the vast bulk of the population, than it has been for the last quarter of a century. For many Americans, the last twenty-five years have been exceptionally difficult. Stagnant or falling living standards, for those in employment, have had to be offset by much longer working hours. For others, the bare necessities of a civilised life have been stripped away as costs have risen far more quickly than ability to pay. The US now has 40m people who are not covered by any kind of medical insurance. Were there really no alternative policies available, within the ambit of practical politics, which could have avoided this deterioration? If so, why were they not adopted?

These questions provide pointers to the third major strand to the thesis which is set out in the pages which follow. It explains why countries which have established supremacy, particularly economic leadership, so often throw it away, allowing others to overtake them. Economic success provides enormous advantages, both externally, in terms of diplomatic and military power, and internally, in terms of the domestic benefits of high living standards and rising prosperity. One might therefore expect that preserving the conditions which created them would be given top priority by those in power, not least because in many ways these people have the most to lose.

This is not, however, the experience in any of the economies which have achieved pre-eminence since the start of modern history. Spain, initially bolstered by New World treasure, fell into decline in the seventeenth century and only began to recover from abject poverty, compared to the rest of the developed world, in the latter half of the twentieth century. The Netherlands, the most prosperous nation – at least per head of the population – in the eighteenth century, was overtaken by Britain during the time of the Napoleonic Wars. Britain faltered during the second half of the nineteenth century, allowing the US to forge ahead, with Germany catching up. With the disruptions of war and slump behind it, the second half of the twentieth century has seen the American lead whittled away, although not yet fully eroded, by Japan. Meanwhile, astonishing rates of economic growth have been achieved in China and in some other parts of the Pacific rim during the last two decades, which may be checked only briefly by the 1997 currency and banking crises. Differential rates of economic growth, with all their consequences for the distribution of power and prosperity in the world, are clearly by no means matters only of the past and not of the future. Is the US going to be eclipsed during the twenty-first century, perhaps by China or Japan, or possibly, in a hundred years' time, by some other state, which now appears backward, but which might leap ahead?

The way that the future will unfold turns on what are, or ought to be, the central questions with which economics is concerned. What are the conditions which allow and encourage economic growth to take place, and how are they created? How can we combine full, or at least nearly full, employment with reasonably stable prices? Can the necessary conditions be created by policy changes, or are they beyond the reach of practical politics? If so, what kind of new policies are needed? These are questions which this book sets out to answer. Its objective is to convince you that there are changes to the way the US runs its economy which could and should be made, which might not provide a solution to all the major problems of the US, but which would go a long way towards doing so. The concerns of many Americans about their country's present condition and its future do not present an insoluble puzzle. On the contrary, some reasonably simple and entirely feasible changes could be made, mostly to do with macro-economic policy, which would transform America's prospects. The following chapters describe these changes.

THE CASE FOR ECONOMIC GROWTH

The case put forward in this book depends heavily on there being substantial positive net advantages to a higher rate of economic growth, and the fuller use of all the available resources thus entailed. This is not to deny that rapidly increasing output can also bring disadvantages; it is to argue that, on balance, more problems are solved than created by faster growth, and that, therefore, if there is a price to be paid, it is a price worth paying.

This is not, however, an argument which is universally accepted. There is a substantial coalition of people who are opposed to higher rates of growth, even if they could be achieved. Some point to the problems of sustaining high and rising levels of industrial output, reflecting the concerns expressed by the Club of Rome in the early 1970s. Others express doubt as to whether higher living standards would make everyone happier, arguing that a less complicated and stressful life would be better than the pressures of consumer-driven societies. Another form of scepticism challenges whether economic growth statistics really measure anything meaningful at all, because of the difficulties of comparing one year with another at a time of rapid technological and cultural change.

There has always been an anti-growth tradition, harking back to Rousseau's simple savage. The romantic movement never liked factory regimentation and the break with established and hallowed practices which the Industrial Revolution inevitably entailed. More recently, particularly from the left of the political spectrum, scepticism about the benefits of economic growth has materialised in a steady undertow of criticism of the same ilk. Targets have been the impersonality of modern production relationships, the alienation and loneliness of late-twentieth-century life-styles, the vapidness of much contemporary culture, and the unfairness in the distribution of the wealth and income which economic growth is alleged to produce.

No-one can deny that there are valid concerns about the impact of indus-trialisation and increasing output. This is a different matter, however, from putting forward a compelling case that humanity as a whole would have been better off, or would have preferred, given the choice, not to have had the benefits which the economic changes in the developed countries have produced. There is no evidence at all that most people would prefer a lower rather than a higher standard of living, as conventionally measured. On the contrary, it is overwhelmingly clear that being better off in material terms is a high priority for almost everyone. Elections are won or lost on economic issues. The world abounds with pressure for migration from poor countries to those which are richer. Almost everyone wants a higher wage or salary.

A reasonably high rate of economic growth is therefore clearly what most people would select, given the choice. Nor are the benefits to be secured, of course, private only to individuals. There is a large public dimension as well. Increased output generates the tax base to pay for a wide range of goods and services which are more sensibly and practically provided collectively than individually. It makes it possible to run the kind of social security programmes which are the hallmark of cohesive communities. It provides the wherewithal for the construction and running of public facilities – schools, libraries, roads, parks, airports and museums, for example – which are necessary and widely appreciated components of modern societies.

Contrary to what might appear to be the position at first sight, economic growth also provides the only realistic way to pay the costs of avoiding the degradation of the environment that a rising population would otherwise entail. The most pressing ecological issues across the world are the provision of clean drinking water, the building of adequate sewage facilities, and the removal and processing of rubbish and waste. Protecting water supplies and the water table, in both the Third World and the developed countries, is expensive. So are all the steps which need to be taken to stop waste building up and the environment being polluted.

In fact, as living standards rise and the economy becomes more advanced, there is a tendency for the raw material content of finished output to fall. This happens as products become more sophisticated and services become a larger component of final output. The result is that, with reasonably competent management, the average economy's capacity to cope with environmental problems can be made to rise faster than its tendency to cause ecological damage. Rising living standards also tend to entail lower population growth, again improving the trade-off between expansion and ecological pressures. There is therefore no convincing case against growth on environmental grounds.

On the other hand, leaving aside the clear preference which almost everyone has for higher living standards, both in terms of private consumption and public provision, there are other reasons for believing that a reasonably high rate of economic growth is overwhelmingly important as a political and social objective. These overlapping considerations concern unemployment, social strains, fiscal imbalance and America's place in the world.

The unemployment issue is simple and straightforward. There is a marked tendency for the average level of productivity of everyone in employment to rise. This stems from a variety of causes, all of which are likely to continue. They include increased use of computers, better management techniques, competitive pressures on manning levels, better and more focused training and education, and technological advances. The impact of these changes is to increase output per person employed in large swathes of the more sophisticated parts of the economy by around 2% per annum on average, even if investment levels are quite low and total output is growing slowly or not at all. The result, however, is a very mixed blessing. It means that a rate of economic growth of about 2% per head per annum is required in any developed country just to keep all the existing workforce in employment, with living standards rising in line with the growth rate. If the growth rate falls below this level, one of two outcomes is certain: either unemployment will increase or the productivity of those competing especially at the bottom end of the labour market will be forced down, as labour is shaken out of higher productivity occupations. If the potential workforce is growing, as indeed it has been in the US at a rapid rate, an increase in effective demand of considerably more than 2% is required to stop either unemployment rising or a marked increase in productivity dispersion occurring.

The situation in most of Europe illustrates one variation on this theme. For many years, the European Union (EU) economies have not been growing at 2% per annum plus about 0.4% per year to allow for the increasing size of the labour force. Indeed, since 1979 the average growth rate has been 1.7%, a full 0.7% less than a reasonable estimate of the increase in productivity. With substantial social security structures in place, greatly reducing the pressure on the population to accept low-paid jobs, the effect has been to increase unemployment by something like 0.7% per annum cumulatively for the whole of the period, as the gap between growth and productivity has failed to close. This is why in the EU both the claimant count registered unemployment figure – currently about 11% – is so high, and also so many other people have dropped out of the labour force. In total, some 17% – more than one in six – of all those potentially capable of working in the EU are not doing so at present.

In the US, where unemployment benefits are far scarcer, the fast growth of the potential labour force combined with relatively slow growth in the economy as a whole has impacted on the labour market not on unemployment but on productivity. The number of people available to work in the US has risen dramatically – from 83m in 1970 to 134m in 1996 – and the number of people in employment has gone up from 78m to 127m. America has created a staggering 49m new jobs in twenty-six years, an increase of 61%. Over the same period, however, the US GDP has risen by just over 33%. The result has been a huge proliferation of low-wage, low-productivity jobs. In 1970, the aggregate income of the poorest 40% of families in the US was 17.6% of the total. In 1995 it was 13.6%. Meanwhile, the proportion going to the top 20% rose from 40.9% to 48.1%. It is not unemployment which has caused this huge increase in the dispersion of incomes – 4.9% of the labour force was out of work in 1970 and 5.6% in 1995. The culprits are low productivity and low pay.

The social impact of low-wage, insecure employment, or no work at all, caused by slow growth, has been enormously damaging. It has produced ghettos, especially in inner-city areas, where almost no-one has a regular job paying a reasonable wage. It is hardly surprising that in this environment crime rates rise, educational standards fall, social cohesion evaporates, anti-social behaviour such as drug abuse proliferates, and high levels of deprivation are passed from generation to generation. It has produced regional imbalances, where the less favoured areas have been unable to attract sufficient economic activity to keep the indigenous population in work. When the pressure of demand is high enough, employers have little alternative to siting their operations in less favoured areas, because the workforces they need are likely to be unobtainable elsewhere. If there is a surplus labour force almost everywhere, no such incentives exist.

Hand in hand with low pay and unemployment goes resentment, particularly towards foreigners. If almost everyone has a good job, it is hard to blame low incomes on those from outside. If many people do not have regular jobs paying a decent wage, it is much easier to attribute lack of employment opportunities to strangers, particularly if they are willing to work for wages and in conditions which the resident labour force regards as unacceptable. It is a relatively short step for this kind of resentment to be channelled by political movements into policies with a heavy xenophobic and racial dimension. There have always been politicians in the US, as in other countries, ready to exploit tensions of this kind, capitalising on the bitterness and frustration which lack of economic opportunities so easily generates.

There are also vital issues concerning the US's place in the world which are intimately bound up with the country's economic performance. In the last analysis, political influence is almost entirely a function of economic power. European countries were pre-eminent in the world in the nineteenth century because they were much more economically developed than those anywhere else, apart from the United States which at that time was little interested in world power. Britain's exceptionally strong position during this period resulted almost entirely from its lead in industrialisation. The outcome of the two world wars in Europe had little to do with the merits of the war aims of the participants, or the nature of the régimes involved, and almost everything to do with industrial and economic capabilities ranged on either side. The hegemony of the United States in the post-World War II period was almost entirely a function of its economic capability.

Power relationships generally change relatively slowly. A difference in growth rate over a year or two of 2% or 3% is barely perceptible. Multiplied over a decade, let alone quarter or half a century, however, the position changes radically. A differential growth rate of 4% will cause one economy to double in size relative to another in about seventeen years. This kind of change in economic weight makes a massive difference to any country's or region's industrial, financial, military and diplomatic power, to its self-respect, and to its ability to look after its interest *vis à vis* other parts of the world.

What will happen to the United States if its growth rate continues to average about 2.4% per annum in the foreseeable future, while the average for the rest of the world continues to be perhaps as much as 4%, and the Pacific rim countries, overcoming their recent problems, achieve anything between 6% and 10%? The outcome is bound to be a major attenuation in the relative status of the US compared to other parts of the world. The US is still an overwhelmingly powerful nation, but it could be overtaken, as were Spain, the Netherlands and Britain in turn, each of which looked impregnable before it happened. Some people argue that the very high growth rates in the Pacific rim countries cannot last, and that their rate of progress will inevitably slow down. For reasons to be discussed later in this book, such an assumption may not be well founded. Even if there is some slowing down, however, the difference in growth performance may still be so large that within a few decades the gap may be closed. The sheer size of the population of China makes it feasible for the total Chinese GDP to exceed that of the US before long, while if Japan could recover even a proportion of its growth record of previous decades, it might overtake the US in GDP per head of the population in a decade or two.

There are thus strong arguments on environmental, social and external grounds for the US increasing its growth rate if it can. Achieving faster growth on a consistent basis, with all that this entails for the standard of living, is also clearly in line with the wishes of a vast majority of the population. For the past decades the US economy has not performed as well as it might have done by a wide margin. The issue, then, is to ascertain the possible underlying reasons for this under-achievement and to use this information to enable more effective policies to be implemented in future.

CURRENT PROBLEMS

In some ways, the US economy has recently appeared to be in better shape than it has been for a long time. According to the 1998 *Economic Report of the President*, the growth rate in 1997 was 3.9%. The number of jobs rose by 3.2m, an average increase in employment of 267 000 per month. Unemployment dropped below 5% for the first time in twenty-four years.

Core inflation – as measured by the consumer price index, excluding its volatile food and energy components – averaged only 2.2%, its lowest rate in over thirty years. The fiscal deficit, which had been as high as $290bn during the 1992 fiscal year, declined to only $22bn in fiscal 1997. The projections for fiscal 1999 are for a balanced budget for the first time since 1969.

The outlook also seemed favourable for continued growth, although at a lower rate than in 1997. There was little sign that inflation was on the increase, or that unsold inventories were accumulating, precipitating a downturn in business activity. Banks and other financial institutions did not appear to be over-extended, as they were at similar points in previous business cycles. Interest rates were stable, largely at the instigation of Alan Greenspan at the Federal Reserve Bank. Although they were still relatively high by international standards, they were not increased, despite anticipation that this might happen. Investment had picked up sharply. Non-residential expenditure on plant, machinery and buildings rose by 11% between 1995 and 1997. The rather tighter labour market had evidently benefited the least well off. Those with the lowest 20% of incomes had seen their real incomes rise by 2.2% per annum during the period 1993–96 – a faster rate than any other quintile.

This is a better picture than might have been expected a few years ago. Are there, therefore, still grounds for concern, or should Americans now believe that they are doing as well as can reasonably be expected in a world in which perfection is unattainable? The answer is that while on the surface much is going reasonably well, and 1997 in particular saw good results in many respects, there are significant problems which have not been resolved. There is still much to be done to enable the American economy to achieve its full potential.

In the first place, although the increase in output achieved by the US economy in 1997 was the best for a decade, the average growth rate has for a long time been well below results attained elsewhere in the world. 1997 appears to have been the peak year in the business cycle, and the general view is that growth will be considerably lower in subsequent years. Even the 1997 US output increase was still substantially less than the average of 6% per annum currently being achieved by developing countries, and marginally below the recent average of about 4% for the world as a whole. If America could choose a higher growth rate, as this book will argue it could, it seems probable that it would choose a figure closer to a cumulative 4% or 5% per annum rather than about half this figure, which has been the norm actually achieved for the past decades, taking good years and bad together.

Many of the reasons for the relatively low US growth rate are reflected in structural problems with the US economy which the Clinton administration has done little to alter. Their existence makes it unlikely that even the current relatively low rate of economic growth will be sustainable, at least in the absence of substantial policy changes. There are three problem areas of major significance which will have to be overcome if there is to be a sea change in the performance of the American economy.

First, the US balance of trade on goods and services is still heavily in deficit – over $95bn in 1996, and $97bn in 1997. Nor is this deficit offset by other components of the US's foreign transactions. The total balance on current account was a negative $148bn in 1996, and an estimated $160bn in 1997. Most commentators believe that the deficit for 1998 is likely to be much higher, with little prospect of improvement even if growth in the US economy slows down. Although foreign trade represents a much smaller proportion of GDP than for many other countries, with exports of goods and services at 11.9% and imports at 13.1% in 1997, the US has a marked tendency to import more when the economy expands. America also has world-wide military and aid commitments which entail further significant calls on the foreign balance, totalling about $40bn a year, all of which add to the deficit.

It is true that as a proportion of the US GDP, the 1997 total deficit was only about 2%, even though the absolute size of the gap is large in world terms. The strength and stability of the American economy is such that up to now there has not been a major problem in attracting sufficient of the world's savings to finance the capital inflow which, as an accounting identity, has to match the US's outflow on current account each year. If the total deficit goes on rising, however, these problems may become more acute. At present, much of the deficit is financed by purchases of US government stock and American real assets by governments, institutions, corporations and private individuals in countries with high savings ratios but currently poor investment prospects, particularly in Japan. There must be some doubt as to whether sufficient funds of this type are going to continue to be available, as alternative, more attractive investment prospects may appear. Nor do many Americans, for understandable reasons, feel particularly happy about more and more of the country's stocks and real estate being bought up by foreigners to finance the payments deficit. Furthermore, even if the investment funds are still available, those responsible for them may be likely to become more wary about investing in the US, especially in debt rather than equity. At present, the Japanese are large-scale purchasers of US Treasury Bonds. If the deficit continues to increase, sooner or later this is likely to put pressure on the value of the dollar. If a serious exchange rate risk begins to materialise, the US may have to raise interest rates to continue to attract the necessary funds, which would be bound to have a negative impact on domestic expansion.

Second, the scale of the US foreign deficit on current account mirrors other features of the US economy, which must lead to doubts about its ability to go on expanding as fast as it has done recently. The US has a low savings ratio compared to many other countries, and a correspondingly weak level of net investment. In 1997, the US saved about 17% of its GDP, up a little from the low of 14.4% reached in 1993, but far below the ratios in most of the developed or developing world, which are often twice as high and sometimes even higher. Japan has a savings ratio of around 30%, Korea about 36% and Singapore closer to 40%. The proportion of GDP invested by the US is only a little higher than that which is saved – again about half the ratio seen in economies which have until recently grown fast, or which are still doing so. There is evidence that the efficiency with which US investment is used is significantly higher than in many other parts of the world, which is an important positive factor. Nevertheless, the above average US increase in output achieved from more efficient use of investment than elsewhere is not sufficient to offset its much lower quantum.

Third, the US has a smaller proportion of its economy devoted to manufacturing and a correspondingly larger percentage producing services than any other major country. Manufacturing accounts for 17% of US GDP, but about 30% in Germany and Japan. This, in turn, has two major implications for the future, as well as providing explanations for past problems. The first relates to the fact that domestically manufactured goods still represent about 60% of all US exports of goods and services. Services only account for just over a quarter, the balance being made up mostly of agricultural products and re-exports. Thus, for America to be able to pay its way in the world, the production of goods which can be sold at competitive prices in sufficient quantity is a major requirement, which at present is not being attained. The second is that productivity increases are much easier to achieve in manufacturing than they are in services, and the very slow growth in productivity in the US is closely linked to its heavy dependence on services. While output per head in American manufacturing has continued to grow in recent years cumulatively by about 4% per annum, the increase in distribution has been around half this figure, while in services there has been a continuous and significant fall. The gap in productivity increase is evident despite the widespread application of information technology in service occupations, which might have been expected to produce much better results than it actually has done.

Controversies about the inability of American manufacturing industries to compete successfully with those of other countries have abounded in recent years. At the same time, the rapid reduction in the proportion of the US labour force employed in manufacturing – from 26% in 1970 to 16% in

1995 – has been blamed for the drop in well-paid blue-collar employment, contributing heavily to the widening disparities in the distribution of income. Some of those involved in discussing what should be done to improve US performance have taken the view that government policy has little to contribute other than providing a stable financial environment. Others have advocated various forms of industrial strategies aimed at promoting US performance, particularly in high-tech sectors of the economy, which they believe represent the key to future prosperity and higher earnings. A third school of thought has sought the solution in varying forms of managed trade, shading from voluntary export restraints by the US's trading partners, through selective import constraints, either in the form of tariffs or quotas, to out-and-out protectionism. A common thread to all these approaches has been a chorus of complaint about the unwillingness of some of America's trading partners, pre-eminently Japan, to open up their domestic markets sufficiently to enable the US to compete on level terms. These writers are surely correct in drawing attention to the problems they discuss, which are real and serious. It is not clear, however, that any of them have solutions which are practical and realistic.

Providing a stable financial environment is no doubt helpful but there is no sign that, on their own, low inflation and comparatively low interest rates will generate a major and sustainable increase in American output. Much more than this is required to ensure that there is a sustained increase in demand to which the US economy is capable of responding. Continuing with current government policy is likely to show the US economy slowing up in the coming year or two, particularly as the foreign balance may deteriorate more rapidly than it otherwise would have done, as a result of the instability in the Far East. The devaluations in countries such as Korea, Indonesia and Malaysia may help to lower US import prices and thus keep inflation down, but they are also likely to lead before long to a further worsening of the trade balance, and hence to a more deflationary stance by the Federal Reserve Bank, or 'the Fed'.

Industrial strategies of any kind are also unlikely to play more than a minor role in finding a solution to America's slow growth problem. The history of state initiatives to promote industrial growth all over the world generally makes exceptionally depressing reading. There is no evidence that governments are particularly good at spotting future economic opportunities, or that they are better than the market at assessing which will be the growth industries of the future. Nor do many commentators in the academic world and the media – few with incomes dependent on the correctness of their assessments – appear to have track records indicating any better judgement. High-tech industries in particular have an allure and mystique with a fatal attraction for people who are more interested in their glamour than their capacity for making money, let alone their ability to provide the backbone for the industrial future. There is in fact remarkably little evidence that they are a better bet for future prosperity than the output of more humdrum products, which actually comprise the majority of international trade.

As for protectionism, there is a large and convincing corpus of literature which demonstrates that free trade ought to be the optimum policy for any country, even if its competitors are protectionist. There is, however, a vital caveat which needs to be added to any panegyric on free trade. The full benefits will only be secured if the exchange rate for any free-trading economy is correctly positioned. If it is not, the case for protection as a second-best option rapidly gathers strength, and the further away the exchange rate is from where it needs to be to produce a multilateral trade balance, the stronger the case for protection becomes. This is a key issue that will be discussed in more detail later on.

The case against current American economic policy is not, therefore, that it is doing exceptionally badly. Most people think it is doing reasonably well. The problem is that present policies may not be doing well enough. The deficiencies are clear to see. They are not producing as fast a rate of growth for the US as that prevailing elsewhere. American savings and investment ratios are dangerously low, and although they have crept up recently, they are still far below those in most other parts of the world. The US is not producing good enough jobs for all the potential American labour force. The quantity may be there, but there is a serious quality problem at the bottom end of the income distribution. Finally, current policies leave untouched the deteriorating foreign balances, and they have few components likely to repair America's weakened industrial base. These are the problems which need to be solved.

HISTORY AND IDEOLOGY

When World War II ended in 1945, the US was in an overwhelmingly powerful position in the world. US GDP per head of the population was far higher than anywhere else – $11 722 in 1990 dollars, compared with $6737 for Britain, $4326 for Germany and $1295 for Japan. In 1950, with post-war recovery under way, the stock of plant and machinery per head of the population in the US in 1990 dollars was $15 150, compared with $2325 in France, $3948 in Germany and $3234 in Japan. Americans were then far better educated than those in other countries, with the average US citizen having received over two years' more schooling than his or her Japanese equivalent, and a year more than the average in Western Europe.

With these major advantages to hand, why did Americans allow other countries' economies to grow so much faster than their own? It is sometimes argued that it was inevitable that the US economy would grow more slowly than others, because, as the US economy was the most advanced in the world, it was natural that other countries would catch up. Examined closely, however, this is an odd and unconvincing argument. There was no shortage of demand at any time for the vast range of goods and services which American businesses were capable of producing. There was no sign that the American people were at any stage satiated with consumption at the income levels they then had, which were far below those they have now. Obviously, there were reasons why the American economy grew considerably more slowly than the world average, but it stretches credulity well beyond breaking point to believe that this happened just because American living standards were higher than those elsewhere in the world. Indeed, if being in the lead position automatically produced slower growth than elsewhere, how could the US have ever overtaken Britain to become the leader in the first place?

The real reasons why the US economy grew more slowly than the average were connected with its leading position, but not simply because US GDP per head was higher than elsewhere. The US did have a technical lead, but there is no reason why this could not have allowed the American economy to grow at least as fast, if not faster, than its competitors, had appropriate policies been pursued. The US in fact grew more slowly for two main reasons. One was that those running the country at the time had many other policy issues with which to contend, so that achieving a higher growth rate was not a major target. The second was that even if it had been, there was no clearly articulated policy available to show how this objective could be achieved.

Part of the explanation lies in the fact that the world leadership position in which the US found itself post-World War II left it with major obligations. In consequence, the US agreed to shoulder substantial military and other international burdens, which on balance probably had a significant negative influence on its growth rate. The strength of the American economy meant that the dollar inevitably took over from the pound sterling as the currency in which most world trade was conducted, and the major reserve currency for the world's banking and monetary system. This provided the US with important advantages, but also responsibilities, which, especially towards the end of the Bretton Woods period, tended to pull down the performance of the US economy. The most important reasons why the US economy grew relatively slowly, however, almost certainly had little to do with explanations of even this more plausible kind. The most significant reasons lay embedded in the culture, the intellectual climate and the social structure of the US, on the one hand, and, on the other, the failure of economists to provide convincing answers to a number of key questions.

In 1982, Mancur Olson published a seminal book on economic growth, stagflation and social rigidities in which he argued that the longer a society enjoys political stability, the more likely it is to develop powerful special interest lobbies that in turn make it less efficient economically. This is a powerful and convincing thesis. Olson, however, was primarily concerned with demonstrating the importance of his ideas in explaining why the performance of economies tends to deteriorate as a result of the impact of special interest groups in an essentially micro-economic sense. He showed how what he called 'distributional coalitions', such as cartels, professional associations and trades unions, whatever the benefits to their members, would always tend to put their own interests before those of the community at large. The overall result was misuse and misallocation of resources on a sufficient scale to cause a significant deterioration in national economic performance. The longer the period of stability lasted, the more acute the sclerotic condition of the economy tended to be.

It is not difficult to extend these ideas so as to consider their impact not just on the micro-economic world of cartels and lobbies, but also at the macro-economic level. In 1945, as a result of a huge military effort, the US had just won a major war. The inevitable result was a powerful armed forces lobby, which naturally saw the deployment of US military power as the most important use to which the strength of the American economy could be put. Much more important, however, was the broader picture in US society. The stability which the US had enjoyed, lasting in the northern states since the arrival of the *Mayflower*, and in the southern states at least since the end of the Reconstruction period, had allowed a substantial coalition of the well-off to develop, with naturally conservative views, because they had much to lose. It is no coincidence that Britain, in a parallel but weaker position than the US at the end of World War II, exhibited very similar characteristics, leaving the British economy with the lowest growth rate of any developed country for the next half century. The contrast with the performance of those nations which were defeated in World War II, or those countries which had been invaded and over-run, even if they finally emerged on the winning side, could not be more stark.

The US has always had a strong pro-business culture which has never allowed the deprecating attitude to trade and manufacturing to develop, still widely prevalent in countries such as Britain. Nevertheless, the accretion of large amounts of wealth in the hands of established families, and the accumulation of substantial savings entrusted to financial institutions, has tended to strengthen the hands of the financial community *vis à vis* trade and industry. The power and profit of banks and related financial organisations have been inclined to colour people's perceptions as to where most influence lies, and which role models are the best to follow and to emulate. The result of all these forces has been to establish a powerful financial and social establishment with a natural inclination to preserve the status quo and to favour old money against new, the interests of the rich against those of the poor, established businesses against upstarts, and, on the whole, clean, modern services as against old, ugly manufacturing.

This combination of social forces, strengthened by prestigious universities, clubs, associations and friendship networks, all helping to reinforce the view of the world which seemed to suit the ruling establishment in the US best, had a powerful influence on the way the economy was run. The pattern of growth and output was undoubtedly to a significant extent subordinated to the requirements of the military and other branches of government charged with upholding America's world role. More importantly, however, the strength of the US economy, combined with the reserve role of the dollar, meant that for the whole of the 1950s and 1960s, the American establishment paid little attention to the fact that other countries were growing much more quickly than the United States. The inevitable consequence of these disparities in growth rates, however, was that the US lead was whittled away. The US share of world trade went down from 11.5% in 1950 to 9.7% in 1973 as investment in plant and machinery, leading to fast-increasing exports, grew much more rapidly in other parts of the world than the US, first in Europe and later in the Far East.

It was this process of rapid industrialisation elsewhere, combined with relatively unimpressive growth in manufacturing output in the US, which was responsible more than anything else for reducing the American lead. Its consequences were slow US productivity growth, sluggish export performance and increasing import penetration. Much of the rest of this book is about the process which caused this to happen. It is still remarkable, however, that at the time, and even now, these chains of causation are remarkably poorly understood. For this, the economics profession must take much of the blame. If there had been clear prescriptions available to the US leaders during the post-World War II period – or indeed at other times – setting out how to achieve higher growth, or indeed any chosen growth rate, it is unlikely that they would have been ignored. There might have been an effective antidote to the conservative pressures which militated against faster growth. Unfortunately, despite a huge increase in its numbers, the economics profession failed to do this.

The problem with economics as it is now taught in most countries, and widely accepted by those involved in forming policies and commenting on them, is that it has not produced answers to some of the most important questions with which it ought to be concerned. Over the last half-century it has strayed from dealing with practical issues and providing clear guidance to policy makers. Some of it has become increasingly concerned with abstract matters, for example those thrown up by pushing the assumptions made in supply and demand theory well beyond those which correspond to real world relationships. Some of it has become increasingly arcane, depending on complicated mathematical models, too often with unrealistic assumptions and little prescriptive value. Where it has been concerned with practical matters, much of the output – monetarist doctrine being the prime example – has been extremely ineffective at solving the problems faced by governments throughout the world. The general development of economics since World War II, as a body of theory, has served those responsible for running economic policy remarkably poorly.

Economics, on the contrary, needs to be able to explain clearly how to deal with pressing practical issues. What makes economies grow, and what has to be done to enable any country to achieve whatever rate of economic growth it believes is desirable and acceptable? What level of unemployment is unavoidable, and how should policies be framed to stay as close to this minimum level as possible? How can high growth and low unemployment be combined with tolerable levels of inflation? How can a relatively even distribution of income – if this is accepted as a legitimate goal – be coupled with acceptable economic performance? Why do some economies manage to perform so much better than others? What steps need to be taken to enable the laggards to do as well as the star performers?

The fact that some countries have done so much better than others is not obviously attributable to the clear-sightedness of those governing them, however much those in charge may feel inclined to claim that it is. On the contrary, it appears that much of the contrasting performance has resulted not from the difference in policies which have deliberately been pursued, but from luck and happenstance. Strong evidence for this proposition is provided by the fact that many of the countries which did best in terms of growth and full employment for long periods after World War II, such as Germany, Japan and France, are all now in difficulties. If the people running these economies really knew why they had previously been so successful, it is hard to believe that they would have deliberately changed their policies to produce the much worse results currently apparent. The inability of economists to provide clear guidance to policy makers is not a problem confined to the US.

There is thus a large vacuum in the middle of economics as a branch of study. It has a lot to say about the micro aspects of the way economies run, but surprisingly little about a number of key major macro issues. It has much to maintain about competition and monopolies, tariffs and free trade, monetary policy and the business cycle. There is of course also the Keynesian legacy, stressing the importance of effective demand, and the role of government in promoting stable conditions by fiscal action to offset booms and depressions. There is still, however, a lack of answers to major central questions. How can any economy achieve whatever rate of economic growth it would like to set as a target? How can it employ to full advantage all those who would like to work? How can high growth conditions be combined with a tolerable level of inflation? These are the key questions which need to be answered, and which this book sets out to address.

CHOICES FOR THE FUTURE

Despite the problems there have been, the US has maintained its position as the most prosperous country in the world. It still has the highest GDP per head of the population. The collapse of the Soviet system has left America with unrivalled military power. The growth rate has been better than previously, with a peak in 1997 after a recovery from the shallow depression of the early 1990s. Inflation is low. Unemployment is falling. Self-confidence is high. Is there really any real cause for concern?

The issue is not whether America has done well. In many respects, although not in all, it has. The question is whether it could do better and, if so, whether it needs to do so. This books suggests that it could, and it should. It argues that there is a surprisingly large gap between the output the US economy is currently achieving and its potential. It also contends that the US growth rate is considerably lower than it needs to be, and that changes in macro-economic policies which would be comparatively simple and easy to implement could substantially increase the US's long-term growth rate. If these policy changes were made, solutions to many of the other problems which exercise both the public and the US government would begin to fall into place.

The trade deficit would right itself, so that the US would no longer have to borrow large sums from abroad every year. The government's finances would become significantly easier to manage without there being a shortfall between income and expenditure. Productivity, especially among those with lower incomes, would improve cumulatively each year, allowing a compound increase in real wages to occur into the future, as has not happened for the past quarter of a century. The distribution of income would become less uneven, alleviating a substantial proportion of the poverty which disfigures American society. For these benefits there might be a small inflationary price to pay, but not one which should cause any undue concern, and in particular, one which should not cumulatively become more difficult to manage.

These are large claims, and to support them the chapters which follow deal systematically with different aspects of the problems to be tackled. Chapter 2 provides a summary of US economic history through to the end of the 1960s, highlighting the most significant developments and the key policy issues. Chapter 3 reviews the changes which occurred as oil shocks and other events slowed down world growth in the 1970s, and monetarism took over from Keynesianism. It then summarises the main events affecting the US economy which occurred from the mid-1970s to the late 1990s, and the impact which changes in fashion in economic ideas had on policy implementation.

The next three chapters then review international experience and ideas about the major issues with which economic policy needs to be concerned. Chapter 4 is about economic growth. It discusses the conditions needed to achieve and sustain it, and the most important reasons why it can cease to occur. Chapter 5 covers employment issues. It looks at the causes of both unemployment and under-employment of the labour force, and reviews the steps which need to be taken to produce rising productivity and real wages across all income bands. Chapter 6 deals with inflation. It is concerned with both the causes of price rises and the steps which can be taken to moderate them without prejudicing the achievement of other economic objectives. Chapter 7 then pulls the threads together and sets out the steps which US policy makers need to take to enable the US economy to achieve the dramatic improvement in its performance potentially available to it.

The US is in a strong position, but not one which is impregnable. It needs to guard against complacency and settling for standards of economic performance which are well below its capability. It is not in the US's interests to see other countries overtaking its standard of living, or even the absolute size of its economy. Given reasonably competent management, this need not happen in the foreseeable future. With poor management, it easily could. The problem is that the trends of the last twenty-five years, and particularly those since 1980, are not in America's favour. They need to be reversed.

Explaining how this might be done is not particularly complicated. It does not involve algebra and impenetrable hieroglyphics. Nor does it require complex mathematics, although the case set out is one which is strongly quantitative as well as qualitative. Anyone interested in current affairs will understand the arguments put forward. Economics does not need to be abstruse; it ought to be clear, intelligible, interesting, and occasionally entertaining. Hopefully, you will find that the pages which follow meet these tests.

2 The Historical Setting

'One of the uses of history is to free us of a falsely imagined past. The less we know of how ideas actually took root and grew, the more apt we are to accept them unquestioningly, as inevitable features of the world in which we move.'

Robert H. Bork

Industrialisation might have started during the period of the Roman Empire, but it failed to do so. There is some evidence that in China during the fifteenth century something close to the beginning of an industrial revolution did occur, but it was snuffed out by the country's leaders who turned back to traditional ways. India, on the other hand, never showed any more signs of sustained industrial development than the Romans, despite the ability of the Mughal culture to build the Taj Mahal, its high point of excellence in both design and execution. Nor were smaller empires. significant though they may have been at the time, any better at producing sustained economic growth. On the contrary, it was in Europe, divided into a large number of relatively small states, that there began to be a sustained increase in living standards, starting early in the second millennium, which eventually produced the Industrial Revolution.

The conjunction of circumstances required to trigger off industrialisation turned out to be remarkably complex. Certainly, both a well-developed trading system and a trustworthy banking network were required, in addition to a legal and political system capable of ensuring that financial surpluses could not be usurped at will by those in political control. There also needed to be sufficient stability and peace to make it worthwhile for entrepreneurs to take substantial risks, with the prospect of recouping their investment outlays over periods of years rather than months. Sufficient technical knowledge and scientific theory was required to enable the development of new processes to be guided by well-established knowledge and scientific principles rather than by guesswork and trial and error. All these requirements, however, had been met, at least to a substantial degree, in other places, but had failed to produce results. What was different about Europe?

A key theme running through this book is that breaking new ground in the commercial and industrial world is difficult and requires exceptional ability. Once it has been done, it is comparatively easy for others to see how it occurred, though not necessarily obvious how to break in against established competition.

The societies which successfully initiated the Industrial Revolution, and those who have been most effective at sustaining it, are therefore ones where a significant proportion of their most talented individuals were immersed in the manufacturing and commercial worlds. The Industrial Revolution began in Europe rather than elsewhere because there was a sufficient number of exceptionally able and gifted people who were interested in industry and commerce. It is not kings or queens, politicians or professionals, churchmen or academics, soldiers or diplomats, who create economic resources. Only to a limited extent, too, do traders and bankers perform a significant role in wealth generation. Most of the increase in output which is achieved by modern methods of producing goods and services, at least in the early stages, comes from manufacturing, with agriculture making an important subsidiary contribution.

The unique contribution which Europe made, and particularly the Netherlands and Britain during the early stages of the Industrial Revolution, was to generate circumstances where sufficient able people began to apply themselves seriously, and on a reasonably large scale, to employing new industrial technology and to improving agricultural methods. Slowly the notion that there might be continuing opportunities to expand output, raise living standards and increase productivity began to spread. Once this happened, the history of humanity was irreversibly established on the path of industrial advance. Compared to most others, those who moved across the Atlantic from Europe to establish a new life in North America were thus exceptionally well equipped with both knowledge of the world and ideas about how governmental institutions should be run. These were assets which were to make an enormously important contribution to the US's future economic successes.

US ECONOMIC HISTORY UP TO WORLD WAR I

When the first settlers arrived in North America from Europe, they brought with them immeasurable advantages over the indigenous population. Even before the Industrial Revolution got under way in Europe in the eighteenth century, producing much higher cumulative increases in output than the world had ever seen before, major technological and intellectual advances had been achieved. Printing, clocks, reading glasses, improvements to ship design and navigation, sophisticated working of metal and other materials, and many other technical advances, not least in agriculture, were in widespread use. The Renaissance had led to important developments in mathematics, astronomy, medicine and the use of scientific method. There were well-established legal systems, particularly in Britain, and the beginnings of democratic institutions. Literacy and numeracy, although by no means universal, were common. The early settlers in the US were thus by all historical standards exceptionally well endowed with their European legacy when they reached their destination, as indeed were many of those who subsequently followed in their steps.

Nevertheless, the life of early settlers in the US, and for many years subsequently, was tough and arduous. The country was enormous, and communications were extremely primitive. Internal transportation was difficult and expensive, and sea-borne traffic provided the only practical solution to the movement of goods and people, producing a strong incentive for the development of efficient sailing ships. The population was overwhelmingly rural. Even as late as 1790, when the population numbered approximately 3.9m, of whom almost 700 000 were slaves, there were only seven places with a population of over 5000 and only twelve with a population over 2500–5000. In these circumstances, manufacturing on anything but the smallest of scales was impractical, because internal transport problems so severely limited the size of the potential market. Almost all US export trade was in raw materials, primarily cotton, tobacco and wheat flour.

The Declaration of Independence in 1776, followed shortly by the Napoleonic Wars, where the US was not a direct participant, and then the 1812 war with Britain, produced both opportunities and disadvantages. Trade was disrupted, but domestic manufacturing was encouraged, and exports grew dramatically, if erratically. Overall, the value of exports which had been $20m in 1790 had grown to $52m by 1815, while imports rose from $24m to $85m. Part of the growth in output in the US was attributable to its rapidly rising population which had reached 7.2m by 1810 and 9.6m by 1820. The really explosive growth in the number of US citizens did not start until about 1830, however, when the population was almost 13m. By 1860 it was 31m. The peak for immigration during this period was 1854, when 428 000 people moved to the US.

As early as 1820 the US was among the richest countries in the world, judged by GDP per capita. Estimates produced by the OECD show the US a little over 25% below the British living standard of the time, a little under 20% behind the Dutch and Australians, and roughly on a par with Austria, Belgium, Denmark and France and Sweden. By 1850, Britain was still well ahead, but the gap was closing. The disruption of the American Civil War held back the US for a few years, but by 1870, the US growth rate was poised for the rapid increase in output achieved over the period between 1870 and 1913. During the fifty years between 1820 and 1870, the US economy had grown much faster than those on the other side of the Atlantic. Between 1820 and 1850, the US economy grew cumulatively by 4.2% per annum, although the increase in output per head was much lower at 1.3% per annum, close to the British figure for the period of 1.25%. This was now to change. During the forty-three years from 1870 to 1913, the US economy achieved a cumulative growth rate of 4.3% per annum. Allowing for compound population growth of 2.1% per annum, US GDP per head rose by 2.2% per annum. Only Sweden did better over this period, at 2.3%, though Denmark came close with 2.1%. Germany achieved 1.8%, and Britain only 1.3%. The average annual growth in output per man-hour was also higher in Denmark and Sweden than in the US. Otherwise Europe lagged well behind. Between 1870 and 1913, British GDP grew by a cumulative 1.9% per annum, France's by 1.7% and Germany's by 2.8%. Owing to differences in population growth, the cumulative annual increases in GDP per head figures per annum over the same period were only 1% per annum for Britain, 1.5% for France and 1.6% for Germany.

A differential in growth rates either in GDP or GDP per head of 1% or 2% per annum may not sound significant taken a year at a time, but the cumulative effect over a period such as the forty-three years between 1870 and 1913 is huge. If two economies start at the same size at the beginning of the period, one which is growing 2% faster per annum than its rival will be 134% larger forty-three years later. Even if the differential is only 1%, it will be 53% bigger at the end of the period. The results of the differential growth rates which occurred between the US and most of Europe in the late nineteenth and early twentieth centuries thus presaged a seismic shift in world power. By 1913, the US had overtaken Britain in living standards, leaving all the rest of Europe well behind. Only Australia and New Zealand were still ahead of the US, but with much smaller populations and GDPs. By this time the US had not only a high GDP per head but also a large population to go with it. By 1890 the US population was 63m, and by 1913 it was 98m. As a result, the US economy was by then well over twice the size of its nearest rival, Britain, and more than four times that of Germany. Japan, which had grown by a respectable 2.8% per annum during the previous three decades, had an economy only about 13% the size of that of the US in 1913.

These figures set the achievements of the US economy in an important context. It is often assumed that the rapid growth rates in the US were the results of exceptional natural endowments, and a tough but on the whole beneficent environment for enterprise, thrift and accumulation. Of course, these characteristics did play an important part, but they cannot be the whole explanation. If they were, how would we account for the achievements of Denmark and Sweden, both of which lacked the expandable territories and the varied resources in which the US abounded? Nor were Sweden or particularly Denmark well known for their rampant capitalism. The key figures then, as now, were not so much the growth in the total GDP. The real test was the growth in GDP per head. As the figures above show, large increases in the population meant that American living standards grew much more slowly than the American economy as a whole during the decades running up to World War I. The exceptional performance of Sweden and Denmark, in increasing their GDP per head faster than the US, was a remarkable achievement.

It has sometimes been said that the cause of rapid American growth in the nineteenth century was the large increase in the population that took place, providing an expanding market and rising demand. No doubt this was an important factor, but having a rapidly rising population is a mixed blessing. It inevitably means that the available capital infrastructure has to be shared among a larger number of people. Offset against this in America's case, however, is the fact that much of the increase in population during the period from the end of the Civil War to the outbreak of World War I came from immigration. During these years 26m people migrated to the United States, most of them educated, of working age, and with well-developed work ethics. This was a bonus by any standards. Perhaps the disbenefits from capital dilution as a result of immigration were roughly offset by the arrival of millions of mostly young, hard-working and reasonably well-trained people. In any event, although the US economy might have reacted to huge population increase by allowing the capital stock per head of the population to decline, this did not happen. On the contrary, during the latter years of the nineteenth century and the early 1900s, gross domestic investment as a proportion of GDP was much higher in the US than it was in other countries. It averaged nearly 20% of GDP for the whole period, compared with about 7% for Britain, but 11% for Sweden and 14% for Denmark. Achieving a high investment ratio was as important in the nineteenth century as it is now, and the US also used its investment more efficiently than the average, thereby gaining an important additional advantage.

The overall growth achieved by the US in the nineteenth century was therefore unprecedented. By 1900 the American economy was about twenty-five times as large as it had been in 1820. By 1980, another eighty years later, by comparison, the increase was to a little over thirteen times the 1900 figure. The key period for expansion of the US economy, however, started during the decade before the Civil War when mechanisation and industrialisation really got into their strides. Between 1830 and the beginning of the 1865, manufacturing output increased nearly tenfold, while the population rose to about three times its 1830 figure. In the final decade before the Civil War began, steam engines and machinery output increased by 66%, cotton textiles by 77%, railroad iron by 100%, and hosiery goods by 608%. As

Reconstruction got under way, and the opportunities for a wide range of new technologies were exploited, improving communications and the quality of manufactures, the economy took off. The US gross stock of machinery and equipment increased by almost 400% between 1870 and 1890, and by 1913 it had nearly trebled again.

It is no coincidence that it was the advent of large-scale increases in industrial output which triggered the rise in the US growth rate. The proportion of US GDP deriving from industry was on an upward trend throughout the nineteenth century. The evidence shows that not only was the US during this period reinvesting a well above average proportion of its GDP; because it was also using the investment efficiently, it achieved unusually high returns from it. This is a characteristic which the US economy still maintains, although the proportion of the US economy's output derived from industry is now much lower than it was, down about 10% from the 27% average achieved during the peak post-World War II period.

It is often alleged that a stable financial environment is the key to economic growth, and that low interest rates and low inflation are required to ensure high levels of investment and increases in output. It is hard to square this view of the world with the experience of the US economy in the nineteenth century. For most of the century, the US had no Central Bank at all. The charter of the first Bank of the United States expired in 1811, when it was not renewed by the Jeffersonians then in power. The Second Bank of the United States, established in 1816, was wound up shortly after the re-election in 1832 of President Andrew Jackson, who bitterly opposed its existence. Thereafter, until the establishment of the Federal Reserve system in 1913, there was no central control of the US money supply. Credit creation was in the hands of thousands of banks spread all over the country, many of them poorly run, under-capitalised, prone to speculation and liable to fail.

It is hardly surprising that, in these circumstances, US interest rates, prices and credit availability gyrated from boom to bust repeatedly during the nineteenth century. The abolition of the Second Bank of the United States in 1833 was followed only four years later by the worst depression the US had experienced so far, in some ways a worse crash than in 1929. Prices fell 40% between 1838 and 1843, railroad construction declined by almost 70% and canal building by 90%. Large-scale unemployment developed, and serious food riots broke out in New York City. It was not until 1844 that the next upswing started, culminating in the next downturn in 1856, which lasted until 1862. This pattern was to be repeated throughout the nineteenth century, accompanied by bank closures, bankruptcies and widespread defaults every time there was a downturn.

The price level was also unstable during the nineteenth century. Between 1815 and 1850, the wholesale price level fell by 50%, with substantial fluctuations in intervening years. It increased by a modest 11% during the 1860s, despite the Civil War, before the delayed impact of the Californian gold rush on the money supply caused a major inflation to take place. By 1870, the price level had risen 45% compared to ten years previously. Thereafter prices fell until, by the turn of the century, they were 35% lower than they had been in 1870. They then climbed again about 16% during the years to 1913, mainly because the development of the cyanide process for extracting gold in South Africa led to another major increase in the world's monetary base.

Since World War II, promoting freer trade has been a major plank of US policy, also in sharp contrast to the high tariff protection promoted by successive administrations during the nineteenth century. Some import duties were imposed partly for revenue raising purposes, as they were the major source of government income at the time, but industrial protection was also a factor from the beginning. The tariff of 1816 imposed duties of 20–25% on manufactured goods and 15–20% on raw materials. Thereafter the tariff level fluctuated, with the trade cycle, as always, playing a major role. The depression of 1837, for example, stimulated a new wave of protectionism as American industrialists blamed high unemployment on cheap imported goods. The major shift to a much more protectionist policy came in 1861 with the Morrill Tariff, designed to make the importation of most mass produced goods into the US completely uneconomic. Import duties were not to be lowered again until 1913 under Woodrow Wilson, although even then they still stood at about 25%. Wool, sugar, iron and steel, however, were added to the free list.

A distinguishing feature of the US economy has always been the low proportion, by international standards, of US GDP involved in foreign trade. Exports averaged about 11.5% of GDP during the period up to World War I – much the same as now. Imports ran then at under 8%, compared with about 13% at present. Part of the reason for these low ratios has always, of course, been the sheer size of the country and its ability to supply a high proportion of its needs from domestic sources. There is little doubt, however, that in the circumstances of the years up to 1913, the high tariff barrier helped the US develop its manufacturing industries, unhampered by competition from abroad. Goods which might have been purchased from Europe were produced in the US. The high level of demand, albeit subject to severe fluctuations which the unregulated credit and banking system generated, provided opportunities which US manufacturers were quick to seize. Under the Gold Standard régime, which the US joined in 1878 when bimetallism was abandoned, it would have been difficult for the US to have lowered its prices internationally sufficiently to have held off growing import penetration. The competitiveness of European exports at the time is amply demonstrated by the high proportion of their output which the European economies were capable of selling overseas during the nineteenth and early twentieth century. In 1900, about 25% of all British GDP was exported, and about 16% of all Germany's. Even in 1913, Britain was still exporting more goods and services than the US, although its economy was almost 60% smaller.

The lessons to be learnt from the US's economic history up to 1913 are just as relevant now as they were then. If the economy is to grow fast, advantage needs to be taken of the ability of industry, and particularly manufacturing, to generate high rates of growth of output. By 1870, a quarter of the US GDP came from industry, and by 1913, almost 30%. The growth in productivity in manufacturing – and agriculture – during this period was about 50% higher than it was in the service sector – a ratio which has widened since then. As the proportion of the US economy devoted to manufacturing rose, so growth increased in the place where it really counts, which is not the size of the national income, but GDP per head. We shall see later, in quantified form, just how important this requirement is, and how hugely damaging it is to let any economy's manufacturing base fall into decline.

BOOM AND DEPRESSION: FROM WORLD WAR I TO WORLD WAR II

For three years after World War I broke out in 1914 the US was not directly involved in the war as a belligerent. The immediate effect on the US economy was nevertheless to precipitate a fall in output between 1913 and 1914 of some 7%, but this ground was rapidly made up. By 1918 the economy had grown by almost 16% compared to 1913. Prices rose by about 50% between 1915 and 1918, but inflation was much less in the US over the war period than it was in other countries. Britain's price level rose nearly 80%, France's doubled, and Germany's increased by 200%.

Up to 1913, the Gold Standard régime had been reasonably successful in holding movements in the price levels in all countries within the system roughly in line with each other. The very different rises in prices in major countries during World War I were, however, only the beginning of the problems which hit the world economy as the war came to an end. The US suffered a comparatively minor 3% drop in GDP between 1919 and 1921 as a result of large-scale reductions in government expenditure on war materials. Unemployment in consequence shot up from 1.4% in 1919 to 11.7% in 1921.

By contrast, a combination of destruction during the war and a much deeper slump when it finished, produced far worse results in Europe. France's industrial production dropped by over 40% between 1913 and 1919. It was 1927 before German GDP rose again to its 1913 level. Britain did not do so badly, with its GDP staying more or less constant during the war, although it fell heavily, by about 20%, when the war ended.

Instability was greatly compounded by the Treaty of Versailles, negotiated between the powers which had won the war and the humiliated Germans. The US insisted on the large debts run up by Britain and France for war supplies being repaid. Britain and France, in turn, looked to Germany to make huge reparations, partly to pay their debts to the US, and partly on their own accounts. Leaving aside the extent to which the German economy was already languishing as a result of the damage done to it by the war, the only feasible way for the Germans to pay the reparations bill was to run a large export surplus. In the fragile state of the world economy in the 1920s, no country was prepared to tolerate a large German trade surplus, even if it could have been achieved. Payment of reparations on the scale demanded, whatever its electoral appeal or the determination of the US to see its debts settled, was never therefore a remotely realistic prospect. The German government struggled to meet the terms imposed on it, but by 1923, unable to raise sufficient revenue through the tax system to meet its obligations, it resorted to the printing press to create the money it was unable to raise in any other way. The result was hyperinflation and the total collapse of the Reichsmark, wiping out the resources of everyone who had savings in cash or interest bearing securities.

While the 1920s saw most European economies recovering from deep post-war slumps, leaving their populations with significantly lower GDP per head than they had enjoyed before the war, the US economy surged ahead. Recovering quickly from its 1919–21 setback, during most of the remaining 1920s a major and sustained boom developed. Between 1921 and 1929 the US economy grew by 45%, achieving a cumulative 4.8% rate of growth during these eight years. From 1920 to 1929 industrial output rose by nearly 50%, while the number of people employed to achieve this increase in output remained almost constant, reflecting an enormous increase in manufacturing productivity, which rose cumulatively by nearly 5% per annum as factories were automated. The use of electricity in industry rose dramatically – by 70% between 1923 and 1929. Living standards increased by 30%, although those on already high incomes gained much more than those further down the income distribution ladder. Investment as a percentage of GDP rose from 12.2% in 1921 to 17.6% in 1928. Meanwhile, the price level remained remarkably stable, consumer prices being on average slightly lower in 1928 than they were in 1921.

The confidence engendered by such economic success was reflected not only by an almost tripling of consumer credit during the 1920s, but also on the stock market. A bull market began to build in 1924. It surged ahead with only minor setbacks for the next five years. The Dow-Jones Industrial Averages, whose high was 120 in 1924, reached 167 in 1926, soared to 300 in 1928, and peaked at 381 on 3 September 1929, a level not to be exceeded for another quarter of a century. Speculative fever reigned in a largely unregulated market. Much of the increase in the value of stocks was financed by increasingly risky but lucrative loans. As the boom gathered strength, those buying shares often had to put up only as little as 10% of the cost themselves, the balance being provided as 'brokers' loans'. These were provided initially by banks, but later increasingly by corporations which found the potential returns irresistible, resulting in many of the major American companies increasingly investing their resources in speculation rather than production. Brokers' loans, which had been about $1bn during the early years of the decade, had risen to $3.5bn by the end of 1927, to $6bn by January 1929 and had reached $8.5bn by October 1929. The huge demand for such loans forced the interest rate on them up and up. By the time the stock market peaked in the late summer of 1929, 12% interest rates were not uncommon at a time when there was no inflation.

The initial falls from the stock market peak were modest, but by late October 1929, confidence was draining away. A wave of panic on 24 October was followed by 'Black Friday', 25 October, and a frenzy of selling on 29 October 1929. In the first half-hour that day losses ran at over $2bn, and by the end of the day they were $10bn as the Dow-Jones fell thirty points, reducing the value of quoted stocks by 11.5%. Worse was to follow. Despite periodic rallies, the market moved inexorably downwards until, by July 1932, the Dow-Jones stood at 41, nearly 90% below its 381 peak. United States Steel shares fell from 262 to 22, General Motors dropped from 73 to 8, and Montgomery Ward plummeted from 138 to 4.

The collapse of prices on the stock exchanges had a devastating effect on the rest of the economy. The huge sums which had been lost caused a wave of bank failures from coast to coast, dragging down countless businesses with them. As both consumer and industrial confidence evaporated, sources of credit dried up, and demand disappeared for many of the goods and services which the US economy was amply capable of producing. Between 1929 and 1933, US GDP fell by 30%. Industrial output went down by nearly half in just three years from 1929 to 1932. By 1933, a quarter of the American labour force was out of work. Nearly 13m people were unemployed.

The financial traumas experienced in the US were rapidly transmitted to Europe. A fragile recovery had taken place in Germany during the 1920s when some reparations payments had been made. The ability of the German economy to meet these payments, however, did not rest on German export surpluses, but on borrowings from abroad, largely from the US. With the collapse of the US stock market, new loans to Germany dried up. Aided by bank failures and singularly inapposite policies of retrenchment by the Brüning government, the German economy also plunged into a slump which was as bad as that of the US. This precipitated the rise of Hitler and his Nazi Party, opening the way to World War II.

The German economic record after 1933, however, provides some important lessons. Whatever distaste one may have for the racist and fascist policies pursued by Germany from 1933 onwards, the remarkable Nazi economic record repays examination. Unemployment, which stood at over 30% in 1932, was reduced to just over 2% of the working population by 1938. Over the same period, industrial production rose over 120%, a cumulative increase of 14% per annum. GDP rose by 65%, a cumulative increase of nearly 9% a year. A substantial proportion of the extra output was devoted to armaments, but by no means all. Military expenditure, which had been 3.2% of GDP in 1933, rose to 9.6% in 1937. It then almost doubled to 18.1%, but only as late as 1938. Between 1932 and 1938, consumers' expenditure rose by almost a quarter. Nor were these achievements bought at the expense of high rates of inflation. The price level was almost stable in Germany in the 1930s despite a large increase in the money supply and widespread deficit financing, based on bank credits. Consumer prices rose by a total of only 7% between the arrival of the Nazi régime in 1933 and the outbreak of war in 1939.

There were also lessons to be learnt from the experiences of other European countries over this period. Britain, which during the 1920s had pursued heavy deflationary policies to get back to the pre-World War I parity between the pound and the dollar, went off gold in 1931, adding tariff protection to a devaluation of 24%. The result was the best growth performance between 1932 and 1937 ever achieved in any five-year period in Britain's history, again accompanied by very little inflation. France, and the other countries in the gold bloc régime, by contrast, refused to devalue until the election in 1936 of the French Popular Front. The result was that from the onset of the slump until 1936, far from achieving any recovery, the condition of their economies continued to deteriorate. French GDP dropped steadily in real terms almost every year from 1930 to 1936, falling by a total of 17% over these six years. Industrial production fell by a quarter. Investment slumped. Unemployment rose continually. The results of the battles in Europe in 1940 at the beginning of World War II were largely predetermined by the economic policies pursued by the countries involved during the previous decade.

In the US, the condition of the economy reached its nadir in 1933. Meanwhile, in 1932, Roosevelt had ousted the hapless Hoover as President in a landslide vote, initiating a New Deal for the American people, designed to tackle the slump. The policies implemented by the new Democrat administration fell into two main parts. The first was a substantial increase in the role of the state. More financial help was provided to those hardest hit by unemployment. The Federal Emergency Relief Act provided $500m in direct grants to states and municipalities. New agencies were established, some of them designed to act in a counter-cyclical way, increasing demand by using the borrowing power of the state to provide funding. The Tennessee Valley Authority provided regional energy and flood control. The National Recovery Administration assisted with industrial revitalisation. The Agricultural Adjustment Administration had as its goal the regeneration of the weakened farming sector of the economy. The result of these initiatives was probably as much in terms of increasing confidence that something was being done by the federal government to improve conditions than in their direct impact, although expenditure on these schemes no doubt had some reflationary impact.

Much more significant in terms of causing the economy to revive were other steps taken on the macro-economic front. In 1934, the dollar was devalued by 41%, adding to the substantial protection for American industry which had already been achieved by the Smoot–Hawley Tariff in 1930, a major step towards the economic nationalism which was a thorn in America's side in the 1930s. One of the Roosevelt administration's early steps had been to stabilise the financial system by declaring a bank holiday, and then allowing the Treasury, under emergency legislation, to verify the soundness of individual banks before allowing them to reopen. Ten days later half of them, holding 90% of all deposits, were back in operation. The result was that thenceforward deposits exceeded withdrawals as confidence in the banking system was restored, thus increasing the availability of credit. The Fed also encouraged recovery by allowing the money supply to rise as the economy picked up. M1 rose from just under $20bn in 1933 to a little less than $30bn in 1936, generating a major increase in the underlying credit base.

The result was that by 1936 the US economy was in considerably better shape than it had been three years earlier. In these three years real GDP grew by 32%, while unemployment fell by nearly a third, from 25% to 17%. Industrial output rebounded, growing 50%. Corporate net income moved from being $2bn in deficit to $5bn in profit. There was little change in the consumer price level. Despite these striking achievements, Roosevelt, who, notwithstanding all the New Deal rhetoric, had never felt wholly comfortable with borrowing to spend, became alarmed by the fiscal deficit which reached $3.5bn in 1936. As a result, he ordered a cutback in federal spending. This coincided with both a reduction in the competitiveness of US exports as the gold bloc countries devalued, and the deflationary impact of the promised new social security tax, another part of the New Deal, which was introduced at the same time. The consequence was a sharp recession. GDP fell by 4% between 1937 and 1938, industrial output fell back nearly a third, and unemployment rose from 14.3% to 19%.

By then, however, the start of World War II was imminent, transforming the prospects for the US economy. Although the US did not become a belligerent until December 1941, following the Japanese attack on Pearl Harbor, the lend-lease arrangements agreed with the Allied powers at the start of the European war rapidly provided a massive stimulus to US output. Between 1939 and 1944, US GDP grew by an astonishing 75%, a compound rate of almost 12%. Over the same period, industrial output increased by over 150%, while the number of people employed in manufacturing rose from 10.3m to 17.3m, an increase of just under 70%. The difference between these two percentages reflected a huge further advance in manufacturing productivity, which rose cumulatively by some 8% per annum. Prices increased by an average of less than 5% per annum, a far better outcome than had been achieved during World War I. By the end of World War II, the US was therefore in an extraordinarily strong position *vis à vis* the rest of the world. Most developed countries had suffered invasion and defeat at some stage in the war, and in consequence their economies had been severely disrupted and in some cases devastated. Between 1939 and 1946, Japan's GDP fell by almost half, and Germany's by just over 50%. Even countries such as Britain, which had avoided invasion and had finished on the winning side, did nothing like as well as the US. The British economy grew by only 10% between 1939 and 1946. No wonder that in 1945 the US economy looked supreme.

The post-World War II period was to produce some unexpected outcomes too, however, but the inter-war years constitute a particularly important period in the world's economic history because it contains such instructive contrasts in performance. It showed only too clearly the appalling results achieved by gross deficiencies in demand, particularly in the US and Germany, which suffered worst of all major countries from the slump. The fact that these two economies were hit so severely reflected the particular unreality of the financial conditions under which they both laboured during the 1920s, albeit for different reasons. The experience of France and the other gold bloc countries is also an object lesson in the disadvantages of financial rectitude in inappropriate circumstances. Nothing was gained from the resulting long period of deflation, while the loss of output, rising unemployment and feeble investment record in these countries undermined their social cohesion, lowered their living standards and weakened their military capacity at a critical period.

The inter-war period also produced some remarkable success stories. These included the large increases in output achieved in the US during the 1920s, and in the mid-1930s once recovery from the slump began. The economic achievements of both Germany and Britain in the 1930s are also highly instructive. Above all, the record of the US during World War II is an outstanding example of what can be accomplished when appropriate economic policies are applied, directing demand and purchasing power to where they can achieve the biggest response. If, when challenged as it was then, the US economy could attain such impressive results, why should it not be able to do so now?

PROSPERITY POST-WORLD WAR II

The years immediately following the end of World War II saw a substantial slackening of demand on the US economy as government procurement for the war effort fell away. In 1944, government purchases represented just over half of all US GDP. By 1947, they were 16%. Although consumer expenditure rose in the immediate post-war years – by nearly 20% between 1944, the peak war-time year, and 1947, as did housing construction, which grew even faster – their impact was insufficient to fill the gap. As a result, US GDP fell over 17% over these three years and unemployment rose from 1.2% to 3.9% – still a low figure. Nevertheless, the level of output achieved by the US economy in 1944 was not to be regained until 1951.

While the US was in an extremely strong position after 1945, however, it did face a number of problems. First, its victorious position left it with heavy international commitments, which greatly increased US unilateral transfers abroad. The most substantial of these was expenditure on major military presences in Europe, the Far East and elsewhere, whose cost increased sharply with the advent of the Cold War, with an additional peak caused by the Korean War which broke out in June 1950. Very significant sums were also paid out in various aid programmes, not least Marshall Aid. This extraordinarily generous initiative, peaking at 3% of US GDP, greatly assisted the war-torn countries in Europe to recover.

Aid programmes also went some way towards helping to deal with the second problem with which the US had to contend – trade imbalances. Although there was a large potential demand for US exports which would have helped to boost the US economy, the rest of the world was extremely short of dollars with which to pay for them. Marshall Aid helped fill the gap, not only by assisting recovering economies directly with aid on soft terms, but also by providing them with payment in dollars, which in turn could be used for buying American goods and services. There was still, however, a substantial 'dollar gap' which could only be filled when the recovering economies had got themselves into a strong enough position to trade on equal terms with the US. One of the major US policy goals in the immediate post-war period was to see artificial barriers to trade and international payments removed, allowing the world to return to something like nineteenth-century conditions as opposed to those of the inter-war period. Although, as we have seen, American tariffs in the period up to World War I were very high, the US authorities now recognised that in the interests of the world as a whole, protectionism was not the way ahead. Freer trade and multilateral payments were not, however, achievable unless all the economies concerned could participate on manageable terms.

These considerations led to the third problem, which in the long term proved to be the most serious. The victorious Allied powers at the end of the war were anxious that the defeated nations should not indefinitely require succour and subsidy. They therefore ensured that their shattered economies should have some chance of speedy recovery by providing them with exceptionally competitive parities for their currencies. In particular, both the Deutsche Mark, following the currency reforms of 1948 and the DM devaluation of 1949, and the yen, after similar financial reforms carried out at the same time by the MacArthur administration in Japan, were given very competitive exchange rates.

These two erstwhile enemies, therefore, soon began to surge ahead with remarkably rapid recoveries. At the same time, other developed nations which had been over-run during the war also began to perform much better than they had done previously. Some of this performance was due to recovery from the war-time devastation, but other causes were almost certainly even more important. Nearly all the leaders of these countries exhibited a new determination to run their economies more successfully, learning from the mistakes of the inter-war period, fortified by the doctrines of Keynes and his associates. Old élites were swept away, discredited by war-time failure or collaboration, leaving the field open to fresh talent. Opportunities opened up by rapid growth in the post-war recovery period sucked able people into those parts of the economy where the scope was greatest, in manufacturing and exporting. As a result, strong and influential social and political groupings were established, determined to safeguard industrial and trading interests.

With these advantages, almost all the economies of Western Europe began to grow much more rapidly, and for a much longer sustained period, than they had ever done before. The whole of continental Western Europe achieved a growth rate in the 1950s and 1960s which averaged just under 5% per annum. Unemployment was almost non-existent, and inflation low. Japan did even better, with a compound growth rate in the 1950s and 1960s of 10% per annum. These rapid increases in output were attained because all the economies which secured them had highly competitive exports, triggering off cumulative expansions in investment and output. Significantly, the economy which did conspicuously worst of all those in the developed world during these two decades was Britain, with a compound increase in GDP of only 2.8% per annum. The reasons for this poor performance were that the British suffered from all the problems faced by the US, but in a more acute form. This left the British economy exceptionally and cumulatively more uncompetitive, which was, albeit to a somewhat lesser extent, the fundamental problem confronting the US. As a result, the US did not do much better than Britain, with a compound increase in output of 3.6% per annum which was well below the world growth rate for the period, which averaged a cumulative 4.8% per annum.

Again, it is important to remember that the impact of differential growth rates, which may seem small viewed a year at a time, has a huge compound effect over any reasonably long span of years. During the twenty years between 1950 and 1970, the ratio between the size of the British economy at the end of this period compared to the beginning was 1.7, for the US it was 2.0, for the Western European economies it was 2.6, and for Japan it was 6.8. Allowing for population growth, the disparities in the changes of living standards caused by these differences in growth rates were even more marked. By 1970, another massive change in the distribution of world economic power had taken place. Whereas up to 1945, however, the underlying trend had been to increase the relative strength of the US economy *vis à vis* the rest of the world, for all of the first quarter of a century after World War II the US was in relative decline, a trend which has continued ever since.

Why did the leaders of the US in the decades immediately after the end of World War II allow this trend to establish itself? There appear to be four main reasons, all of them to a greater or lesser extent still relevant to the condition of the US today.

First, taken year on year, it was not so obvious that a long-term tendency towards relatively poor US growth performance had established itself. There were fluctuations in the US growth rate, and those of other countries, which made the long-term trends more difficult to confirm than would have been the case if all economies had grown at a steady pace throughout the period. Furthermore, during the 1950s and 1960s, the US economy was not only vastly more productive per head of the population than that of other countries, it was also growing richer almost every year, even if more slowly than elsewhere. As a result, the leaders of the US did not, on the whole, worry greatly about the overall performance of their economy in terms of its aggregate output. Their concerns were directed more to matters such as containing inflation within reasonable bounds, and all the innumerable issues concerning taxation and expenditure which determined which national interests obtained larger or smaller slices of the federal cake.

There was some concern that the Soviet Union might be growing exceptionally fast, and could therefore pose a military as well as an economic threat to the hegemony of the US. The point in time, however, at which this might conceivably happen seemed some distance away, even in the 1960s, and the Soviet bloc was never a sufficient economic threat to galvanise the US government into taking radical action to head it off. There were also concerns about the outstanding performance of Japan, which obviously was growing very fast, but at least until well after 1970 the Japanese economy was still much smaller than that of the US, with a much lower GDP per head. Furthermore, the US had no difficulty in running a balance of payments surplus, often substantial, every year from 1945 to 1971, so the exceptional success of other countries in building up their economies did not appear to be a direct threat to American interests. On the contrary, increasing prosperity elsewhere, particularly in Europe and Japan, was welcomed as a development likely to lead to a lightening of US international burdens, providing other countries with opportunities to take a larger share in military expenditures and other international commitments such as aid programmes.

Second, the relatively slow growth rate of the US in the 1950s and 1960s was not a matter of major concern to those leading the country because it was not a significant electoral issue, or one which greatly stirred public opinion. The huge size of the US and its substantial self-sufficiency, combined with its prosperity and power, left most American citizens more than content with the country's international performance. The US has never had a period when either imports and exports involved as much as 15% of GDP, and in this sense the US economy is much more isolated from the rest of the world than most others. Furthermore, even as late as 1965, almost 80% of US imports were still raw materials and semi-manufactures, down from 84% in 1960, and 97% in 1950. Imports of this type were not a threat to US manufacturing, and the hollowing out of the US industrial base, which was to happen later, had hardly begun. By 1970, however, the proportion of finished goods in US imports had gone up from 21% to 39%, as US industries began to face mounting problems in competing with manufactured imports at the end of the 1960s. Until this process was well under way, however, there were still plenty of high-paying jobs in US industry. In 1950, 26% of the US civilian labour force was employed in manufacturing, and still 25% in 1970.

Third, the US's world leadership role put substantial constraints on its ability to make the kind of changes which would have ensured that the US economy grew faster. From the end of World War II onwards, the dollar provided the keystone to the world's financial system, established at Bretton Woods in 1944. The dollar was established as the world's reserve currency, and maintaining its stability was an essential component of the post-World War II financial system. This depended on exchange rates being kept within tight fixed bands, with parity changes only taking place relatively rarely when currency values were clearly fundamentally out of line. Devaluing the dollar to make US output more competitive, encouraging the type of export-led growth in the US which was fuelling the rapid output increases in Europe and Japan at the time, would have been severely disruptive in the 1950s and 1960s, as indeed it was when it eventually happened in 1971.

Nor was the US lead role only concerned with financial issues. To maintain its military hegemony, large outlays were required on procurement of materiel for the armed forces and payment for the current costs of maintaining millions of people under arms, with much of this expenditure being incurred in foreign currencies. During the decades after World War II, the US also undertook a high proportion of the world's aid expenditure, as well as paying a substantial proportion of the costs of a variety of international bodies. The result was that for every year from 1945 onwards, the US balance of payments had to bear a cost of billions of dollars in unilateral transfers overseas. Nevertheless, despite the relatively slow growth in US exports during the 1950s and 1960s – 6.2% cumulatively, compared to 8.4% on average for the major European economies, and 15.4% for Japan – the US did not have a major problem with its foreign payments. This was partly because imports were so low, and partly because of a substantial and sustained surplus on investment income from abroad during this period. The result was that the drain on resources from leadership commitments, though significant, was never large enough to require a major shift in economic policy to enable them to continue to be supported.

Fourth, during most of the 1950s and 1960s, the US was a largely conservative and contented country. At least until the advent of serious opposition to the Vietnam War, and the student campus troubles and the battles over desegregation which occurred at about the same time, American society was generally at ease with itself. The rhetoric of the Kennedy era did not do a great deal to disturb the status quo, and even the more disruptive developments of the late 1960s, during the Johnson presidency, affected only a minority of the population. With stability and satisfaction with existing conditions, all societies tend to become more complacent and less keen on radical change. The power and influence of those in established positions tends to grow over time. The cumulative effect of successive good years strengthens conservative financial interests. Those who have done well are seldom interested in seeing changes made involving upheavals which might allow others, until then less fortunate, to catch up in wealth and status. The strong conservative bias in American society during the post-World War II period was perhaps the most important reason of all why no vigorous action was taken to change the trajectory of US economic policy for a quarter of a century after 1945. Events were occurring, however, which were soon to overturn the contentment of the 1950s and 1960s. As times became more turbulent and troubled; what seemed in retrospect to have been for most American people a golden age slipped into history.

GATHERING CLOUDS

During the late 1960s, the prospects for the American economy began to darken rapidly. There was no one single cause. A variety of different developments occurred, all of which combined to topple the dollar from the pre-eminent position it had enjoyed for the previous quarter of a century, and to produce a period of much greater instability, slower growth, higher unemployment and greater inflation than had prevailed for the previous decades.

A major cause of these upsets was the combination during the late 1960s of escalating expenditure on the Vietnam War with the rapidly rising costs of implementing the Great Society programme, which the Democrat President, Lyndon Johnson, had close to his heart. Successive reports from the military in charge in Vietnam, particularly General Westmoreland, each suggesting that a further comparatively modest increase in expenditure would turn the outcome of the war decisively in the US's favour, had turned out to be false. As a result, the cost of the war had steadily mounted. Total defence expenditure rose from $50bn in 1964 to $79m in 1968, an increase as a proportion of GDP from an already high 7.8% to 8.9%. The Great Society programme was both a cherished big government Democrat programme in its own right, and a response to the civil rights campaigns of the 1960s, which in turn had drawn in other disadvantaged groups. Its cost, however, was also high. Expenditure on income support, social security, welfare, veterans' benefits and housing and community services, which had been $40bn in 1964, had risen by 1968 to $66bn, an increase from 6.2% of GDP to 7.5%. The combined cost of both the war and increased social expenditure therefore involved an increase in expenditure of 2.6% of GDP in three years.

A shift of this magnitude might not have been a problem if taxation had been raised to pay for it, but this did not happen. Federal receipts as a proportion of GDP rose between 1964 and 1968 by only 0.4%, from 19.4% to 19.8%. The result was highly reflationary as government expenditure rose rapidly, financed largely by borrowing from the banking system, generating a fiscal deficit which peaked at $12.7bn in 1967. This occurred at a time when the US economy was already booming. Between 1960 and 1968, the cumulative growth rate was 4.6%, a much better figure than had been achieved previously. Unemployment fell below 4% but investment lagged. Despite the more rapid growth in GDP, gross private fixed investment as a proportion of US GDP never rose during the 1960s to much more than 15%, a very low figure by international standards. By the end of the 1960s, the average age of US plant was eighteen years, compared to twelve in West Germany and ten in Japan. The overall result was that the economy became progressively more over-heated and its output less internationally competitive. Consumer price inflation, which had averaged 1.3% per annum between 1960 and 1965, reached 5.8% in 1970. The balance of trade on goods and services, which had been in surplus for almost every year since 1945, moved into deficit in 1968. Imports of motor vehicles and parts alone rose from $0.9bn in 1965 to $5.9bn in 1970, a real increase of nearly 450%, while over the same five years, imports of consumer goods, excluding vehicles, rose from $3.3bn to $7.4bn, almost doubling in real terms.

When President Nixon took over the White House in early 1969, he therefore faced an increasingly difficult economic situation. The Vietnam War was wound down and government expenditure was cut, but inflation persisted despite rising unemployment. The wage and price control programme, introduced by the new President, helped to bring the rate of increase in the consumer price index down from 5.8% in 1970 to 3.3% in 1972, but at the cost of increasing unemployment to 5.6% by 1972, up from 3.5% in 1969.

Meanwhile, on the external front, the situation was also deteriorating. Having moved back into surplus in 1970, the balance of trade showed a $3bn deficit in 1971, to be followed by $8bn in 1972. It became clear to everyone that the dollar was seriously over-valued. The result was a conference, held in 1971 at the Smithsonian Institution in Washington DC, at which the US announced that the link between the dollar and gold, which had underpinned the Bretton Woods system, could no longer be kept in place. The dollar was then devalued, and the Bretton Woods fixed exchange régime broke up. With the dollar no longer available as an anchor reserve currency, all the major currencies in the world began to float against each other.

By 1972, the dollar had fallen 16% against the yen, 13% against the Deutsche Mark, 4% against the pound sterling and around 10% against most other currencies. As a result, by 1973 the US balance of trade showed signs of recovery. The absence of exchange rate constraints for the first time for decades, however, left policy makers throughout the world without familiar landmarks to guide them. Shorn of accustomed restraints, most countries began to reflate simultaneously. Credit controls were relaxed, and the money supply greatly increased, partly fuelled by an increasing pool of Euro-dollars, themselves the product of the US deficit. World output soared, growing 6.7% in 1973 alone. The impact on commodity markets was dramatic. After years of falling prices caused by excess capacity, demand suddenly exceeded supply. The prices of many raw materials doubled or trebled. Then, in 1973, the Yom Kippur War broke out between Israel and the surrounding Arab countries. It ended with a resounding victory for the Israelis, but at the cost of the West seriously alienating the Arab States, many of them major suppliers of oil to the Western nations, particularly the US, which had supported Israel during the conflict. Shortly afterwards, OPEC, the oil producers' cartel, raised the price of oil from around $2.50 to $10 per barrel.

The consequences of all these events for the developed world were disastrous. The increased cost of oil, although it only represented about 2% of the West's GDP, presented oil importers with a new and highly unwelcome blow to their balance of payments. Almost all tried to shift the incidence elsewhere by a process of competitive deflation. At the same time, the quadrupled price of oil, accompanied by the doubling and trebling of the cost of other commodity imports, greatly increased inflationary pressures. Growth rates tumbled, and unemployment rose all over the world as inflation moved to unprecedented levels. Mirroring similar developments in other advanced countries, the US economy, far from growing, shrank by 1% in both 1974 and 1975. Unemployment rose to 8.5% in 1975, while the year-on-year increase in the consumer price level peaked at nearly 11% in 1974.

The severe economic difficulties and disruption facing the world in the mid-1970s did not, however, affect only rates of inflation, growth and unemployment. They also had a profound effect on the intellectual climate. The consensus around the ideas of Keynes and his associates, which appeared to have guided world economic policy so successfully in the 1950s and 1960s, was shattered. Demand management did not appear to provide any satisfactory solutions to the problems faced by those confronted with the severely unstable conditions with which they now had to cope. Into the vacuum thus created moved an old economic doctrine in a new guise to take the place of discredited Keynesianism. Monetarism arrived on the scene as the intellectual underpinning of economic policy formation in a world which had lost fixed exchange rates and the discipline they provided as the anchors for decision taking.

3   The Monetarist Era

'The experience of being disastrously wrong is salutary; no economist should be denied it, and not many are.'

John Kenneth Galbraith

It is no coincidence that the prevalence of monetarism is highly correlated with failure of economic performance. Those most convinced by monetarist doctrines are to be found at the helm of the slowest growing economies. There are interlocking reasons why this is so. It is partly that monetarist prescriptions lead to slow growth, and partly that the cultural attitudes which breed monetarist opinions flourish especially strongly in slow-growing economies. Monetarism is the intellectual component of the vicious spiral of import-led stagnation from which poorly performing economies suffer.

This is a problem which afflicts not only the long-standing slow-growing economies such as the United States and Britain, although monetarist doctrines have a particularly strong hold in both. The same ideas have also managed to get their grip on the whole of the European Union, leading to the determination, exemplified in the provisions of the 1991 Maastricht Treaty, to put monetary stability before prosperity. The loss of confidence in Keynesian policies after the rising inflation and international dislocation of the early 1970s led to policy changes in a monetarist direction, particularly in Germany and France. These have changed the EU bloc from being one of the world's fastest growing regions into an area of exceptionally slow increase in output, accompanied by painfully high levels of unemployment. Countries which give monetarist prescriptions less priority, on the other hand, both in Europe and elsewhere, continue to grow apace. Norway, a prime example, outside the European Union, achieved the highest rate of GDP per head within the OECD between 1973 and 1992, just ahead of Japan, increasing the population's living standards by 80%. The Norwegians succeeded in combining this achievement with one of the better OECD records on inflation, especially recently, and an unemployment rate now barely one third of the EU average. Over the same period Britain and the US, both countries strongly influenced by monetarist ideas, achieved GDP per head increases of only 36% and 34% respectively. The EU as a whole achieved 48%.

Monetarist prescriptions, stripped of their theorising and rhetoric, are familiar to anyone who has studied economic history. Their hallmarks are relatively tight money, high interest and exchange rates. These conditions slow down productive enterprise, and make it harder to sell abroad and easier to import. They discriminate against manufacturing investment and drain the talent out of industry. Monetarism, and the devotion to balanced budgets and financial conservatism which was its predecessor, have never been far below the surface in the US, especially during the second half of the twentieth century. In particular, post-1973, and especially in the 1980s, monetarism created macro-economic conditions in the US which were almost wholly responsible for the low growth, and hence low productivity increases of the subsequent quarter of a century. It is also directly accountable for the huge widening of incomes there has been over the last twenty-five years, with which the attenuation of US manufacturing capacity, itself a direct result of monetarist policies, is heavily bound up.

We will turn to monetarist theory in the next section. As a precursor, it is worth looking again at how a combination of self-interest and social attitudes can produce an environment where monetarist ideas can take strong hold even if they are weak in intellectual coherence and undermined by prescriptive inadequacies. Why should mature, stable, slow-growing economies be particularly prone to producing a climate of opinion where such ideas can flourish?

The answer is that the implications of monetarist policies are far from unattractive to large sections of the population, especially in slow-growing economies where lenders tend to be in a strong position and borrowers in a weak one. Those who have achieved success in finance rather than manufacturing tend to move into positions of influence and political power. As they do so, the monetarist doctrines which appeal to people with financial backgrounds become increasingly predominant. The attitudes of those whose business is lending money, who have an obvious interest in high interest rates and scarcity of the commodity they control, become politically significant; not least because their opinions have a self-fulfilling quality. If there is great fear that losing their confidence will lead to a run on the currency, this places those in a position to keep the parity up by their decisions in a very powerful position. Those whose incomes depend on high interest rates – pensioners and many others – are also naturally inclined to support a policy which seems so obviously in their favour. Bankers, financiers and wealth holders are the immediate beneficiaries of monetarist policies, buttressed by those who can see no further ahead than obtaining the immediate benefits from low-cost imports and cheap holidays abroad. The losers are those engaged in manufacturing and selling internationally tradable goods and services.

When the economy grows slowly, the power and influence of finance increases against that of industry. This is partly a result of the process of accumulation of capital wealth, much of which tends to be invested abroad rather than at home because slow growth in the domestic economy creates better opportunities overseas. This was the story of Britain in the nineteenth century and the United States for a long period post-World War II, while Japan has now moved into a similar role. This process produces profound effects on social attitudes and political power, particularly if these conditions prevail for a long period of time, as they have in the US.

If the economy is run with relatively tight money, high interest rates and a high exchange rate, the inevitable consequence is to produce adverse trading conditions for manufacturing industries exposed to international competition. Adequate returns on investment become much harder to achieve. It becomes increasingly difficult to pay the going wage or salary rates for the calibre of employees required. Of course there will always be exceptionally efficient companies, or even industries, which buck the trend, but they are not critically important. It is the average which counts, and here the results are impossible to dismiss. The profitability of large sections of US manufacturing became insufficient for it to be worth while for them to continue in business. This is why the proportion of US GDP derived from manufacturing has fallen so precipitately over the last three decades. By 1983, half of all US imports were manufactures, compared to just over 20% only twenty years previously. Between 1960 and 1982, Japanese car production rose from 0.5m to 11m per annum, while US output fell from 6.7m to 5.0m. Over the same period, Japanese crude steel output increased from 22m to 111m tons per annum, while US output dropped from 90m to 68m. The same trends affected swathes of other industries. Meanwhile in countries which gave their industrial base a better deal, fortunes were made in manufacturing, and the rest of the economy struggled to keep up.

The most able graduates from US universities nowadays go decreasingly into industry. The easiest money and most glittering careers beckon in the professions, on Wall Street and in the media. The academic world, politics, government service increasingly look more attractive than industry, and for those bent on a career in mainstream business, distribution or retailing offer more security and prospects in most cases than manufacturing. If the most able people choose not to go into industry, but instead become lawyers or bankers or television personalities, the educational system responds accordingly. The subjects of most use to those engaged in making and selling are downgraded in importance compared to those required for other careers. Science subjects fall in status compared to the arts. Commercial studies come to be regarded as second-rate options compared to professional qualifications. Practical subjects, such as engineering, become perceived as less glamorous and attractive – and potentially less lucrative – than the humanities. There was a precipitate fall in freshman enrolments in business studies and engineering from the mid-1980s to the early 1990s, coinciding with the bloodletting of manufacturing which took place at the time. Those planning to pursue business studies fell from 27% to 16% of the total, while the proportion choosing engineering fell from 11% to 8%. At the same time, the share aiming for professional qualifications rose from 13% to 20%. These figures provide clear evidence as to how the educational system itself then becomes part of the cultural conditioning process, as peer pressure, career prospects and the priority and prestige accorded to different subjects, determine where the nation's talent directs its energies.

A significant consequence of the social bias which runs through the whole of this process is that it determines the background of people most likely to reach the peak of their careers running major companies, especially in manufacturing. An interesting contrast between countries such as the US, which has grown slowly, and those economies which have grown fastest, is that quite different people tend to become chief executive officers (CEOs). In slow-growing economies, chief executives are often professional people such as lawyers and accountants. Where the economy is growing fast, they tend to be engineers and salesmen. No doubt both cause and effect are operating here. If the most able people in the commercial field are in the professions, they will finish up at the top of big companies where their particular talents will be especially in demand in dealing with powerful financial interests. In fast-growing economies, where financial interests are often less immediately pressing and the most able people are not in the professions, engineers and salesmen tend to hold the top positions. It is hardly surprising that companies which are run by accountants and lawyers are particularly concerned with financial results, while those run by salesmen and engineers are more orientated to markets and products.

Nor is the low status of industry only a financial or social matter. It also has a large impact on the political weight of manufacturing interests as against those of other parts of the economy. Exercising political power requires talent, takes time and costs money. All are in increasingly short supply in American industry and the results are clear to see. Few members of Congress have any significant hands-on manufacturing experience. The role models to whom the younger generation looks are nowadays not those with manufacturing industry as their goal. Law practice and investment banking look much better bets. In these circumstances it is small wonder that economic ideas which promote finance over manufacturing tend to find favour. It does not follow, however, that these ideas are well founded. Still less is it true that they are in the best long-term interests of the economy as a whole, or even of those in the financial community itself. In the end, those concerned with finance depend as much as everyone else on the performance of the underlying economy, and in particular on its capacity to hold its own in world markets.

MONETARIST THEORY AND PRACTICE

The appeal of hard money has a long history. Those with established wealth have always been keen that it should earn a high return. High rates of interest and low rates of inflation have an obvious appeal to them, a view of the world almost invariably shared by those with a banking background. A sense of prudence militates against deficit financing and easy money. Making life easy for manufacturers and exporters by having low interest and exchange rates and plentiful credit somehow seems a less obvious way to encourage their operations than submitting them to the rigours and discipline of a much less easy economic environment.

Nor, as we have seen, is it just the well-off who are inclined to favour the financial environment which monetarist policies generate. Many poorer people, particularly pensioners on fixed incomes, favour high interest rates and therefore the relative scarcity of money which is necessary to ensure that they can prevail. A high exchange rate, which runs with high interest rates and a restrictive monetary policy, provides the benefit of lowering the cost of imports and making travel abroad cheaper, reinforcing the widely held view that people should be proud of their currency if it is perceived to be 'strong' rather than favouring a low, but competitive, international value.

Predilections of this sort were therefore widely prevalent before monetarist orthodoxies became fashionable. The change in intellectual view which occurred was the result of a number of important works, not least those of Professor Hayek and other Chicago associates, who had always had serious reservations about the Keynesian revolution. Monetarist ideas, in their standard form, would not have become accepted as widely as they were, however, without the theoretical and statistical underpinning provided by Milton Friedman and his associate, Anna Jacobson Schwartz, in their seminal book, *A Monetary History of the United States, 1867–1960*, published in 1963. In this book, they made three important claims which had a major impact on economic thinking all over the world. First, they said that there was a clear association between the total amount of money in circulation and changes in money incomes and prices, but not economic activity until approximately two years later. Changes in the money supply therefore affected the price level, but not, except perhaps for a short period of time, the level of output in the real economy. Second, these relationships had proved to be stable over a long period. Third, changes, and particularly increases in the money supply, had generally occurred as a result of events which were independent of the needs of the economy. In consequence they added to inflation without raising the level of economic activity.

The attractive simplicity of these propositions is easily recognised. The essence of the monetarist case is that increases in prices and wages can be held in check by nothing more complicated than the apparently simple process of controlling the amount of money in circulation. Ideally, a condition of zero inflation is achieved when the increase in the money supply equals the rise in output in the economy. Since both wage and price increases can occur only if extra money to finance them is made available, rises in either wages or prices cannot occur unless more money is provided. Thus, as long as the government is seen to be giving sufficient priority to controlling the money supply, everyone will realise that it is in his or her interest to exercise restraint, reducing the rate of inflation to whatever level is deemed acceptable.

These ideas have been summarised by an eminent economist, Professor Sayers, in the following terms:

> First, past rates of growth in the stock of money are major determinants of the growth of Gross National Product in terms of current prices. It follows from this that fiscal policies do not significantly affect GNP in money terms, though they may alter its composition and also affect interest rates. The overall impact on GNP in money terms of monetary and financial policies is for practical purposes summed up in the movements of a single variable, the stock of money. Consequently, monetary policy should be exclusively guided by this variable, without regard to interest rates, credit flows, free reserves or other indicators.
>
> Second, nominal interest rates are geared to inflationary expectations and thus, with a time lag, to actual inflation. Although the immediate market impact of expansionary monetary policy may be to lower interest rates, it is fairly soon reversed when premiums for the resulting inflation are added to interest rates.
>
> Third, the central bank can, and should, make the money stock grow at a steady rate equal to the rate of growth of potential GNP plus a target rate for inflation.
>
> Fourth, there is no enduring trade-off between unemployment and inflation. There is, rather, a unique rate of unemployment for each economy which allows for structural change and job search, but which cannot be departed from in the long term. Government policy will produce ever-accelerating inflation if it persistently seeks a lower than natural rate of unemployment. If it seeks a higher rate, there will be an ever accelerating deflation. The natural rate of unemployment cannot be identified except

through practical experience. It is the rate which will emerge if the proper steady growth policy is pursued.

These prescriptions have attracted much support to the monetarist banner, although it has always been clear that the monetarist case had severe deficiencies. To start with, the theory begged the fundamental question as to the appropriate way to measure the money stock when so many different ways of determining it were available. It was, in any event, well known that the ratio between the stock of money, however defined, and the volume of transactions could vary widely, as the so-called 'velocity of circulation' altered. More recently, in addition, there has been widespread criticism of the methodology used by Friedman and Schwartz in their analysis of the relationship between money and prices in the US, indicating that the statistical basis from which their conclusions were drawn was unsound.

As with so much else in economics, there is a major feedback problem with much of the monetarist position, making it difficult to distinguish between cause and effect. It may be true that over a long period the total amount of money in circulation bears a close relationship to the total value of the economy's output. It does not follow, however, that the money supply determines the money value of the GNP, and hence the rate of inflation. It may well be, instead, that the total amount of money in circulation is a function of the need for sufficient finance to accommodate transactions. If this is so, then an increase in the money supply may well accompany a rise in inflation caused by some other event, simply to provide this accommodation. It need not necessarily be the cause of rising prices at all.

Common sense tells us that changes in the money supply are only one of a number of relevant factors determining rises or falls in inflation. Monetarists, however, reject this proposition, alleging that all alterations in the rate of price increases are caused by changes in the money supply some two years previously. They also claim that the future course of inflation can be guided within narrow limits by controlling the money stock. Empirical evidence demonstrates that this contention is far too precise, and greatly overstates the predictive accuracy of monetarist theories.

For this amount of fine tuning to be possible, an unequivocal definition of money is required. It is one thing to recognise a situation where clearly far too much money, or, more accurately, too much credit is being created. Monetarists are right in saying that if credit is so cheap and so readily available that it is easy to speculate on asset inflation, or the economy is getting overheated by excess demand financed by credit creation, then the money supply is too large. This is a broad quantitative judgement. It is quite another matter to state that small alterations in the money supply generate correspondingly exact changes in the rate of inflation. Yet this is the claim which monetarists put forward.

This claim is implausible for a number of reasons. One is the difficulty in defining accurately what is money and what is not. Notes and coins are clearly 'money', but where should the line be drawn thereafter? What kinds of bank facilities and money market instruments should also be included or excluded? Many different measures are available in every country, depending on what is put in and what is left out. None of them has been found anywhere to have had a strikingly close correlation with subsequent changes in the rate of inflation. Often, different measures of the money supply move in different directions. This is very damaging evidence against propositions which are supposed to be precise in their formulation and impact.

Another major problem for monetarists, referred to above, is that there can be no constant ratio between the amount of money in circulation, however defined, and the aggregate value of transactions, because the rate at which money circulates can, and does, vary widely over time. The 'velocity of circulation', which is the ratio between the GDP and the money supply, is far from constant. As can be seen from Table 7.1 on page 154, in the US the M3 velocity fell 17% between 1970 and 1986, but by 1996 it had risen 22% compared to ten years earlier. It has been exceptionally volatile in Britain, where it rose by 7% between 1964 and 1970, and by a further 28% between 1970 and 1974, only to fall by 26% between 1974 and 1979. Since then it has risen by 82%. Other countries, such as the Netherlands and Greece, have also had large changes in the velocity of circulation, particularly during the 1970s.

Some of these movements were caused by changes in monetary policy, but a substantial proportion, especially recently, have had nothing to do with alterations in government policy. They have been the results of radical changes to the financial environment, caused by the effects of deregulation on credit creation, and the growth of new financial instruments, such as derivatives. Variations like this make it impossible to believe in the rigid relationship that monetarism requires. In fact, the statistical record everywhere on the money supply and inflation shows what one would expect if there was very little causation at all at work. Except in extreme circumstances of gross over-creation of money and credit, changes in the money supply have had little or no impact on the rate of inflation. The need to provide enough money to finance all the transactions taking place has, over the long term, proved to be much more important a determinant of the money supply than attempts to restrict it to control inflation, although some countries have certainly had tighter monetary policies than others. In the short term, there is no systematic evidence that changes in the money supply affect subsequent inflation rates with any precision at all.

It is not surprising, therefore, that the predictions of monetarists about future levels of inflation, based on trends in the money supply, have turned out to be no better, and often worse, than those of other people who have used more eclectic, common-sense methods. Monetarists have not kept their predictions, however, solely to the future rate of inflation. There are three other areas of economic policy, as we can see from Professor Sayers' synopsis of their views, where their ideas have had a decisive effect on practical policy over the last quarter of a century: unemployment, interest rates and exchange rates.

The monetarist view of unemployment is that there is a 'natural' rate which cannot be avoided, set essentially by supply-side rigidities. Any attempt to reduce unemployment below this level by reflation will necessarily increase wage rates and then the price level. This will leave those in employment no better off than they were before, while the increased demand, having been absorbed by high prices, will result in the same number of people being employed as previously. Increasing demand only pushes up the rate of inflation; it will not raise either output or the number of people in work.

At some point, as pressure on the available labour force increases and the number of those unemployed falls, there is no doubt that a bidding-up process will take place and wages and salaries will rise. This is an altogether different matter, however, from postulating that unemployment levels like those seen in the US during the 1980s, or the widespread prevalence of low-skilled, low-productivity labour now evident in the US, are required to keep inflation at bay. Nor is it plausible that supply-side rigidities are the major constraint on reducing unemployment. There is no evidence that these rigidities are significantly greater than they were in the 1950s and 1960s, and on balance they are almost certainly less. If, during the whole of these two decades, it was possible to combine reasonably high rates of economic growth with low levels of either unemployment or underemployment in the US, while inflation remained stable at an acceptable level, why should we believe that it is impossible now for these conditions to prevail again? One of the unfortunate triumphs of monetarism has been to condition people to tolerate much higher levels of unemployment or low-productivity work than would otherwise have been considered economically desirable or politically acceptable.

Monetarism has also had a considerable influence on interest rates. The tight control of the money supply which monetarists advocate can only be achieved if interest rates are used to balance a relatively low supply of money against the demand for credit which has to be choked off by raising the price of money. As we can see from Professor Sayers, however, this requirement is made to seem less harsh by suggesting that a positive rate of interest will always be required to enable lenders to continue providing money to borrowers. It is alleged that any attempt to lower interest rates to encourage expansion will fail as lenders withdraw from the market until the premium they require above the inflation rate reappears.

Yet again, we have a proposition much more strongly based on assertion than on evidence. For years on end, in many countries including the US, real interest rates paid to savers have been negative, sometimes even before tax. Lenders, of course, have never regarded negative interest rates as fair, and frequently complain bitterly when they occur. There is, however, little that they can do about them. Their ability to withdraw from the market is generally limited. Shortages of money can in any event always be overcome by the authorities creating more money to replace any which has been withdrawn. It is undoubtedly the case, however, that high positive rates of interest are a discouragement to investment, partly directly but mostly because of their influence on driving up the exchange rate.

This is particularly paradoxical in relation to the third major impact of monetarist ideas on practical issues, which has been on exchange rate policy. It is argued that no policy for improving an economy's competitiveness by devaluation will work, because the inflationary effects of a depreciation will automatically raise the domestic price level back to where it was in international terms. This will leave the devaluing country with no more competitiveness than it had before, but with a real extra inflationary problem with which it will have to contend.

This proposition is one which is easy to test against historical experience. There have been large numbers of substantial exchange rate changes over the last few decades, providing plenty of empirical data against which to assess the validity of this monetarist assertion. The evidence is overwhelmingly against it. As we shall see, there are plenty of examples to be found of devaluations producing no sign at all of automatically leading to excess inflation, wiping out all the competitive advantage initially gained. On the contrary, there is ample evidence to indicate that exactly the opposite conclusion should be drawn from experience both in the US and elsewhere. Devaluing economies tend to perform progressively better, as their manufacturing sectors expand and the internationally tradable goods and services which they produce become cumulatively more competitive.

Countries which have gained an initial price advantage therefore tend to forge ahead with increasingly competitive import-saving and exporting sectors. Rapidly growing efficiency in the sectors of their economies involved in international trading gains them higher shares in world trade, providing them with platforms for further expansion. High productivity growth generates conditions which may even allow them, with good management, to experience less domestic inflation than their more sluggish competitors. In practice, monetarist policies have had pronounced effects on the exchange rates of the countries where they have been most effectively imposed, but invariably their impact has been to push the exchange rates up. The economies concerned then suffer the worst of all worlds – a mixture of sluggish growth, low increases in output to absorb wage and salary increases, and sometimes higher price inflation than their more favoured competitors.

Monetarist theories start by appearing simple and straightforward, but end by being long on complication and assertion and short on predictive and practical prescriptive qualities. They pander to the prejudice of those who would like to believe their conclusions. They lack convincing explanations about the transmission mechanisms between what they claim are the causes of economic events, and the effects which they declare will necessarily follow. Where they can be tested against empirical results, the predictions their theories produce generally fail to achieve levels of accuracy which make them worth while.

Monetarist theories have nevertheless reinforced everywhere all the prejudices widely held in favour of the cautious financial conservatism which monetarism so accurately reflects. In practice, monetarist policies are almost indistinguishable from old-fashioned deflation. By allowing themselves to be persuaded by these misguided doctrines, it becomes all too easy for those responsible for running the nation's affairs to acquiesce in accepting levels of low growth and high unemployment which they would never have tolerated if they had realised how unnecessary they were.

The result has been that policies which should have been rejected have continued to be accepted, although they failed to work. Because expectations have been lowered, the deflationary consequences of high interest rates, restrictive monetary policies and over-valued exchange rates, have not caused the outcry that might have been expected and which they deserved. The American people, except perhaps those in the top income-earning brackets who have tended to benefit substantially from monetarist policies at everyone else's expense, have been lulled into accepting levels of economic performance far below those routinely attained elsewhere in the world. If higher levels of achievement are going to be reached, a much less complacent attitude is going to be required, to ensure that the changes which are needed are put in place.

THE YEARS WHEN MONETARISM REIGNED

The later years of the 1970s saw a return to substantial growth rates after 1974 and 1975, which were both years of contraction. The US economy bounced back, growing at around 5% per annum in 1976, 1977 and 1978, as the real value of the dollar fell a further 10% between 1974 and 1978, stimulating an impressive export performance. Bringing inflation down, however, proved stubbornly difficult, adding to the appeal of monetarist disciplines. The consumer price index, having dropped to 6.5% per annum in 1977, rose to 11.3% in 1979 and 13.5% in 1980, mainly because of the massive international increase in the price of oil which occurred in 1979. By 1979, unemployment had fallen to 5.8%, although it subsequently started to rise again as the US economy moved into another year of falling output in 1980.

Compared to many other countries, nevertheless, the US weathered the 1970s reasonably well. Years of small reductions in output in 1970, 1974 and 1975 were offset by substantial growth in other years, producing an erratic but, nevertheless, in the circumstances of the time, tolerably satisfactory outcome. Real GDP growth averaged 3.2% per annum for the decade, a little below the 3.8% average for all the developed countries in the OECD. US GDP per capita, however, grew by a more modest compound 2.1% per annum. An encouraging sign was that non-residential gross investment rose faster than GDP, at 5.6% per annum on average, albeit from a low comparative level. The cumulative increase in consumer prices, at 6.6% per annum, was well below the OECD average of 9.1%. The reduction in the dollar's post-Smithsonian parity, augmented by the US's better than average performance on inflation, gave those parts of the US exposed to international trade an increasing edge. As a result, exports of goods and services, net of inflation, rose cumulatively by 7.3% per annum compared to total imports which only increased at a compound rate of 4.9%.

Unfortunately, however, this relatively good performance was heavily undermined by adverse movements in relative costs. In particular, during the 1970s the price of oil rose hugely, with the major price increase in 1979 following the earlier one in 1973. By 1980, the US was spending $79bn a year on oil imports, compared with only $3bn in 1970. As a result the balance of trade in goods and services began an alarming deterioration. A surplus had been achieved in 1975, caused mainly by a much more substantial increase in the value of manufactured exports compared to imports – no doubt the consequence of the dollar devaluation earlier in the decade. In the late 1970s, however, the further rapid increases in the value of oil imports began to swamp the surplus earned on manufactures. From 1976 onwards, the US has had a trade deficit every single year.

To maintain a high rate of growth in the 1980s, the US therefore urgently needed a considerably more competitive exchange rate. By increasing the country's exports of manufactured goods, it would have been possible to offset the heavy burden across the exchanges occasioned by the extra cost of oil imports. Unfortunately, exactly the opposite policy was put into operation and, as a result, the US's growth in GDP during the 1980s fell back to a cumulative 2.8% per annum. Because the population was growing fast, GDP per head grew at only 1.8% per annum. It was from then onwards, and particularly during the early years of the 1980s, that the major problems from which the US still suffers began to materialise in earnest. The years of the Reagan and Bush presidencies did very serious damage to the US economy, leaving a legacy which the Clinton administration has failed, in a number of key fundamental respects, to reverse. This is why US economic policy is still so urgently in need of reform.

By any standards, the performance achieved by the US economy from 1980 onwards was far below what it could have been. Why did this happen? Fundamentally, the explanation is that the major defect perceived by most commentators on the record of the US economy in the 1970s reflecting the preoccupations of those increasingly attracted by monetarist ideas, was the relatively high rate of price increases during this decade. The real problem, however, was elsewhere. It was in the weakening of the US trade position, in which monetarists were much less interested. Plentiful evidence from other developed countries suggests that inflation would have subsided in the US during the 1980s without the anti-inflationary monetarist policies pursued by the Reagan administration, which did so much damage to the economy's ability to hold its own in trading terms, and hence to its ability to grow as fast as it could have done.

It is not, of course, surprising that the Republicans, with their strong links to old money and the financial community, should have taken to monetarist doctrines with more enthusiasm than the Democrats. It was clear from the beginning that they would benefit the rich at the expense of everyone else, as indeed they did. Faith in monetarism, which took hold of both the academic and the wider worlds, therefore provided the intellectual underpinning for the Reagan economic programme. There is no question, however, but that the policies which were then implemented were directly responsible for the massive deterioration in the American economic condition from 1980 onwards.

It is true that there was still a significant inflationary problem at the end of the 1970s. The need to get inflation down was widely perceived to be a prime requirement. Controlling rises in the price level, above all, was the policy area in which the claims of the monetarists were most forcefully expressed, and where they appeared to many people to be most convincing. When the Reagan presidency got into its stride, therefore, bringing down inflation, using monetarist remedies, was treated as a major policy objective.

Monetary policy had already tightened sharply at the end of the 1970s, precipitating the 1980 fall in GDP which contributed to the Republican presidential victory that year.

With Reagan elected as President, a further tightening took place in 1981 and 1982, particularly of M1 and M2, though M3 proved harder to contain – itself a sorry commentary on the precision which monetary control is supposed to exemplify. Interests rates were raised sharply. The federal funds rate, which had fallen to just over 5% during the boom years of the late 1970s, reached over 16% in 1981. The inevitable result was that the dollar soared on the foreign exchanges. With 1973 equalling 100 as the base, and thus already allowing for the 10% post-Smithsonian devaluation, the trade-weighted value of the US dollar had fallen to 83 by 1979. This trend was then dramatically reversed. By 1982 the index had reached 112, and by 1985 it was 132. In six years, the dollar had sustained a real appreciation of almost 60%. Furthermore, this increase took place at a time when, by all rational calculations, the dollar really needed to fall rather than rise, to keep US exports sufficiently competitive to support all the economy's import requirements in the 1980s, combined with maintaining the labour force fully employed and at full stretch. The results were catastrophic.

What is more, while recognising that prices were rising too fast in 1980, it is hard to see, even by monetarist standards, that the policies pursued to remedy this condition made sense. There was no evidence that lax monetary policies had made any contribution to the immediate inflationary problems of the early 1980s. Much of the rise in the consumer price level at the end of the 1970s was caused by the second OPEC oil price increase, a factor over which monetary remedies had no influence at all. The rate of increase in consumer prices did come down, from 13.3% per annum in 1979 and 12.5% in 1980, to 3.8% in 1983, and a low of 1.1% in 1986, before starting to rise again to an average of around 4% per annum. Similar results, however, were achieved by almost all other advanced countries at the same time, but without the bloodletting to which the US economy was subjected. As can easily be seen from the world's economic history over the last fifty years, given reasonably competent management the world's advanced economies have exhibited a remarkable capacity to absorb inflationary shocks. This objective is most easily and painlessly achieved by using expanding output and productivity increases to soak up excessive price rises. The very different policy pursued in the US, mirroring a similar and equally disastrous experiment with extreme monetarism that began in Britain a little earlier, had the same results as those achieved in Thatcher's Britain. Inflation fell, as it almost certainly would have done anyway, but the method used for getting it down, both in the US and Britain, hugely damaged the real economy and its capacity to provide all, or almost all, its citizens with well-paid and secure jobs.

Entirely predictably, the proportion of US GDP derived from manufacturing fell heavily. Between 1980 and 1993, it dropped from 23.4% of GDP to 17%, a relative reduction of more than a quarter. The number of people employed in industrial occupations also fell slightly in absolute numbers, but much more steeply as a proportion of the total labour force. Of those in employment, the proportion working in manufacturing dropped from 22% to barely 16%. The problem was then the familiar one, which is that productivity increases are much more difficult to secure across the board in the service sector of the economy than they are in manufacturing. The decline in industrial output as a proportion of GDP thus contributed directly and heavily to the low growth in overall productivity which was such a key negative characteristic of this period in American history.

Reflecting the decline in manufacturing and the incidence of the policies pursued by the Reagan and Bush administrations on the growth rate, both the US savings and investment ratios fell heavily from the none too impressive levels achieved previously. In 1980, gross savings represented 19.4% of US national product, close to the average for the two previous decades. By 1986, this ratio had fallen to 16.2%, and by 1993, it had reached a nadir of 14.4%, a drop of just over a quarter from the 1980 level. Total investment fell almost as precipitately – from 20.6% in 1980 to 15.3% in 1993 – with the financing gap being made up by borrowings from abroad. Over nearly all of this period, the US continued to generate too little saving of its own to pay for the still low – by international standards – proportion of the national income it reinvests.

Table 3.1 shows the picture sector by sector, dividing the US economy's output between the main classifications used in US statistics. In the twelve years from 1980 to 1992, output per person employed in manufacturing rose cumulatively by 3.1% per annum. Mining and the wholesale trade also put in creditable performances, at 5.1% and 3.9%, while output per head in agriculture, forestry and fishing rose by a compound 8.1% per annum, as the labour force fell rapidly from 3.7m in 1980 to 2.8m in 1992. In the rest of the economy, however, the results were dismal, particularly for finance, insurance and real estate, the retail trade, and services. All produced cumulative increases of 1% per annum or less, while services showed a fall of nearly 0.8% a year – a cumulative reduction in output per head of 8.8% over the whole twelve-year period. Those employed in finance, insurance and real estate, though earning far larger amounts on average than the rest of the working population throughout the period, achieved a total increase in productivity over the whole twelve years of only 4%, equating to a compound rate of barely 0.3% per annum – a humiliatingly poor record by any standards.

Table 3.1: Changes in Output per Head of the Working Population
between 1980 and 1992

1980	Value (constant 1992 $bn)	Labour Force (000s)	Output per Head ($)		
Manufacturing	822.6	20 285	40 552		
Construction	214.7	4 346	49 402		
Mining	82.0	1 027	79 844		
Sub total	1 119.3	25 658	43 624		
Agriculture, Forestry & Fishing	58.2	3 699	15 734		
Transport & Utilities	385.0	5 146	74 815		
Wholesale Trade	226.0	5 292	42 706		
Retail Trade	374.5	15 018	24 937		
Finance, Insurance & Real Estate	862.8	5 160	167 209		
Services	810.8	17 890	45 321		
Statistical Discrepancy	44.5				
Not Allocated	−14.9				
Government	748.8	16 241	46 106		
1980 GDP	4 615.0	94 104	49 041	*Output per Head Percentage Changes from 1980 to 1992*	
1992				*Total Change*	*Average Annual*
Manufacturing	1 063.6	18 104	58 749	44.9	3.1
Construction	229.7	4 492	51 135	3.5	0.3
Mining	92.2	635	145 197	81.9	5.1
Sub total	1 385.5	23 231	59 640	36.7	2.6
Agriculture, Forestry & Fishing	112.4	2 810	40 000	154.2	8.1
Transport & Utilities	528.7	5 718	92 462	23.6	1.8
Wholesale Trade	406.4	5 997	67 767	58.7	3.9
Retail Trade	544.3	19 356	28 120	12.8	1.0
Finance, Insurance & Real Estate	1 147.9	6 602	173 872	4.0	0.3
Services	1 200.8	29 052	41 333	−8.8	−0.8
Statistical Discrepancy	44.8				
Not Allocated	−				
Government	873.6	18 645	46 854	1.6	0.1
1992 GDP	6 244.4	111 411	56 048	14.29	1.12

Source: *Economic Report to the President*, February 1998, Tables B.13, B.46, B.100.

These broad averages, however, inevitably disguise a wide distribution of productivity increases within each sector. In some parts, output per person hour did go up fast, and incomes rose rapidly as a result. Across the board, in the more sophisticated part of the service industries, productivity was increasing at probably about 2% per annum. This was, however, considerably faster than overall output per head was rising. The result was the major shake out of labour from commercial companies and other organisations all over the country, which was such a characteristic feature of the 1980s. All these people, plus millions of new additions to the labour force, had to find jobs somewhere, as the vast majority – about 60% – had no unemployment compensation on which to fall back. For most of them, therefore, the choice was whatever work they could find or abject poverty. They finished up in huge numbers in insecure, low-paying, low-productivity jobs across the nation, working increasingly long hours.

The result was that, between 1980 and 1993, the first full year of the Clinton presidency, although the economy grew cumulatively by 2.7% per annum and GDP per head rose on average by 1.4% a year, none of these benefits worked their way through to the average worker in terms of compensation per hour. On the contrary, across the board average earnings per hour fell. For the whole American economy, in real terms, income per hour peaked in 1973, at $8.55 measured in constant 1982 dollars. By 1980, the rate was $7.78. After a marginal increase to $7.81 in 1986, it dropped to $7.39 in 1993. Thus, over the twenty years between 1973 and 1993, earnings per hour for the average American dropped in real terms by a staggering 13.4%. Against the background of the steady rise in real earnings per hour in the US economy in the 1950s and 1960s of a little under 2% per annum – about 18% per decade – who, predicting in 1973 a fall for the next twenty years, would have been given a hearing?

How did this manage to happen, however, if the economy was growing? A number of factors were responsible. First, the US population was increasing rapidly during the period 1980 to 1993, as was the labour force, and this explains why the increase in GDP per head, averaging 1.4% per annum, was only just over half the growth rate of 2.7%. Between 1980 and 1993, the civilian labour force rose from 107m to 134m. Excluding the unemployed, the increase was from 99m to 120m. Second, the proportion of the US GDP paid out as compensation to employees fell as higher proportions of the national income went in other directions, including profits, rent and transfer payments, which rose significantly faster than GDP. These mostly involved increased pension payments, as the population aged. Transfers to the poorest sections of society, such as the Family Assistance and government unemployment insurance benefits, on the other hand, fell as a proportion of GDP. Third, the reduction in income received per hour was offset by a large increase in the proportion of the female, though not male, population in employment, combined with an increase in the number of hours worked. Between 1980 and 1993, the proportion of women of working age in employment rose from 51% to 58%. The number of hours per week worked in manufacturing, including overtime, rose from 42.5 to 45.5. Despite extra participation in the labour force, and working longer hours, the consequence for blue-collar workers across the nation was that their living standards stagnated. They stayed roughly static for the twenty years from 1973 to 1993. Those at the bottom end of the income profile did even worse.

It was the catastrophic fall in real hourly earnings, barely offset by a higher labour force participation rate and longer working hours and aggravated by a tougher line being taken on social security payments, which caused the distribution of income, even before tax, to become much more uneven. Up to 1980, the proportion of aggregate income going to the bottom 40% of income earners had been roughly stable at about 17%. By 1993 it was 14%. For the bottom quintile, the drop was even more precipitate, from 5.3% to 4.1%, making the whole of this vast swathe of the American population – well over 50m people – about 8% worse off on average in 1993 than they had been in 1980. The percentage of children brought up below the poverty level rose from 15% in 1970 to 22% in 1993. The number of families in poverty rose over the same period from 6.2m to 8.4m, an increase of over one third. Meanwhile, at the other end of the spectrum, those in the top 5% of income earners saw their share of total incomes rise between 1980 and 1993 from 14.6% of the total to 20.3%. As a result, their incomes increased in real terms by about two thirds.

After tax, the distribution of income became even more uneven as tax rates on the rich were cut. The theory behind this was that the government revenues ought to increase if tax rates were lowered, both because there would be less incentives for avoidance and because lower tax rates would stimulate more enterprise and hence more revenues. The 'Laffer Curve' approach to tax policy – one of the more egregious elements of the 'supply-side' economic policies fashionable at the time – never came near improving the overall federal collection rate, however, although it certainly served its purpose in justifying lower tax payments rates by the rich. The result was one of the reasons why the US fiscal deficit began to widen.

The other major reason was a vast increase on defence outlays. In 1980, defence costs represented 5.3% of US GDP, down substantially from their 8.9% peak during the Vietnam War. By 1984 they were 6.4%, as expenditure jumped from $143bn to $233bn, a real increase of 30% in just four years. The result was that the overall government's fiscal stance, including both federal and state levels which had been $9.4bn in surplus in 1979, plunged into deficit, reaching a negative $134bn by 1983. The federal government record was even worse, with its deficit touching over $200bn for the first time in 1983. For the next eleven years it averaged $210bn a year. Hardly surprisingly, an immediate repercussion from the deterioration in the fiscal balance was a large increase in the value of outstanding federal debt. In 1980, the gross federal debt had been just under $1000bn, representing 33.4% of GDP. By 1993, it was $4351bn, equivalent to 67% of GDP, and still rising.

One of the consequences of the heavy increase in military spending during the Reagan years was that a higher proportion of the relatively weakening US industrial base was drawn into defence work, exacerbating problems on the trade balance, which also hugely deteriorated over the same period. By 1980, the total US foreign payment position was back in balance, after deficits in the late 1970s, with the surplus on investment income offsetting a $15bn deficit on goods and services. From then onwards, the position went from bad to worse. By 1984 the trade deficit was $103bn, and by 1987 it was $143bn. Most of this huge deterioration was the result of a catastrophic turnaround in trade in manufactured goods. Even as late as 1980, the US had a reasonably healthy $21bn surplus in trade on manufactured goods, but by 1984 this had turned into a deficit of $29bn, and $116bn by 1988.

There is an inexorable accounting identity which applies to foreign trade. Any deficit on current account has to be made up by exactly corresponding capital borrowing. To pay for the multi-billion dollar deficits which accumulated, the US therefore had to become a major net borrower from abroad and a major net seller of investment assets to foreigners. The result was a drastic change from the US being by far the world's largest creditor, to its being much the biggest debtor. In 1980 the US's net international investment position at cost was a positive $392bn. By 1990 it was negative $251bn, and by 1993 it was negative $503bn. Nor is this a trend which is currently improving. By 1995 the deficiency was $814bn, and it is still rising fast.

This deficit is connected to perhaps one of the most significant of all the changes there has been in the US since 1980, which is in the distribution of wealth. The self-help ethic, which permeated US society from the beginning of European settlement in North America, has always been relatively tolerant of wealth accumulation and the disparities in asset holdings between the rich and the poor which is its inevitable consequence. This sits reasonably comfortably with the egalitarian tradition in the US, where equality of opportunity is stressed more strongly than equality of outcome, and where rewards to hard work and successful risk taking are not generally resented.

The period from 1980 onwards, however, saw an enormous increase in the wealth of the US's better-off citizens where in very many cases they had to do little, if anything at all, to become very much richer. The Dow-Jones, which was 891 in 1980, reached 1793 by 1986, 3794 in 1993, and in December 1997 it was 7903. Over a period during which the US GDP grew in money terms to 3.2 times its previous size, the stock market had risen to almost nine times where it had been seventeen years previously. The returns to financial institutions have risen particularly quickly, reflecting the increasing opportunities to make money out of financial activities rather than making or selling products. At the other end of spectrum, as the deflationary impact of monetarist doctrines hit hard those not already well heeled, the business failure rate rose by leaps and bounds. In 1980, there were 42 failures per 10 000 listed business enterprises. By 1986 there were 120, and still 109 in 1993. A further cause of rising wealth inequality stems from the value of residential accommodation, which has also risen far more rapidly than the nominal value of GDP, increasing the net asset position of the well-off, and raising the rents payable by those not fortunate enough to be owner-occupiers.

The reason why the balance of payments deficit is relevant to the huge increase in asset values which has taken place in recent years is that the gap between US domestic savings and investment has been quite small. For most years between 1980 and 1997 the value of investment within the US has been higher than saving, but only by a few billion dollars. The exceptionally high demand for US stocks and other assets has not, therefore, come from domestic sources. It has been fuelled by the massive inflow of capital funds to the US, which mirrors the current account deficit. For most of the years since 1985, this has been well over $100bn, and this is another problem which shows little sign of disappearing. With a trade deficit of well over $100bn per annum, net unilateral transfers abroad of $40bn, and with a rapidly disappearing net investment income to act as an offset, as more and more US net assets are sold to foreigners, the total deficit, and thus capital inflow to the US, in 1997 may well top $160bn. Most commentators believe that the figures for 1998 and 1999 may well be much higher.

The reduction in the performance of the US economy below what it might have achieved during the Reagan and Bush presidencies was thus enormous, and the legacy left to the incoming Democrat administration much worse than it should have been. The US is still a powerful country, and the underlying strength of the US economy is such that despite all the mistreatment meted out to it between 1980 and 1993, its powers of recuperation are still immense. The Clinton administration certainly came to power with the intention of tackling the inheritance left to the American people from the years when monetarism ran riot in the US. There are major questions, however, as to whether the reversals in policy direction which have taken place so far will bring the US back to anywhere close to its full potential.

CLINTON AND THE 1990s

While, as always, there were other factors at play, there is little doubt that a major reason for the support achieved by the Democrat candidate for the presidency in 1992 was the widespread dissatisfaction with living standards which never seemed to rise, even for many of those in regular work. 'It's the economy, stupid', was not for nothing the watchword of the Clinton campaign. The new President came to power, therefore, well aware that getting the economy to perform better had to be high on the list of policy priorities. How well has the Clinton administration done?

During the middle years of the Bush régime the economy had faltered, growing by only 1.2% in 1990, and contracting by almost 1% in 1991. No doubt this contributed to the Republican defeat in 1992, although by then the economy was starting to pick up again. The downturn reduced the current account balance of payments deficit, which fell from over $100bn in 1989, to only $6bn in 1991, a much better outcome than had been achieved since 1981. The trade deficit also fell to a more manageable $31bn from the much higher figures in the immediately prior years, aided by a fall in the value of the dollar. By the start of the Clinton administration's term of office, the trade-weighted value had come down a long way from the stratospheric levels of the mid-Reagan era to a considerably more realistic index of 86 in 1990 and 83 in 1992. Unemployment rose to 7.5% in 1992, following the impact of sharp interest rate increases in 1989 on the level of business activity. The consumer price index, which had shown a rise of 6.1% in 1990 – well above the increase in the immediately preceding years, although in line with the average experience of other OECD countries – had dropped back to 2.9% in 1992. The economy inherited by the Clinton administration therefore brought with it all the structural imbalances which the monetarist era had wrought upon it, combined with considerable room for bouncing back from the shallow depression in 1990 and 1991.

Between the spring of 1993, when the Clinton administration took over, and the end of 1997, there have been some small improvements, but not nearly enough to counteract the impact of the Reagan and Bush policies on the American economy. The growth rate has averaged a compound 2.7%. This is slightly higher than the 2.5% achieved between 1980 and 1993, but not much more, and largely attributable to an almost inevitable recovery from the Bush depression. Between 1993 and 1997 the population grew by an average of almost exactly 1% per year, so that during those four years, GDP per head grew at 1.7% per annum, again an improvement on the cumulative 1.4% per annum achieved by the Republican administrations, but not a very large one. Most observers predict that the better growth rate achieved in 1997, at 3.9% for the year, is not likely to be sustained in 1998 and beyond. The general consensus is that the growth in output for the next year or two is likely to be closer to 2.5% per annum. On the bright side, the rise in consumer prices was only 1.7% in 1997, a very good figure, although comparable to the outcome in most other OECD countries. Unemployment fell to 4.7% in December 1997, the lowest figure since the end of the 1960s, but increased numbers of people working, accompanied by only a relatively small rise in output, indicated continuing very low increases in productivity. This outcome is borne out by average hourly earnings which, in real terms, had gone up by only just over 0.5% per annum in the five years to the end of 1997, rising in constant 1982 dollars from $7.41 in 1992 to $7.54 in 1997. Increases in earnings were largely achieved by working even longer hours – up nearly 14% between 1992 and 1996, a very large rise.

Table 3.2 shows the details in the same format as the previous table covering the years 1980 to 1992. Again, there is a relatively strong performance from manufacturing and mining, both showing output per head increasing cumulatively by more than 5% per annum. Agriculture, forestry and fishing show a small decline in output per head, mainly because the reduction in the size of the labour force – a major influence in the 1980–92 period productivity increase – had ceased to be a factor from 1992 onwards. The performance of all the service economy, with the exception of the wholesale trade which showed a cumulative increase in output per head of 2.9%, is again dismal. Transport and utilities, finance, insurance and real estate, and the retail trade all produced increases in output per head of between only 1.2% and 1.6%, and services showed an even larger reduction in output per head per year, at –1.4%, than the –0.8% achieved between 1980 and 1992. If results as bad as this were achieved when the economy was growing relatively quickly, what is likely to happen when growth falls off towards the end of the current decade?

Between 1992 and 1996, there was a significant shift back to manufacturing activity which rose as a percentage of GDP output from 17% in 1992 to 19.1% in 1996. This change was reflected in an increase in the proportion of GDP devoted to investment. Non-residential private gross fixed investment rose as a percentage of GDP from 8.9% in 1992, a very low figure compared to previous years, to 11.1% in 1996. The business failure rate dropped back from 110 per 10 000 to 80. Much of this success had to do with the policy pursued by the Fed on interest rates, which consistently stayed considerably lower than they had done during the Republican years. Between 1980 and 1992, the average interest rate had been 9%, while the compound rise in the consumer price index had been 4.5% per annum. Even the Fed was therefore charging a very high average real interest rate for the whole of this period

Table 3.2: Changes in Output per Head of the Working Population
between 1992 and 1996

1980	Value (constant 1992 $bn)	Labour Force (000s)	Output per Head ($)		
Manufacturing	1 063.6	18 104	58 749		
Construction	229.7	4 492	51 135		
Mining	92.2	635	145 197		
Sub total	1 385.5	23 231	59 640		
Agriculture, Forestry & Fishing	112.4	2 810	40 000		
Transport & Utilities	528.7	5 718	92 462		
Wholesale Trade	406.4	5 997	67 767		
Retail Trade	544.3	19 356	28 120		
Finance, Insurance & Real Estate	1 147.9	6 602	173 872		
Services	1 200.8	29 052	41 333		
Statistical Discrepancy	44.8				
Not Allocated	–				
Government	873.6	18 645	46 854		
1992 GDP	6 244.4	111 411	56 048	*Output per Head Percentage Changes from 1992 to 1996*	
1996				*Total Change*	*Average Annual*
Manufacturing	1 323.7	18 457	71 718	22.1	5.1
Construction	264.3	5 400	48 944	–4.3	1.1
Mining	101.9	574	177 526	22.3	5.2
Sub total	1 689.9	24 431	69 170	16.0	3.8
Agriculture, Forestry & Fishing	111.7	2 842	39 303	–1.7	–0.4
Transport & Utilities	608.9	6 261	97 253	5.2	1.3
Wholesale Trade	493.3	6 483	76 091	12.3	2.9
Retail Trade	648.5	21 625	29 988	6.6	1.6
Finance, Insurance & Real Estate	1 258.5	6 899	182 418	4.9	1.2
Services	1 342.9	34 377	39 064	–5.5	–1.4
Statistical Discrepancy	–51.3				
Not Allocated	–48.1				
Government	874.1	19 447	44 948	–4.1	–1.0
1996 GDP	6 928.4	122 365	56 621	1.02	0.25

Source: *Economic Report to the President*, February 1998, Tables B.13, B.46, B.100.

of 4.5%. For the five years from 1993 to 1997 the Fed's interest rate averaged 4.8% against a compound increase in consumer prices of 2.7% per annum, producing a lower but still significantly positive real interest rate of 2.1%. The US gross savings ratio as a percentage of GDP rose, but from the exceptionally low level reached at the end of the Bush presidency. In 1992 the ratio was 14.5%, and by 1997 this had climbed to a little over 17%. Personal saving, however, actually fell over this period as a percentage of disposable income, from 6.2% to 3.8%.

The Clinton record on the federal deficit was also much better than those of his two immediate predecessors. A combination of contained expenditure and rising tax revenues reduced the deficit, which had peaked at $290bn in 1992, to $22bn in 1997, with a balanced budget projected for 1999. The gross federal debt at the end of 1997 was $5370bn, however, and the interest charges on this large sum were an additional drain on the government's current resources.

By far the largest fundamental problem facing the Clinton administration at the beginning of 1998 was the foreign balance. By 1997, the trade-weighted value of the dollar had risen from an index of 83 in 1992 to 96 in 1996. A combination of devaluations in the Far East and the weakening of most of the major currencies in Europe had left the dollar dangerously exposed. As the US growth rate has climbed during the 1990s, so the overall balance of payments deficit on current account worsened, from $56bn in 1992 to $133bn in 1994, $148bn in 1996, and almost certainly more than $160bn in 1997. The projections are that, without a major change in policy this deficit will continue to widen.

The US economy despite its travails may still be immensely powerful, but the borrowing required to finance a deficit on this scale is beginning to look daunting. As a percentage of US GDP the sums involved are not unmanageable, but in relation to the US foreign earnings position they are considerably more difficult to handle. The US is already a major net creditor to the rest of the world. In consequence the net investment income which used to buttress the US foreign payments position had been reduced by 1997 to a small fraction of its previous size. In subsequent years it is almost bound to turn negative. Other adverse developments may worsen the situation, not least a possible rise in the price of oil and other commodities which the US imports in large quantities, and whose prices are currently at historically low levels. There must, therefore, be an increasing exchange rate risk for those purchasing US fixed interest stocks, as the dollar looks more and more over-valued in relation to the US's current and future commitments.

If the dollar does come under pressure, the Clinton administration is going to be faced with difficult choices. If it is not going to allow the dollar to fall, the consequences are bound to be rising interest rates and domestic deflation to try to keep the foreign payments deficit within bounds. This will inevitably threaten many of the other policy objectives which the administration has set itself, and thus weaken its electoral appeal. There is, of course, an alternative, which is to let the dollar fall, and the results which might be achieved by either passively allowing this to happen, or actively encouraging it to do so, will be discussed in later sections of this book.

In the meantime, the huge flow of investment funds coming into the US as the counterpart to the foreign deficit is still helping to sustain the Dow-Jones. Property values are rising. The rich are getting richer much faster than the increase in incomes of the poor, who are working longer and longer hours to achieve modest increases in earnings as, for the vast majority of them, their productivity stays flat or falls marginally. The US can do better than this, and the following pages set out how this might be done.

4   Economic Growth

'The slogan of progress is changing from the full dinner pail to the full garage.'

Herbert Hoover

The economic history of the developing world since the start of industrialisation has been remarkably patchy. Britain experienced a long period of rapid growth in the first half of the nineteenth century, but then slowed down between 1850 and 1900. The US grew rapidly during the whole of the nineteenth century and, more intermittently, through to 1945, but then slowed relative to new challengers. Germany and the Netherlands did much better during the second half of the nineteenth century than the first, and better still during the early years of the twentieth century leading up to World War I. The 1930s were a particularly interesting and important period, with the US and France languishing, Britain doing far better than previously, and Germany surging ahead at an astonishing pace. There have been decades when most of the main economies were expanding very quickly, as they did in the 1950s and 1960s, although the US did not grow as fast as others during these decades. After the post-war boom, in the 1970s, increases in output slowed generally. The world's growth rate of 5.2% per annum cumulatively between 1950 and 1973 slowed to 2.8% per annum from 1973 to 1992.

Why did these changes in relative performance occur? Why was growth so much faster in some periods than others, and what can policy makers do to create the conditions where growth takes place? How can they avoid it slowing down? The objective of this chapter is to set out an explanation for the causes of economic growth, and the processes by which it takes place. If we can understand why some economies grow fast and others slowly, and why some succeed in employing their resources of labour and other factors of production more fully than others, much will be revealed. It then becomes possible to see not only the reasons for past history, but what might be done to alter the course of events in the future.

The starting point is to understand the circumstances which allow and encourage economic growth to take place. Growth is achieved by creating conditions where the output of goods and services rises. Essentially, this can be done in two ways. One is to increase inputs – to employ more labour, to educate and train it better, and to use more capital equipment, land and buildings. The second is to achieve more output in relation to inputs than

69

was attained before – increasing what is called total factor productivity. This is done by improved management, better design and enhanced production efficiency. Any convincing explanation of the way output can be increased needs to take account of all these components to the growth process.

It is often said, or implied, that achieving economic growth is mainly a matter of increasing productivity, at least among the existing workforce. Higher total output entails greater average productivity per person if the same number of people are employed to produce more output. The same increase can be achieved, however, if the number of people working goes up without any extra output per person. Furthermore, if productivity increases in isolation from a general expansion of the economy, it will not contribute to raising the growth rate. On the contrary, if total output stays constant, more output per head among some people will inevitably be counterbalanced by rising unemployment elsewhere. This important point, which has wide policy implications, runs through all the arguments which follow. The key to achieving high growth rates for the economy as a whole is to create conditions where increases in output will take place across the board, keeping all factors of production fully employed. This will then cause average productivity to rise, without increasing unemployment, which is the key combination of objectives which needs to be attained.

High growth rates are achieved by keeping all the factors of production, particularly labour and capital, in use as intensively as possible. The growth in output thus achieved will be reflected in increased output per head, which is how productivity is raised. At the level of the individual enterprise, this is accomplished in three principal ways. The first is by investing in machinery and equipment which makes it possible for the existing labour force to achieve increased production. The second is by better management and training of the workforce, and enhancing its skills and experience. The third is by increasing sales, so that all the available resources of labour and capital are used to maximum capacity.

The potential for improved production as a result of capital investment is a familiar concept. The power, dexterity and speed with which machinery operates made the Industrial Revolution possible. During the past two centuries, the development of a huge range of machines has been matched by many other inventions and technological developments which can be used to increase output, from internal combustion engines to electronics, from steamships to airliners, from new building techniques to plastics. All these developments make it possible to produce goods and services of greater value per labour hour. We shall see, however, that there is a huge variation in the return on investments. Some types of investment are very much more productive, and therefore conducive to high rates of economic growth, than others. One of the ways of increasing economic growth, and making it much easier to achieve, is to create conditions in which the economy is biased towards the most highly productive investment.

The quality of management is extremely important in producing greater output. Many improvements in working practices which lead to more production, or changes in output designed to make it more attractive to consumers, involve little capital outlay but a great deal of management skill. Some of this comes from good education and training. An even more important factor is ensuring that the best available managerial talent is concentrated in those areas of the economy where it can be used most effectively to improve economic achievement. Where talent is actually concentrated depends critically on economic rewards and the social status which follows behind them. The second element in improving economic achievement is to shift both rewards and social status towards those involved in running the parts of the economy where good management has the best chance of increasing performance.

The third vital component is to create enough pressure of demand on the economy to ensure that all the available resources of capital and labour are, as far as possible, fully utilised. To achieve most from capital equipment, it needs to be used as intensively as possible. To get the best out of the labour force, it needs to be fully employed. When there is a shortage of jobs, it may make sense to increase output by using relatively low-productivity machinery and more employees. As supplies of labour run short, this no longer becomes a viable option. There is then no alternative to labour-saving equipment. At the level of the enterprise, a full order book at profitable prices is needed, with highly productive machinery used to capacity to produce goods which the market is hungry to buy, operated by a well trained and motivated labour force, led by able managers. Despite recent setbacks, these are the conditions which still exist over much of the economy in Korea, Taiwan and the fast-developing parts of China, which is why these economies are expanding so rapidly. They were also replicated in Germany, France and Italy – indeed, over most of Western Europe in the 1950s and 1960s – when all these countries were growing much faster than they are now. In some parts of the US economy these conditions are still to be found. The American problem, however, is that throughout too large a proportion of US economic activity they no longer apply.

COMPETITIVENESS

What are the conditions which enable economies to prosper? How is an environment created which encourages increases in economic output to take place? What can those responsible for the performance of the US economy do to ensure that its growth performance is as good as that achieved with comparative ease in many other countries? It is often claimed that the solution is to concentrate on the supply side of the problem. The way to higher growth, it is said, is to improve competitiveness by better education and training, by higher levels of investment, and by improving productivity. This will make US output more competitive, and increase the productive capacity of American companies, allowing more growth to take place. The problem with this approach, however, is that improving efficiency will not necessarily result in lower prices and greater competitiveness. It depends on the price charged to the rest of the world for the economy's output. Nor does increasing productivity necessarily result in rising total output.

A variation on the supply-side theme is to blame poor growth performance on production techniques and design sophistication which are not as advanced as those available elsewhere in the world, perhaps compounded by ineffective salesmanship, late deliveries and inadequate after-sales service. This has certainly been a well-recognised problem in the past. The automobile industry is a particularly obvious example, but there are many others to which the same strictures could have been, and were applied. Nowadays, in the US, there is much greater awareness of the need to set high standards to compete internationally. The problem is that at present there is still too little that the US is capable of producing which the rest of the world wants to buy at the prices at which it is on offer.

Of course, productive efficiency has some bearing on competitiveness, but actually surprisingly little. The higher the level of productivity, the more efficiently goods and services will be produced, but it does not necessarily follow that they will then be internationally competitive. High output per head is closely associated with high standards of living, but very poorly with competitiveness. This is why there is no observable correlation between the growth rates of rich and poor countries. It is, nevertheless, true that in any economy which is growing, productivity will be increasing. This leads many people to conclude that concentrating efforts on raising output per head will push up the growth rate.

Unfortunately, this conclusion is not correct. Productivity is not the same as competitiveness. There are many examples of countries round the world where output per head is increasing quite rapidly, but growth in total output is slow. The result is the rising unemployment and unused resources which is such a conspicuous feature in the European Union. In the US, on the other hand, unemployment is low, and rapid increases in productivity in some parts of the economy produce a different problem. With insufficient effective demand to generate enough high-quality jobs for everyone, rising productivity among some sections of the labour force is inevitably reflected in low or negative rises in output per head among large sections of the remaining working population.

Striking confirmation of these propositions is provided by comparing the position of the United States and the Tiger economies of the Far East during the period since World War II. After 1945, the US labour force was vastly more productive than the largely peasant workforces of Taiwan and Korea. The levels of training and education in the US were far superior to those in most other countries in the world, while significant proportions of the Taiwanese and Korean labour forces were illiterate. The value of capital per head in the US was many multiples of the almost non-existent industrial capacity in Taiwan and Korea. Despite all these huge advantages, the US has been completely outpaced in the growth race since World War II by these economies.

It is not, therefore, productivity which is the key to making economies potentially capable of growing fast. It is competitiveness. It is the prices charged for the economy's output to buyers both in the home and export markets, compared to foreign suppliers, which count. This is partly a function of how productive the domestic economy is, but it is also a question of how much its exporters charge the rest of the world for their output, whatever the level of productivity. This is determined by the exchange rate. Even if productivity is very low, and everything is wrong with the output of the economy, if it is cheap enough, a fair proportion of it will sell. However high the quality of the output, if it is too expensive, market share will be lost. In the end it is price which balances out all the other quality factors. This is why the exchange rate is so critically important.

Other things being equal, the lower the exchange rate, the less the domestic economy charges the rest of the world for its labour, land and capital, and the more competitive, compared with the rest of the world, the domestic economy will be. This condition bears directly on the three requirements identified earlier for increasing both productivity and output. First, for all those economic activities which require capital investment to secure increase in output, the lower the associated labour and interest costs, measured in international terms, the higher the profitability of the capital investment, and the more of it will be undertaken. Second, the greater the competitiveness of the output produced, the easier it will be to sell larger quantities at a profit, and the greater the capacity utilisation. Third, the higher the profits thus generated, the more those sectors of the economy which are engaged in producing internationally tradable goods and services will be able to attract the most talented people into management positions. Exceptional profitability will also enable them to employ and make best use of the most competent people available to staff every level of the operations concerned.

Just as a company's competitive position is heavily disadvantaged if its costs are far out of line with the rest of the market, the same is true for the whole economy. There is, however, one further important difference between companies and economies. If the exchange rate is too high, reducing it is an even more potent way of cutting costs across the board than anything an individual company can do. All companies have fixed costs which are difficult and sometimes impossible to cut significantly. This is not true of the economy as a whole. Changing the exchange rate carries with it the costs of every factor of production. No wonder countries with over-valued exchange rates suffer so grievously, and those with under-valued exchange rates do so well.

The relationship between productivity and competitiveness is therefore the reverse of what is often supposed. It is not increasing productivity which produces greater competitiveness. It is greater competitiveness which generates the conditions where increased productivity is most easily achieved, and with the greatest advantage. This is not a trite conclusion. It has profound implications for determining the conditions which will make economies grow, and the policies which need to be pursued to make this happen.

The significance of these exchange rate issues to the US is that for the whole of the period since shortly after the end of World War II, the output of the goods and services produced by US companies has not, on average, been sufficiently competitively priced in world terms. As a result, the share of the US home market taken by imports, particularly manufactures, has risen dramatically, while simultaneously the share of world trade achieved by US exporters has fallen heavily. As late as 1963, the US imported 8.6% of the world's manufactures and exported 17.5% of them. By 1994, imports were 17.5% of the world total, and exports 13.1%. In 1950, manufactured goods represented only 7.5% of all US merchandise imports. By 1960 the ratio was 20%, by 1983 it was 50% and in 1996 it was 56%.

As a result of these persistent trends, the US has foregone the direct benefit which would have been secured by having a larger proportion of GDP devoted to manufacturing, where, in the right conditions, increases in output and rising productivity are so much easier to achieve than they are in other sectors. The US economy has also been exposed to persistent balance of payments problems, which have constrained the capacity of successive administrations to expand the economy as fast as they might otherwise have chosen. It has therefore been impossible for buoyant consumer demand and high rates of investment to fill the gap left by sluggish foreign trade performance. The combined impact of these major influences provides the fundamental explanation for the relatively slow growth the US economy has achieved since the war.

PROTECTIONISM AND FREE TRADE

It is often proposed, particularly by those suffering from price competition which they find hard to combat, that the way to create favourable conditions for growth is through measures designed to shield domestic producers from world competition. In the US, protectionist interests have for long periods been dominant. American economic history is replete with examples of high tariffs being imposed to keep out foreign goods, particularly during the late nineteenth and early twentieth centuries, and during the 1930s. The economic nationalism of the inter-war period, however, changed the minds of American policy makers. After 1945, the US swung round to being one of the strongest protagonists for moves to freer trade. Nevertheless, despite all the support which the US has given since World War II to successive rounds of negotiations to reduce tariff levels throughout the world, the pressures for more protection in America are still strong.

Difficulties in competing with consumer products from the Far East and other developing countries have already led to significant restraints on trade. The Multi-fibre agreement, covering a wide range of clothing and apparel, was one of the earlier examples. Restrictions on the imports of Japanese cars is another. Other major areas of the US economy which are protected from outside competition are steel, semiconductors and agriculture. If there needs to be more investment in American industry, and better rewards for those employed in it, then some degree of protection, it is claimed, is the best way of ensuring that these objectives are achieved. If this cannot be attained openly by raising tariffs or quotas, then covert protection, making importing difficult in other ways, may be the solution. This approach has led, in particular, to leaning on foreign governments, especially the Japanese, to restrict their exports in sensitive areas such as cars and electronic components. 'Orderly marketing arrangements' and 'voluntary export restraints' then become the appropriate euphemisms.

Buttressing these arguments are others which have been the common coin of economic debate for centuries. By imposing a tariff, the domestic economy can tax the foreigner to its advantage. Because those selling to the domestic economy will have to lower their prices to compete in its protected market, the terms of trade will improve. The domestic economy will then obtain more imports per unit of exports than it did before the tariff was imposed, thus making itself better off. Furthermore, if the effect of putting on import duties is similar to reducing the exchange rate, having higher tariffs on some commodities than others may give the domestic economy advantages that would not be obtained by a devaluation. For example, if import duties are imposed on finished goods but not on raw materials, the domestic economy may be able to protect its manufacturers without raising their costs.

The arguments in favour of free trade are nevertheless extremely strong, provided certain essential conditions are fulfilled. In modern conditions, there is an impressive and persuasive case against reverting back to a protectionist approach, and indeed for moving further towards opening up the US market to foreign competition wherever possible. America is more likely to improve the prosperity of its citizens by looking outwards rather than inwards. The arguments for free trade and keeping the US economy open to foreign competition are as important now as they ever were, provided they are not undermined by inappropriate exchange rate policies, which can all too easily generate protectionism which politicians find difficult to resist.

First, there are the traditional comparative cost arguments for foreign trade. The relative costs of producing a wide range of output vary from country to country. It pays countries to trade with each other if they swap those products where their relative costs are low for others produced elsewhere which could only be made at a relatively high cost domestically. It is important to note that the case for international trade for comparative cost reasons is independent of absolute levels of productivity. Countries with such low productivity that they produce everything relatively inefficiently can still trade to their advantage with countries which produce everything more efficiently. It is the variances round the norm which make this trade worth while.

Second, there is the spur to efficiency produced by competition from abroad. Most people prefer a quiet life and do not relish the prospect of having to adapt constantly to changing tastes and fashions, to new technology and methods of distribution. Provided it is not overwhelming, foreign competition keeps them on their toes. A copying process results as those who are behind the times replicate the trends set by the market leaders. They buy in or duplicate foreign technology and equipment, management techniques and sales methods. It is possible to achieve high rates of growth behind tariff barriers, as for example Spain did for decades during the Franco régime and Japan has done in different ways for decades. The output produced in these circumstances, however, tends to lack the quality of the goods and services available in countries which are more exposed to the world economy. Japanese manufactured goods may be superb but much of the domestic economy in Japan, particularly in services, is a byword for inefficiency and wasteful use of people in low-productivity jobs. The informal protectionism which is Japan's speciality has been, in some obvious ways, extremely expensive for its citizens.

Third, there are great advantages in producing competitive exports if all the raw materials, intermediate goods and other inputs which have to be bought in from abroad can be obtained at the lowest possible price. One of the problems with either import tariffs or quotas is that they generally increase the costs of domestic production. It is now more difficult than it was to draw a clear distinction between raw materials and finished goods, with tariffs imposed on the latter but not the former. If the key to long-term improved economic performance is to increase the competitiveness of US producers of goods and services at home and abroad, it does not help to raise domestic production costs more than can be avoided, or to restrict access to raw materials and components at the best available prices.

Fourth, tariffs or quotas have a fundamental flaw if they are employed to deal with an underlying lack of competitiveness. The problem is that while it is conceivable that there should be relatively low import duties, or a limited number of products subject to quotas, as soon as the height of the tariffs gets beyond a fairly low level – about 20% – the distortions they entail become more and more difficult to justify. Administrative problems also mount rapidly when quotas increase in complexity. It is not possible to keep on raising tariffs or tightening quotas indefinitely without dramatically diminishing returns setting in. Economic distortions get worse, evasion becomes an increasing problem, and complicated appeals procedures are difficult to avoid.

If the root problem, however, is lack of competitiveness on the export market, as much as too much import penetration – and of course the two go together – then either the tariffs will have to be increased or quotas will have to be tightened beyond any realistic point. Alternatively, the real remedy needed, which is changing the exchange rate, will have to be adopted. This is because tariff protection will not increase exports, but a growing economy will need more imports. There is no way out of this problem short of eventual autarchy, which forces the protected economy to produce more and more of its needs in the home market, even though it would be much cheaper to buy them from abroad. Because of its size and diversity, the US economy may appear to be in a better position to adopt this approach than many others, but it still does not follow that it is in the US's interests to do so.

There are, therefore, strong arguments for maintaining economies in the developed world as open as is politically feasible, although there may be a practical case for some measure of protection because of the difficulties of ensuring that exchange rates are always correctly aligned. This is the justification for the North American Free Trade Area, for the European Union's Common External Tariff, and for similar arrangements in South

America, the Pacific area and elsewhere. Too many cross-parity rates may be difficult to manage. Achieving equality in competitiveness between economies within a customs union area, which is a vital component of good economic management, may therefore, in practice, be easier to achieve behind a common external tariff high enough to contain an unmanageable volume of foreign competition. It has to be said, however, that even this conclusion is disputed, and in an ideal world regional customs areas would be unlikely to exist.

Nevertheless, in the real world there are arguments for a degree of protection which are difficult to resist. They are weaker for quotas than for tariffs, and there is a stronger case for low tariffs than for high ones. When there is unmanageable competition there is always pressure for protection. The case to be made in these circumstances, however, almost invariably depends on exchange rates being in the wrong position in the first place. Protectionist policies are then all too readily inclined to become the justification for failing to correct the exchange rate fundamentals. There is therefore no valid argument for a retreat into further protectionism as a major plank of economic policy. There is a much more effective way of dealing with the problems of major trade imbalance, for which tariffs and quotas are not the solution. This is to make greater efforts to position exchange rates at the right level, and to allow them to keep adjusting themselves as circumstances change and relative competitive advantage alters so that the need for protectionist measures falls away. This might have been difficult for the US during the 1950s and 1960s, when the international anchor role of the US dollar was pre-eminent. There is no reason why the dollar's parity cannot be changed nowadays, however, if this is what the US economy needs to enable it to perform very much better.

RECAPTURING HOME AND EXPORT MARKETS

So far we have looked at the conditions favourable to economic growth in a static context, but the process we are looking at is far from stationary. It is one where movement and change are essential elements. There are two particular features which need to be highlighted. The first is that rapid economic growth, once established, has a strong capacity to reinforce itself. On the whole, therefore, fast expanding economies tend to stay growing rapidly. The second is that this virtuous circle of fast growth cannot be taken for granted. It can slow down or even stop for a time altogether, as has been the experience across much of Europe since the mid-1970s, and particularly strikingly in the case of Japan since 1991. It is important to be able to explain both what causes growth to accelerate to a fast pace and why it can slow down, stop, or even go into reverse. This means pinpointing the mechanisms involved in both the virtuous circle of import-saving and export-led growth, and the vicious circle of import-led stagnation.

One of the keys to understanding this issue is to appreciate a particularly important characteristic of a large proportion of the investment taking place in those parts of the world economy which produce internationally tradable goods and services. This is the large increases in output which investment of this sort is capable of producing at relatively low run-on costs. Indeed this characteristic provides the main explanation for the enormous growth in international trade which has occurred over recent decades. The result is a special feature of the production costs of internationally traded goods and services. They almost all involve steeply falling cost curves. This means that the expense involved in producing the first batch of any new good or service may be high, but all subsequent output is much cheaper. The average cost of production therefore falls quickly as the volume of output builds up.

This characteristic of internationally traded goods and services is highly significant. Any country with macro-economic conditions making it relatively easy to sell the output from this kind of investment – in particular low interest rates, a plentiful supply of credit and a competitive exchange rate – will achieve rapid output growth. Once the initial investment is on stream, low marginal costs of production lead to high sales and profits, which are then available to finance the risks involved in subsequent waves of investment. High profitability also enables these enterprises to attract and hold the most able people in management positions, making it more likely that the next round of investment decisions will be shrewdly judged and efficiently carried out. The low cost of production makes it relatively easy to keep plants fully occupied as higher output leads to even lower production expenses, and the capacity for yet more competitive pricing.

This virtuous circle thus tends strongly to fortify itself. Higher sales and greater profitability make it easier to finance research and development, and to keep ahead. They also provide the cash flow needed to sustain high selling costs, so that new markets can be penetrated. The competitive position of successful enterprises is strengthened by better design, advertising and selling efforts, and after-sales service, all of which are expensive. On the back of a large volume of profitable sales, however, they can be relatively easily afforded. Profits remain high, making expenditure to produce increased output easy to finance. Both the savings ratio and the rate of investment as a proportion of national income tend to be high and rising in economies with strong export sectors. With substantial rewards in successful enterprises go social status and political power, thus attracting and retaining more and more of the best talent. It cannot be stressed too strongly how important a contribution to achieving sustained growth is accomplished by having a high proportion of the country's most able people involved in making and selling goods and services, especially those involved in foreign trade. Creating the right economic conditions for the virtuous spiral of import-saving and export-led growth may be the precursor to economic success, but there is no substitute for the highest possible standard of efficiency at the level of the firm. This is where management quality is as critical as any other factor, perhaps the most critical of all. Sustained high growth rates can only be achieved by the difficult processes of making good judgements about increasingly complex problems, managing more and more complicated organisations, dealing with rapid and frequently technically intricate change, and assessing and sometimes anticipating accurately market trends, often covering the whole world.

The crucial question then is what makes it possible to break into the virtuous circle of import-saving and export-led growth? What are the conditions which cause import-led stagnation? The exchange rate is the most critical determinant, for reasons which Table 4.1 makes clear. This table shows in schematic, but not unrealistic form, the costs and pricing options available to companies competing in international trade in three different economies, one with a parity in line with the world average, one with an exchange rate under-valued by 20%, and one with an exchange rate which is over-valued by the same percentage. The case covered here involves manufacturing, where the impact of high or low exchange rates are particularly pronounced, but similar results are obtained when considering internationally traded services.

The costs of manufacturing companies are made up of a number of components, some of which are determined by world prices, and some locally. In the table, raw materials are shown as 20% of international prices for the firm's output in the averagely competitive economy. There is a world market for nearly all raw materials, but favourable selling conditions for exporters tend to go with efficient and low-cost raw material suppliers in economies whose manufacturing base is expanding rapidly. There is also an understandable tendency for economies with strong export sectors to lack significant tariffs or other import restrictions on raw material imports, whereas economies with weak balance of payments positions are more prone to try to protect their remaining industries with import constraints. Raw material costs are therefore likely to be lower in highly competitive economies than in those which are uncompetitive. The figures in the table show a 5% spread round the average.

Table 4.1: Options Available to Companies Producing Internationally Tradable
Goods in Economies with Parities at Varying Levels

	Countries with Average Parities	Countries Under-valued by 20%	Countries Over-valued by 20%
Costs fixed in World Prices			
Raw Materials	20	19	21
Capital Depreciation	10	8	12
Total Internationally determined Costs	30	27	33
Costs fixed inDomestic Prices			
Labour Costs)			
Local Supplies)			
Land & Premises)			
Interest Charges)	60	48	72
Total Costs	90	75	105
World Prices for the Company's Output	100	100	100
Trading Profit or Loss at World Prices	10	25	−5

Source: Derived from OECD *National Accounts.*

Second, there are capital costs, which, when depreciated over output achieved in the average economy, are shown as 10% of selling prices. These costs, however, are even more likely to be lower than raw materials in highly competitive economies, and higher in those which are uncompetitive. Not only do fast-growing economies tend to have cheaper and more efficient suppliers for capital equipment than elsewhere, but they also benefit from potentially much higher levels of capacity utilisation. The result is that the cost of capital depreciation per unit of output tends to be much lower in companies in competitive economies than in those which have high domestic costs, a factor further reflected in the figures in the table.

Third, there are all the costs which are incurred locally. An over-valued currency implies that the average wage costs per hour, adjusted for local productivity, are necessarily above the world average by a similar proportion to the over-valuation. Indeed, it is the costs which the domestic economy charges the rest of the world for its labour, adjusted for productivity, which substantially determines whether the currency is over- or under-valued in the first place. Since employee costs make up some 60% of total charges incurred in developed economies, this factor makes a large difference to the prospects for the average company. Higher labour costs per hour, adjusted for productivity, affect not only the employee charges the firm directly incurs, but also the labour component in all the goods and services it buys in from local suppliers. Furthermore, in an economy with an over-valued currency, interest charges will also almost certainly be higher than average, and high interest rates tend to push up the cost to the firm of land and premises, as well as borrowing. Taking all these locally determined costs together, they are shown as accounting for 60% of the selling prices for manufacturing companies in averagely competitive countries. These costs, however, measured against world prices for the firm's output, will be proportionately 20% higher in economies with over-valued currencies, and 20% lower for those whose currencies are under-valued. Finally, the table shows the firm in the averagely competitive economy making a 10% net profit on sales.

Now consider the options available to companies operating in the economy with the under-valued currency. If these companies sell at world prices, even with normal capacity utilisation, they make huge profits. This happens because their locally determined costs are 60% × 20% less than the world average, giving them a 12% cost advantage, in addition to the 10% net profit for which allowance has already been made. An alternative strategy, which would still give them a 10% net profit on turnover, would be for them to sell at prices some 15% lower than the world average, providing them with an enormous cost advantage. They could then use their capital equipment much more intensively, reducing its depreciation charges as a percentage of selling costs by perhaps a fifth, the ratio used in the table. They could do this by relying on the large volume of orders which can be obtained at lower prices to achieve high-capacity working. In practice, the evidence from all the rapidly growing economies is that once reasonable profits on turnover are being made, companies which are highly competitive tend to go for lower prices and higher volumes of sales, rather than trying to keep prices up. This leads to even more rapid export-led growth than would otherwise occur.

The companies in the over-valued economy, on the other hand, face very different prospects. Their higher domestic costs amount to 12% of the world selling prices for their output. These excess charges are more than the 10% net profit made by their competitors in the averagely competitive economies. Their higher locally incurred costs therefore wipe out all profitability for firms in countries with heavily over-valued currencies, if they sell at normal world prices, leaving them trading at a loss. They then have two choices. They can cut their current expenses by paying lower wages and salaries, worsening employment conditions, cancelling investment projects and abandoning research and development programmes. Steps such as these may help in the short term, but are fatally weakening for the future. Alternatively, they can try to sell at higher prices. If they do this, however, unless they are in niche businesses which are not subject to normal competitive pressures, orders are bound to fall away, leading to lower-capacity working and higher depreciation costs per unit of output. To make a 10% net profit on turnover, allowing for lower-capacity working, the firms shown with the cost structure in the table in the over-valued country would have to charge prices nearly 20% above the world average. It is clearly impossible to compete at such high prices, especially against aggressive companies in the under-valued economies. All they can do, therefore, is either to withdraw from the market altogether, or to persevere with prices which are the best compromise they can find between total lack of profitability and holding on to some market share.

It is all too clear which of these three examples is closest to the recent experience of much of US manufacturing, particularly those sectors confronted with competition on consumer goods from the Far East. Faced with the familiar problem of being uncompetitive, however, why cannot these companies increase their productivity to whatever level is required to be competitive with the world average, as all those who advocate industrial strategies and wage restraint are essentially trying to achieve?

Some companies can and will succeed in doing so. These are the ones which will survive even in the harsh conditions portrayed in Table 4.1 for companies in uncompetitive countries. Critical, however, to economies as a whole is not the performance of exceptional companies. It is the average achievement which counts. The required change might be made if it were possible to engineer a sudden huge increase in productivity across the board which competitors could not emulate, without any of the rise in output being absorbed in extra wages and salaries. One has only to look at these conditions, however, to see how completely unrealistic they are. It is far more difficult to increase productivity in slowly growing economies, with depressed levels of investment, low-capacity utilisation and relatively poorly paid staff, than in economies which are already growing fast, and where productivity will inevitably already be increasing rapidly. It is impossible not to share rises in output with the labour force to a substantial degree. What may be possible in isolated companies cannot be done across the board in all companies.

In economies with over-valued exchange rates, the more perspicacious managers of manufacturing companies do not persevere with attempts to improve productivity when they realise that they will never achieve sufficient increases in performance to be able to compete. They conclude that the safest, most profitable and rational strategy is to abandon manufacturing in the domestic economy. Some of them decide to buy from abroad whatever their sales forces can sell, perhaps reinvesting the proceeds from selling off factory sites and installations into manufacturing facilities in other parts of the world. Others sell out to multinational companies, who then use ready made channels to distribute their output. The less perspicacious plough on until their companies go out of business. One of the paradoxical reasons why industrial strategies will always fail in economies with over-valued currencies is that the better the management in industry is at seizing profitable opportunities, the faster the process of deindustrialisation is likely to be. This is why many companies with the best performance records in slow-growing economies are those which have closed down their manufacturing operations fastest, and moved them to other countries where costs at the prevailing exchange rates are much lower.

RETURNS ON INVESTMENT

A characteristic of much of the investment which tends to occur in rapidly expanding economies strongly reinforces the virtuous growth spiral. This investment is found mainly in manufacturing, especially in light industry, and also some parts of the service sector, where the returns are not only high but also tend to be very rapid. This is an extremely important component of the success of fast-growing economies, not least because it explains clearly why some countries have been able to go from being poor economic performers to being extremely successful very quickly. How did Taiwan and Korea manage to move from decades of stagnation to fast growth almost overnight? If it is possible to explain how this happened, and to show that it would be relatively easy for the US economy to recreate the conditions which would allow it to grow fast again, a further important policy plank available to US policy makers will have been laid.

The reason is that the return on nearly all successful capital investment is much greater than the proportion which comes back either as dividends or interest to the people who put up the money to pay for it. The 'private' rate of return on investment, which investors typically receive, is seldom above about 10%, even in those economies which are doing very well. However, it is by no means only investors who benefit directly from the projects for which they put up their money. Many others do as well.

The management and the employees in the enterprises where the investment has been made, whose productivity rises in consequence, almost invariably share in the benefits by obtaining salary or wage rises. The state also obtains a share through increased tax receipts. In addition, the consumer, who is provided with a better product or service, or a lower price, or both, is also a gainer. If the aggregate rather than just the private rate of return is considered, then across a wide swathe of much of the investment in fast-growing economies, the total return to the economy is much higher than 10%. This is not a particularly difficult ratio to calculate from national accounts. For those familiar with them, it is the reciprocal of incremental capital to output ratio. It is often 40% or 50% per annum, and sometimes higher still.

From the point of view of the investor, the build-up period for an investment is not normally particularly important. This is the time between when the investor starts to forgo the alternative uses to which his or her financial resources could be put, and when the investment comes on stream, and starts to produce output and income. It is the time taken to build or construct the project into which the money is being put. The investor's concern is that once the project is in operation, it should be able to provide a sufficient return to cover the interest charges during the build-up period as well as to produce a reasonable private return subsequently. For everyone else in the economy, however, and indeed for the economy as a whole, the build-up period provides no return at all because the outlay for the investment is not yet producing anything. There is no additional output to defray the private rates of return, or to contribute to the total rate of return, until the project on which the money has been spent is physically in use.

It is extremely significant that investment projects typically found in rapidly growing economies combine the following characteristics. First, they have a high total rate of return. Second, they have a short build-up period, often of the order of six months or even less. Third, they tend to be used fully once they are in place, because of the high level of demand which fast growth entails. When these three factors are put together, a truly astonishing cumulative rate of return on investment projects of this type becomes relatively easy to achieve. Those which produce a total rate of return of 50% or more in six months or less, if the return on all the new output thus created is saved and reinvested, can produce a cumulative rate of return in excess of 100% per annum. This makes it possible for the whole of that part of the economy where this type of investment is taking place not only to double its output every year, but to generate all the savings required for this to happen. This kind of increase can still be seen, despite the recent turmoil, in some parts of the economies of countries such as Korea, Taiwan and Malaysia and, until recently, Japan, and now in the fast-developing parts of China. The huge returns on investment in the production of internationally traded goods and services, and the tendency for them to be reinvested, explain why rapidly growing economies have such high savings ratios, and why their well run industries have relatively few financing problems.

These large rates of return cannot, however, be attained across the board. It is impossible to obtain 100% returns on outlays in the social infrastructure, housing, public works and the like, except in rare and unusual circumstances.

Many private sector investment projects do not fulfil these qualifications either. Anything which takes a long time to build, whether large-scale infrastructure projects or complex products requiring years of development, will inevitably have a low cumulative total annual rate of return. These are not the projects which produce fast economic growth. Those that do, however, are exactly those with which the most profitable and rapidly growing international trade is concerned.

This is so because they have the same characteristic significant initial costs, with falling cost curves as production builds up and rising productivity comes through. Here, then, is another essential element in the strategy for achieving rapid economic growth. It is to pitch the exchange rate at a parity which enables fast export expansion and import saving to be achieved. This policy is needed not only because it creates and expands sectors of the economy where productivity growth will be very high. In addition, the total rate of return it can achieve is so large that it can generate the whole of the saving required to finance its own expansion, even if this entails doubling its output every year.

Two extremely important conclusions flow from these considerations. The first is that the lower the parity, the more chance there is of achieving not only self-sustaining but also self-financing growth at a high rate. The increase in exports which is thus likely to be achieved is more than sufficient to take care of any increased import requirements there may be. Since any import restraints will make the exchange rate higher than it otherwise would be, the case for as few and as low tariffs as possible is reinforced. The second is that the large increase in productivity and output makes it much easier than might be supposed to deal with the inflationary pressures caused by rapid growth. We return to this important point in Chapter 6.

The hugely varying rates of return to the whole economy achieved by different classes of investment project may also throw light on an important and puzzling economic growth paradox. Compared to the international average, the US achieves a relatively high return on the comparatively low level of investment it undertakes. This is why the growth rate of the American economy has averaged a little over 3% per annum over recent decades despite its low reinvestment rate. By contrast, many of the fast-growing economies in the Pacific rim score very poorly in this respect. Most of their high growth can be accounted for by large amounts of increased inputs – labour, education, and particularly high levels of capital investment. The explanation for the poor returns, particularly to investment, in many Pacific rim countries, surely lies with the mixture of investment projects which are undertaken. Countries like Korea, which have spent, at government instigation, large sums of money on grandiose industrial schemes to produce ships, chemicals, cement, and so on, have a large proportion of their total investment producing low cumulative returns. This balances off the very high compound returns produced in the large Korean light industrial sector to produce an unimpressive average. The US, with proportionately far smaller involvement by the government in industry, has avoided these pitfalls. What could the US economy achieve if its internationally tradable sectors had the competitive advantages which Korean light industry has had, unaccompanied by the cronyism, corruption and waste which the Korean *chaebol* system brought in train?

CHANGING THE EXCHANGE RATE

Is it possible for the exchange rate to be influenced by policy changes? Or is the parity entirely determined, as monetarists claim, by market forces over which governments have little or no control? If it really is the market which controls exchange rates, and governments are powerless bystanders, then attempts by monetary authorities to position the foreign exchange value of the currency where they want it to be are bound to fail, unless they simply ape the market's wishes. If, on the other hand, government policy can have a powerful impact on the parity of the currency, then the scope for using exchange rate policy to shape the performance of the economy generally is much enhanced.

One of the most important tenets of the monetarist school is that the exchange rate for all economies is very largely, if not entirely, fixed by market forces so that no action taken by the government to change it will make any significant difference. Monetarists have built up an elaborate theory which is intended to prove that there is an equilibrium exchange rate towards which every parity has a strong tendency to return. The traditional form of this theory was known as the Law of One Price, and the modern form is sometimes referred to as International Monetarism. It states that if attempts are made by the authorities to move to a parity away from the one established as the equilibrium point by the markets, then differential rates of inflation will soon pull it back to where it should be.

In particular, it is argued that any attempts to make the economy more competitive by devaluing will automatically cause an increase in inflation which will rapidly erode away any increased competitiveness temporarily secured. This will leave the economy not only as uncompetitive as it was before, but with an extra inflationary problem to add to its other difficulties. It is also contended that if, as a result of a temporary disequilibrium, the currency is over-valued this will exercise a strong downward pressure on the price level, thus reducing the rate of inflation without sacrificing competitiveness, except perhaps in the short term. There is little doubt that many people in powerful positions in the US and elsewhere believe this theory to a greater or lesser degree. What is there to confirm that this proposition is correct?

The reasons why devaluations do not always produce a corresponding increase in inflation will be reviewed in detail in Chapter 6. Suffice to say for the moment that the empirical evidence for the monetarists' contentions is extremely weak, and that there are good reasons, both theoretical and practical, for believing that on this issue they are wholly wrong. At this stage, all that needs to be done is to look at the impact on the price level of exchange rates across the world to see whether there is any evidence of an iron law which determines that parities cannot be altered without differential inflation rates at once starting to bring them back to equilibrium again.

All the evidence, which is plentifully available, shows beyond any reasonable doubt that monetarist contentions that exchange rates are entirely a function of market forces over which governments have no control cannot be correct. Without question, governments can and have changed both the nominal and the real exchange rates of the economies for which they were responsible by very large amounts. A conspicuous case was the huge rise in the rate for sterling which took place at the end of the 1970s and the early part of the 1980s. This was a direct result of the tightening of the money supply and the increase in interest rates which began under the Labour government of the time, and which was continued and reinforced by the incoming Conservative government after 1979. As a result, the nominal value of the pound rose on the foreign exchanges from $1.75 in 1977 to $2.33 in 1980, an increase of 33%, and against the Deutsche Mark from DM3.85 in 1978 to DM4.56 in 1981, an increase of 18%. This happened despite inflation being well above average in Britain over this period, thus enormously decreasing the country's competitiveness. In consequence the real exchange rate rose by 25% with calamitous results for British industry.

Another telling example comes from the early part of the Reagan presidency when the US allowed the nominal value of the dollar to rise by no less than 60% against the Deutsche Mark (from DM1.83 to DM2.92) between 1979 and 1985, although the inflation rates in the two countries were similar. A current example of a currency being held at a rate which is far from a market clearing rate is the *franc fort* policy pursued by the French. The cost to the French economy in holding the rate for the franc against the Deutsche Mark has been enormous. Growth has languished, investment has slumped and unemployment has risen to nearly 13% of the labour force, while the economy has had to be forced by deflation to run a balance of payments surplus without which the *franc fort* policy would collapse.

Governments can also bring down the external value of their currencies if they want to do so. Between 1982 and 1989 the nominal rate for the US dollar against the yen fell by an astonishing 45% (from ¥249 to ¥137), while the rate for the dollar against the Deutsche Mark went down by 38% (from DM2.84 to DM1.76) in just four years, between 1984 and 1988. Of course, there is a limit to the extent to which governments can resist market pressures, as the US discovered when the dollar was devalued at the beginning of the 1970s. There is still, however, considerable scope for monetary authorities in any country to choose whether they want to be at the high or the low end of the range of possibilities which the market will accept.

Nor does a longer perspective do anything to improve monetarist theory's credibility. One of the most striking cases of a successful devaluation was that of France at the end of the 1950s. The government of Charles de Gaulle, faced with increasing competition from Germany as the Common Market became established, devalued the French franc twice, by a total of 25%. Inflation in France rose sharply for a few months, but by nothing like as much as the devaluation. Within a year or so it dropped back to where it had been before. French competitiveness *vis à vis* the German economy was established. The result was a long boom which took the French average growth rate to 5.5% per annum for a decade and a half, more than doubling the national income in fifteen years.

The evidence clearly shows that it is well within the power of any government to choose from a spectrum of possibilities where it wants the real exchange rate to be, and over the long term to hold it there within reasonably narrow margins. Of course there will be short-term fluctuations, but these are not important. It is the medium-term trend which counts. There is without doubt a range of policies which any government can pursue to change the exchange rate, and then hold it at or near the preferred level, all of which need to be used in a co-ordinated fashion.

First, and underlying all else, is the monetary stance adopted by the government. There is overwhelming evidence that tight monetary policies, and the high interest rates which go with them, pull the exchange rate up, and that more accommodating monetary policies and lower interest rates bring it down. Study after study has shown that interest rates have a powerful effect on the exchange rate, significantly greater than other changes; for example, alterations in the availability or cost of raw materials such as oil.

Second, the actions and stance of both the government and the central bank in dealing with the foreign exchange market have a major influence where expectations and opinion are almost as important as the underlying realities. If the government has a clearly expressed view that the exchange rate is too high or too low, the market will respond – as it did, for example, in the United States during the 1980s. The operations of central banks in buying or selling foreign currencies can and must be made consistent with other government policies.

Third, the government should have a clear strategy as regards foreign trade balances. In the short term, fluctuations are unavoidable, but in the longer term these can to a large extent be ironed out. If balance of payments surpluses are allowed to accumulate, as has happened in Japan, there will be strong upward pressure on the exchange rate. The converse is clearly the case, reinforcing the arguments for taking a liberal view on protection, and in general avoiding impediments to imports. The balance of payments is also a function of the level of domestic activity. Deflation produces a larger surplus or smaller deficit and upwards pressure on the parity, and reflation the opposite. The strength of domestic demand is therefore a further important determinant of the exchange rate.

Fourth, the government has a considerable degree of control over capital movements, with or without formal exchange controls. Any policy which encourages repatriation of capital and discourages capital outflows – particularly high domestic interest rates – will push up the exchange rate, and vice versa. One of the problems which may occur if a policy of growth based on increased competitiveness is successfully pursued is that capital may be attracted in undesirably large quantities as a result of exceptional investment opportunities. This may make it more difficult to keep the exchange rate down. The answer to this problem is likely to be lower interest rates, if these are feasible, or deliberately deciding not to fund the whole of the borrowing requirement to discourage an inward flow of money. Domestic sources of capital funds can also be encouraged by concentrating economic activity as far as possible in those parts of the economy which can generate their own savings and investment at a high rate. If there are enough domestic savings to finance all the economy's capital needs, there is no merit in stopping any surplus being invested abroad. Still less is it sensible to insist on capital being repatriated which is not required, unless circumstances are such that it is necessary to get the exchange rate up. If the exchange rate needs to be kept down, there are, on the contrary, positive advantages to capital exports.

Finally, allowance needs to be made for the well known 'J' curve effect. If the value of the currency falls, there is a tendency for imports to stay at more or less their previous volume while the domestic revenue from exports decreases because the exchange rate has gone down. This produces a worsening in the balance of payments position until the volume of exports increases in response to lower prices. If the value of the currency falls slowly, a succession of 'J' curve effects flows from each move downwards in the exchange rate, giving the impression that no improvement is in sight. The United States had something of this experience in the mid-1980s. The reverse tendencies are to be found if the exchange rate appreciates, giving the false impression for a few months, until market forces work their way through, that making exports less competitive does not make the balance of payments position worse. Part of the reason for the 'J' curve, however, is the belief by importers that any reduction in the profitability of their imports will shortly be reversed by an appreciation of the exchange rate. If it is clear, however, that a radical change in exchange rate policy has taken place, which is unlikely to be reversed, it is possible to alter the behaviour of importers much more quickly.

With the battery of policy instruments available, governments can therefore determine the level of the exchange rate within wide limits. There is ample empirical evidence of government instigated exchange rate movements which have been successfully accomplished. Obviously it is impossible for all countries to move towards being competitive with each other simultaneously, although it would be possible for the world economy as a whole to adopt more expansionist policies. The evidence shows that it is practical for any individual country to decide where, within wide bounds, on the spectrum of international competitiveness, it wants to be, and, having chosen that position, to stay fairly close to its preferred location.

Is it true, therefore, that the markets can be bucked? They do not need to be. There are internally consistent policies which any government can adopt to hold the exchange rate down at least to a level which allows the current account to be balanced with full employment and a sustainable rate of growth. These include low interest rates, an accommodating monetary strategy, keeping the economy open to imports which are competitive with domestic supplies, and encouraging capital exports. There are also other policies, currently adopted conspicuously by the French, for example, but also, perhaps less obviously, by the US, which will hold the parity at a higher level than it really should be. Provided the markets are satisfied that the government has adopted a policy stance with which it is determined to continue, stability can be achieved over a wide band of different degrees of exchange rate competitiveness. It is not then necessary to buck the market. This is why, by choosing the right policy mix, it is always possible to choose a macro-economic stance which will ensure that external balance is combined with full employment and rapid growth.

POLICY IMPLICATIONS

We have seen that rapid growth takes place in economies which are competitive in world markets and which start with the advantage of costs at least as low as their main competitors. This enables them to expand their exports, without suffering from excessive import penetration, thus providing them with opportunities to grow without the constraint of balance of payments problems. Internal demand can then be kept at a high and rising level, without undue inflationary pressures developing. These conditions were established and maintained for the US during the nineteenth century and some of the first half of the twentieth century, albeit behind high tariff barriers which had other disadvantages. They applied to most of the rest of Western Europe – excluding Britain, which grew much more slowly – during the quarter of a century after the end of World War II and the immediate post-war recovery. At least until the recent instability, the same conditions were to be found in the fast-growing economies in the Far East. The reason why such sustained growth was achieved, why living standards much more than doubled in the course of less than two decades, why unemployment barely existed, and why inflation was in nearly all cases relatively low and stable, was that the macro-economic conditions were right.

To achieve high exports, any economy has to sell at home and abroad both the output of its labour and of its other factors of production taken together at competitive prices. If it does so, it will be able to achieve import-saving and export-led growth. If it fails to do so, especially by a wide margin, it will plunge into import-led stagnation. The only practical way of making any economy competitive is to position the exchange rate correctly. This is why the parity of the currency is so critically important. There is no other feasible way in which any country can change the price it charges for the whole of its output sufficiently to make the necessary difference.

The higher the proportion of any country's GDP involved in world trade, the more obvious it is that its exchange rate needs to be correctly aligned *vis à vis* its competitors. Perhaps one of the illusions under which the US has suffered is that because its foreign trade exposure is comparatively small, the impact on the economy of unmanageable competition from abroad may therefore have appeared to be relatively slight. Whether the parity of the dollar on the foreign exchanges was appropriate for the interests of the domestic economy may therefore have been given less attention than it should have been. In fact, the exchange rate of the dollar against all other world currencies has been as critically important in determining the US growth rate as it has been to all economies exposed to any significant degree of international competition.

The US emerged from World War II in such a dominant position, and in a world so hungry for goods of any kind, making US production so easy to sell, that there seemed to be no evidence of lack of competitiveness in the immediate post-war period. The problem, on the contrary, was a massive shortage of dollars which barred potential purchasers in the rest of the world from buying American goods and services on which they were otherwise only to willing to spend their money. When the countries which had been over-run during World War II began to recover, it was therefore easy for the US to underestimate the competitive advantage which they had then secured, and to fail to see the long-term consequences. During the 1950s and 1960s, the recovery in Europe and Japan, and the rising prosperity that rapid growth achieved, was barely seen as a threat to the US. Rather it was regarded as a welcome sign that former enemies, or the countries which had been the victims of their attacks, had become able to support themselves economically. They had achieved sufficient prosperity to become stable democracies, no longer a threat to world peace. The US, nevertheless, forewent the greatly accelerated import-saving and export-fuelled growth which most of the rest of the developed world achieved between 1950 and 1973. This was responsible for both the US economic lead being whittled down, and the American economy becoming increasingly poorly prepared for the challenges which it met in many respects unsuccessfully from the 1970s onwards.

The devaluation of the dollar in 1971, and the subsequent further fall in its parity during the 1970s, provided the US tradable sector with a breathing space, but not one of sufficient size. By 1970, the impact of the low rate of reinvestment in US industry was becoming clearly apparent. Although the average American worker was backed by much higher levels of capital investment than in other countries, the age of this equipment tended to be much greater. Meanwhile US wages, at the current exchange rates, were high by international standards in relation to productivity. In other words, the wage costs per unit of output in the US economy were on average uncompetitive, and US-produced goods were priced too highly on average for world markets. This was reflected in the quality of American company performance which in many cases left much to be desired. Poor quality production, over-mighty unions, out of date designs and a high average age for capital equipment were all signs of decay. The beginning of the slide in American trade performance was already visible at the end of the 1960s. After some signs of stabilisation in the 1970s, the 1980s saw the overall position go from bad to worse.

Of course, as always, there were some bright spots to be found. Some industries always did well despite the value of the dollar. The American lead in aircraft production was almost impregnable, although Airbus Industries in Europe provided an alternative source of supply, amid allegations and counter-allegations about hidden subsidies. The US never lost its lead in innovation in the computer and semiconductor industries, despite the fact that making enough money out of producing computer components in America to justify the investment and risk involved proved to be difficult, leading to some protection. Fierce competition from overseas, particularly from Japan, drove industries such as automobiles and steel into either facing bankruptcy or making vast improvements in quality, design, service and sensitivity to the market. The positive response which they evinced, helped by restrictions on imports which sometimes raised costs to other producers struggling to meet international competition, was nevertheless impressive. The problem was that in many cases the solution adopted to make companies more competitive was to make them leaner, employing fewer people, rather than to raise their output per head by major increases in sales and production volumes. The inevitable consequence was then the 'downsizing' and 'delayering' which increased the profitability of industrial operations remaining in existence, while reducing substantially the proportion of US GDP in this part of the economy. Productivity grew rapidly in manufacturing, but the proportion of the labour force it employed tumbled.

In truth, much of American industry showed amazing resilience and ability to fight back against very difficult challenges. This is why US manufacturing output has managed to climb back somewhat in the 1990s despite the adverse conditions it has had to face. The proportion of the US economy involved in manufacturing, however, is still very low by international standards, and the consequence for the growth rate is plain to see. So, too, has been the impact of job shedding by industry on the labour market as a whole, involving large numbers of people having to find jobs in sectors of the economy where growth in output and productivity has proved to be exceptionally hard to achieve. This is the subject of the next chapter.

5   Full Employment

'When a great many people are unable to find work, unemployment results.'

Calvin Coolidge

During the past quarter of a century, an extraordinary change has taken place across much of the developed world. It has been the huge growth in unemployment, particularly in Europe, matched by the fatalism with which this has been accepted by most of the population. In early 1998, about 11% of all the EU's labour force was registered as out of work. About 19m people were looking for jobs. In the US, the level of registered unemployment was much lower. In the spring of 1998 it was 4.7% – about 6.5m people. It was a little higher for men than for women – 4.8% to 4.6% – and considerably greater for people under 25 – a total of 11%, again with a rather higher proportion of men than women out of work, 12.1% compared to 9.8%. Across the board, non-white members of the labour force were a little more than twice as likely to be out of work as their white counterparts. All the same, viewed as a whole, the job market seemed to be working much better in the US than it was the other side of the Atlantic. Whether this is a correct perception is another matter, but at least the very high number of people without jobs in Europe has concentrated attention on the availability of good quality jobs in a way which is not true to nearly the same extent in the US.

It is surely right to regard unemployment, especially on the scale currently apparent in the EU, as a major evil. Being without a job is a personal tragedy for everyone who wants to work and to make a useful contribution to society, and who is denied the opportunity to do so. It is an economic disaster for those without work, whose incomes suffer accordingly. It is extremely expensive for taxpayers, especially in countries with major welfare programmes, who have to foot the bill for unemployment and related benefits. The indirect financial costs of having millions of people with no job is also high. Those who are unemployed are much more likely to need the assistance of health and social services, and other welfare benefits, than they would if they were in work.

Nor are the financial costs of unemployment simply to be counted in the payments to those who have no jobs. In addition, the economy forgoes the output that they could have contributed if they were working instead of being idle. In 1997, the average gross value of the output of every person in employment in the US was about $65 000. In the EU it was around $60 000. Even assuming that the average output of those just coming back into a job was rather less than this, the lost production of goods and services from having people capable of working, but not doing so, is very substantial.

There is also a huge social as well as personal and financial cost to be taken into account. Innumerable studies show that there is a correlation between high levels of unemployment and crime, particularly theft. It is hardly surprising that it is difficult to get the more disadvantaged teenagers to concentrate on their studies if there is little prospect of a job when they leave school. It is equally difficult, therefore, to avoid the conclusion that there is a strong association, reflected in international comparisons of educational achievement, between poor job prospects and low levels of literacy and numeracy among a whole generation of young people, many of whom have never been employed at all.

High levels of unemployment cause major fiscal problems, especially in countries with substantial welfare programmes. A large proportion of the taxable capacity of the EU Member States has to be deployed into paying for unemployment benefit, and all its associated costs. At the same time, the tax base shrinks because millions of people, who could be working and paying taxes, are drawing benefits instead. The major reason why governments across the EU have been unable to reduce the proportion of the national product spent by the public sector, and thus to contain or reduce the overall level of taxation, has been the inexorable rise in the cost of social security payments, for which high levels of unemployment are largely to blame.

Furthermore, having millions of people who would like to work makes less and less sense when the demographics of developed countries are considered. The position varies from country to country, but there is a marked tendency everywhere in the developed world for the number of people of working age to decline, particularly in relation to those who are retired. This inevitably means that the burden of supporting non-earning fellow citizens is going to have to rise for those who are in employment. It makes no sense at all, in these circumstances, for there to be large numbers of people of employable age who would like to work but cannot do so. Again, this is a particularly serious problem in the EU compared to the US.

Nor do the published figures with the numbers out of work tell the full story. The headline unemployment rate measures only those who are actively looking for a job. It excludes all those who would like to work, if the opportunity for doing so existed, but who have given up, temporarily or permanently, trying to find a job because the prospects look hopeless, or because they would be no better off in than out of employment. The ratio between active job-seekers and those who could work, but are not trying to do so, varies from country to country. The average for the European Union as a whole, according to Eurostat figures, is that for every 100 people who are registered as unemployed, about another 45 would like to have jobs if they could.

The total number of people who would prefer to work, given a reasonable opportunity to do so with acceptable levels of remuneration, is therefore far higher than the number of registered unemployed. International Labour Organization figures show that there may be as many as 30m people in the EU who could be drawn into employment if the conditions were right. No doubt many of them are currently working in the black economy, so the potential gains may not be quite as large as appears possible at first sight, but they would still be very substantial. So would be the fiscal benefit from bringing them back into the tax system. Furthermore, there is considerable scope for increasing the amount of work done by those who count as being employed, but who are only employed for limited hours and who do not have a full-time job. Some people, especially those with family responsibilities, may prefer part-time responsibilities, but there are many others who would rather work longer hours for more pay.

When contrasted with the position in the EU, whose total economy and population are roughly the same size as that of the US, it is therefore easy to come to the conclusion that the position in the US is very much better than it is the other side of the Atlantic. Undoubtedly, in some important respects, this is a correct conclusion. The US has been much better at creating new jobs over the past decades than the EU. Between 1973 and 1992, the US employed labour force increased by 37%, from 86m to 119m, as 33m new jobs were created. Over the same period, the fifteen countries now in the EU saw the total number of jobs rise from 138m to no more than 148m, an increase of just over 7%. It is true that over this period the US population increased by 20% and the EU by only 7%, but there is still a striking contrast in job creation performance. The availability of jobs in the EU increased almost exactly in line with growth in the population growth, whereas in the US it was much faster.

The reason why the number of jobs needed across the developed world rose considerably more quickly than the size of the population was partly caused by changes in the proportion of the population of working age, but much more significantly by the increasing willingness of women to work. This change, more than anything else, created the requirement for substantial numbers of extra jobs per head of the population. By far the most important reason why the unemployment rate is so much lower in the US than it is in the EU is because America has been much more successful at creating new jobs than Europe. Because the proportion of the potential labour force out of work is so much lower in the US than the EU, and because the US has a much less comprehensive welfare system, the costs to public expenditure of supporting those without jobs is far less. There is also a persuasive case to be made for saying that even if many of the jobs in the US are low paid, it is better for those concerned to be in work than on welfare. When anyone is in employment, the skills needed for holding down a job do not get rusty. Self-respect is maintained. Welfare assistance is not required.

It seems, therefore, that the US has a lot to teach the EU about how to avoid unemployment, and how to combine job creation on a major scale with stable levels of inflation. There are, however, reasons for believing that the US record is not as good as it appears to be at first sight. Unemployment may be lower, but other problems may be more severe. Both the US and the EU suffer from inadequate job opportunities, especially for their poorer and less advantaged citizens. Different fiscal, legal and welfare systems, however, have meant that the results have materialised in varying ways, in some respects worse in the EU, but in others more damaging in the US.

COMPARATIVE EXPERIENCE

In the European Union there is a major and obvious problem with unemployment. 19m people are registered as looking for work which is not available. About another 11m would like to work, but have dropped out, temporarily at least, from the potential labour force. The costs to the governments concerned are enormous, both in benefits to be paid out and in tax forgone. Crime rises with higher unemployment. Alienation increases. Education standards become harder to maintain. Public expenditure as a proportion of GDP tends to rise.

The US appears to have avoided at least the worst of these pitfalls, but the underlying realities may not be so different each side of the Atlantic. The apparently better US performance may be mostly on the surface rather than underneath. This perception flows from the fact that both the US and the EU suffer from similar root problems, for which lack of job opportunities, especially for those lower down the income scales, is a prime symptom. Growth has been slow on both sides of the Atlantic. The advent of computers, increased competition, better training and more professional management have produced distinct improvements in productivity particularly among those at managerial levels in the labour force. Slow growth, especially per head of the population, combined with productivity in much of the economy rising faster than output per head, has inevitably led to job losses.

In Europe, the impact of these developments has been to increase unemployment. Over the nineteen years between 1973 and 1992, the EU compound growth rate was 2.2% per annum. Output per head among those working, allowing for a 7% increase in the labour force between 1973 and 1992, therefore increased at about 2.1% a year. Over the same period registered unemployment in the EU rose from 2.5% to 10.5%, a rise of 8%, or an average increase in registered unemployment of a little under 0.4% per annum. In the EU, Eurostat statistics show that for every 100 people who appear on the unemployment statistics, close to 145 have lost their jobs. The percentage of the potential labour force involuntarily ceasing employment each year is therefore likely to have been somewhere between 0.5% and 0.6%. Assuming that the output per head of those leaving the labour force was roughly the same as those remaining – and as we shall see later this is a reasonable approximation after making various necessary allowances – a first estimate of the shortfall in demand each year to stop unemployment rising over these years was about 0.5–0.6% of GDP. In fact this is likely to be too low. The average growth in productivity in the labour force would certainly have been higher if demand had been greater. Allowing for all relevant factors, probably an increase in GDP of around 3% per annum cumulatively would have been required in the EU between 1973 and 1992 to keep unemployment down to around 3% of the potential labour force. This would have implied an average increase in productivity of all those then working of about 2.5% per annum, or perhaps a little more.

In the US, similar processes have been at work, but with a different outcome. Although the US economy has grown at almost exactly the same rate as that of the EU over the last twenty-five years – 2.2% compound in each case – the US labour force has increased much more quickly – by nearly 1.7% per annum cumulatively, compared to 0.4% the other side of the Atlantic. The result has been the dismally low US increase in output per head, or increase in productivity actually recorded, of only 0.5% per annum. With its labour force increasing as rapidly as it did, the US economy ought to have been able to expand much faster than the results actually achieved. The reason it did not do so, as in the case of the EU, was that there was a substantial shortfall of effective demand in relation to the level needed to soak up the increases in productivity potentially achievable. Assuming that they were roughly equal to those in the EU, allowing for a cumulative increase in output per head of the order of 2.5% per annum given reasonably favourable conditions, the shortfall in demand in the US turns out to be even higher than in Europe. To achieve full potential utilisation of the labour force, mainly because of its rapid growth, between 1974 and 1992 the missing US cumulative increase in demand was closer to 2% per annum compound compared to 1%

for the EU. The US deficiency of 2% each year is calculated as the difference over the last twenty-five years between the actual increase in labour force productivity, which was 0.5%, compared to the potential increase, which from experience in Europe appears to have been at least 2.5%.

The consequences for the EU of the shortfall in demand needed to keep the labour force fully employed has been a well-publicised catastrophic increase in unemployment. In the US, this has not been the outcome, but only because the welfare system is so different. In Europe, being out of work has many well-known major disadvantages, but generally being on the breadline is not one of them. All European states have comparatively generous social security systems which mean that those out of work are still left with benefits on which they can survive without falling into intolerable poverty. Some EU states have even more abundant entitlements, leaving their recipients with up to 80% of their previous earnings for considerable periods. Understandably, in these circumstances, those who have lost their jobs are prepared to wait, if necessary for a long time, until another position comes up which they think would suit them. The pressure to take any job, even if the pay rate is very low, is heavily blunted.

In the US, by contrast, the welfare system is much smaller in overall scale than in Europe, and considerably less orientated, within a smaller total, to unemployment compensation than to other disbursements such as pensions, medical care and help to poor families. Of those unemployed in the US, in 1995 barely a third are covered by state unemployment insurance, down from 44% in 1980. Those who are entitled to compensation for being out of work in the US receive benefits for a much shorter period of time than is generally the case in Europe. As a result, the pressure on those losing their jobs in America to find another job quickly is much greater.

Entirely understandably, those offering employment opportunities respond in different ways to the availability of labour, and its willingness to work, on each side of the Atlantic. In Europe – where protection for those in employment is relatively high, making it expensive to lay off those in work, but unemployment benefits are also high – the labour market is relatively unresponsive. Employers are reluctant to take on labour if they know that it will be difficult and expensive to discharge it if there is a downturn in business activity. The unemployed can afford to be relatively selective about the jobs for which they apply. In the US, on the other hand, where the opposite conditions apply, the labour market is much more fluid. The risks involved in creating new jobs are much lower, and the competition for them correspondingly greater.

The effects of the two different systems on productivity and income distribution then become clear. In the EU, the productivity of those remaining employed has risen by about 2% per annum, while those who lose their jobs make no contribution to national output at all, at least outside the black economy. In the US, almost everyone capable of working has a job, but the extra net output achieved by many of these jobs is very low, and often negative. Labour is relatively speaking so cheap at the lower end of the US market that employers can afford to use it extremely wastefully. Very high manning levels in hamburger bars, plenty of employees available to clean windscreens at filling stations, and rows of people ready to clean shoes, are not signs of a highly productive economy. They are the result of the same financial pressures which force large numbers of people into these kinds of jobs in Third World countries.

To some extent at least, the availability of large amounts of cheap labour also has a self-fulfilling element to the way the economy develops. It does not pay to install so much labour-saving equipment if there is a large pool of people who will work for low wages. Nor does it pay to invest heavily in skill training. The results are reflected in the depressed level of capital investment in the US, and the poor education and training levels achieved by much of the US labour force. In Europe, by contrast, the opposite pressures apply, and investment levels are greater, and the employed labour force tends to be better educated and trained.

The distribution of income is also different in America and Europe. In both areas there has been a marked increase in inequality of earnings during the last quarter of a century. For broadly the same reasons, the rich have become much richer than they were twenty-five years ago, while the poor have seen only a modest increase in income, and those falling through the net are in too many cases significantly worse off than their counterparts in 1973. Within these broad categories, however, there are big differences. In Europe, blue-collar workers still in employment have roughly kept their share of national earnings, so that their real living standards have risen in line with GDP per head. The heavy losers have been those who no longer have jobs, or who have been dependent on benefits which have not risen in line with output per head. In the US, on the other hand, the competition for jobs has depressed real earnings increases to levels much higher up the income scales. This is why blue-collar real incomes have hardly increased at all in the US during the last twenty-five years.

Thus the employment record in the US, though on the surface better than that of the EU, contains major blemishes. Average productivity growth among those in employment has been much lower. The impact of fierce competition for jobs has caused the real earnings of those in the middle ranges to rise much more slowly than in Europe, making the overall distribution of income even more uneven. Excess labour supplies have probably contributed to lower levels of investment and poorer standards of education and training on average than in the EU. There has been a vast waste of human resources in Europe during the last twenty-five years, but the figures suggest that the greatly increased labour supply in the US has been even less gainfully used than in the EU. By a very wide margin, unemployment percentages on their own do not tell the whole story.

The real problem with the labour market in the US is not that the total number of people without a job is excessively high. On the contrary, it is quite low by international standards, though it might be lower still. The major American problem is that a very high proportion of its labour force is grossly under-used. This is why both its output and its growth in productivity are so low, reflected in almost static real incomes and large numbers struggling through life on minimum wages. The problem in the US may not be unemployment, but there is under-employment on a huge scale. What can be done to put this problem right?

FALSE TRAILS

Faced with the fact that in much of the developed world, there are evidently serious difficulties about providing large numbers of people with reasonably secure, well-paid jobs, almost everyone's instinctive reaction is to resort to essentially supply-side explanations for this state of affairs. Many different reasons are advanced to explain the difficulties which advanced economies appear to have in allowing their workforces to compete successfully with other parts of the world. In consequence a wide range of remedies is on offer. It is not at all clear, however, that any of the explanations usually put forward either at the popular, or more policy-orientated level to account for the low productivity of much of the US labour force, or the high level of joblessness in the EU, have any real credibility. If this is so, the solutions they entail are unlikely to do anything effective to resolve the problem.

First, there is a widespread tendency to blame poor job prospects, especially for those on low incomes, on technical progress. It is clearly the case that much modern equipment can replace men and women with machines, which can do the necessary work far more quickly and accurately than any human can manage. Perhaps the greatest fears are of computers, with their ability to replace armies of clerks, accountants and secretaries. It seems logical at first sight that if machines can replace human labour, then the result must be fewer jobs and more people out of work.

This is of course a line of argument which has been current since the beginning of the Industrial Revolution, when mechanisation started. It is wrong because it depends on the 'lump of labour' fallacy. This is the assumption that the total demand for the output of labour is fixed, so that if part of a given amount of work is done by a machine instead of by human labour, lack of good employment opportunities must be the result. There is, however, no reason why the amount of output for which demand is available should be static. On the contrary, the history of the economically developing world has been one of rising demand ever since the Industrial Revolution began. Provided there is a steadily increasing amount of purchasing power available to buy the expanding output from mechanisation and technical improvements, there is no reason why involuntary unemployment or under-employment should increase. The benefit from technical change will then appear as rising productivity and higher living standards. Problems will only occur if inadequate purchasing power is available to mop up all the new output potentially available.

Second, poor job prospects for low-income earners are not caused by the social and economic changes on which they are often blamed. Neither more women in the labour force, nor more part-time workers, nor shifts away from basic industries to light manufacturing, nor from manufacturing to services, nor any other changes in working patterns are directly responsible for low incomes, though the indirect effects of some of these changes are a different matter. It is true that many of the new jobs which have been created recently in the US have been part time, especially in the service sector, and that women have been in some cases more willing to adapt to them, and to work for lower pay than many men have found acceptable. It is also true that the pattern of work available has shifted away markedly from employment where physical strength was at a premium to office and service activity. This has left older male workers with skills and experience which have sometimes been difficult to redeploy into the modern labour market. In this sense, there are mismatches in the labour market between the skills and abilities for which employers are seeking, and those which a significant number of applicants have to offer.

This cannot, however, be a satisfactory overall explanation for the current high levels of under-employment in the US, or unemployment in the EU. The changes which are taking place in the labour market today are not so different from those which were occurring all over the developed world in the 1950s and 1960s when no such problems were apparent, at least to anything like the same degree. The real problem is a different one. It is that there is not enough work to go round. In these circumstances, employers will inevitably choose the people who are most obviously suited to the work they have to offer, who are most adaptable and who will work for the lowest pay. With insufficient work for everyone, those who are least obviously fitted for the available employment, whether because of their locations, skills, ages or attitudes, will inevitably finish up with a low-paid job or no job at all. If there were a much higher demand for labour, these problems would largely disappear.

It is often argued that so many people, and particularly youngsters, are in dead-end jobs or out of work because their educational skills are inadequate, they are poorly trained and lack technical capabilities, and they are not well motivated. There is little doubt that large numbers of younger people in the rich countries of the world lack good education and training. It is hardly surprising that many of them lack motivation if they are brought up in a culture where so many leaving school fail to find steady employment with reasonable prospects. It does not, however, follow from this that they are incapable of holding down demanding jobs. As with other categories of the labour force, the difficulty is that they are not those most obviously suitable for whatever employment is on offer, so they get left at the back of the queue. The problem, again, is that there is not enough work to go round, and in these circumstances the least advantaged are the most likely to finish up with poorly paid, low-productivity jobs or no job at all.

A different line of argument is that lack of good employment prospects for many people in developed countries is caused by their high wages compared to those in many other parts of the world. It is assumed that it is therefore impossible for the American labour force to compete with workers in places like China and Malaysia, where the average standard of living is far below the level in the US. It is, however, a fallacy to believe that work always goes where labour is cheapest. It is also a fallacy to believe that rich countries and poor countries cannot trade together to their mutual advantage, however different their wage rates and productivity levels may be. The critical factor is not the amount that labour is paid per hour, but its cost per unit of output, taking account of how productive it is and the rate at which it is charged out both to home and export markets. If the productivity of the labour force is high enough, it can compete comfortably in the world even though it is very well paid. The fact that wage rates for many Americans are not high by international standards at the lower end of the income scale, but still the companies they work for have problems competing in world markets, simply reinforces the fact that the US has a major low-productivity problem among much of its workforce. We used to be told that it was cheap labour that made the Far East economies competitive. Now, however, the Tiger economies have incomes per head approaching, and in some cases exceeding, those in the West, but their economies are still growing fast. Hong Kong currently has a standard of living which is approaching that of the poorer parts of the US, and its economy was still growing, at least until recently, at about 7% per annum.

Variations in the cost of producing different goods and services explain why rich and poor countries can trade together to their mutual benefit, even if the poor country makes everything less efficiently than the rich one. Rich and poor countries will always produce some goods and services relatively more efficiently and cheaply than other outputs, and these are the ones which they can sell abroad. For example, a low-productivity Third World country may be a much cheaper place in which simple assembly work can be carried out. A rich country, in turn, may well be able to design complex products at far lower cost than might be possible even with the lowest-paid labour in the poor country. It is these so-called variances which make it worth while for both countries to trade with each other. Each gains, and is better off than it would otherwise have been, as a result of the exchanges which trade makes possible.

For trade of this sort to take place to everyone's advantage, however, another important condition has to be fulfilled. The trade has to be in rough balance. Of course, in the modern world where almost every country buys from and sells to every other, it makes no sense to try to make sure that trade between each pair of countries is in equilibrium on a bilateral basis. It is each country's overall trade balance with the rest of the world which counts. If this is out of kilter – in particular because a country cannot sell enough to the rest of the world to pay for its imports and it therefore has to depress its economy to avoid balance of payments problems, thus putting people out of work – then its economy and its people will suffer from poor job prospects. This is not an argument, however, for abandoning the advantages of free trade. It is one for ensuring that the exchange rate is correctly positioned to enable each economy to hold its own with the rest of the world.

A different explanation advanced for high levels of unemployment, though not under-employment, and in consequence much more applicable to Europe than America, is that generous state-run welfare systems have blunted the need to work. Large numbers of people do not, therefore, try to get jobs. It makes more sense to sit at home collecting benefits, the argument runs, than incurring the costs of being at work, especially if the pay is low. There is some truth in this assertion, especially for some people on small incomes. The effects of relatively high levels of income tax on low wages, combined with benefit withdrawal, can produce high effective rates of tax on people at the bottom end of the pay scale. There are also particular problems for married couples, where one spouse working for low pay can reduce family entitlements by more than the income gained if the other remains out of work.

As a general explanation for high levels of unemployment, however, this argument is also implausible. First, large numbers of people who are out of work do not suffer from these kinds of income-trap problems. Second, at least some of these problems arise from the fact that there is so much unemployment in the first place. Many jobs are on offer at low pay because there are large numbers of people competing for the smaller quantity of unskilled jobs available nowadays. Third, and perhaps most importantly, much of the income-trap problem is itself directly the result of the huge cost to the state of having millions of people involuntarily out of work. There is acute strain on the state revenue and benefit system, largely because of the massive loss of income tax revenues from unemployment combined with the heavy costs in benefits of having millions of people without jobs. The resulting high levels of assessments on those with low earnings causes much of the overlap between taxes and benefits for people on meagre incomes.

Even if high welfare benefit levels are not likely to be seen by most people to be a significant contribution in the US to the reasons for poor job prospects for many people, we are left with the other explanations, which look equally unconvincing. They are nevertheless widely believed. This is why many of the policy prescriptions for improving the prospects for those currently doing poorly in the labour market in Western economies are orientated to supply-side solutions. If, however, the disease has been poorly diagnosed, the remedies proposed are unlikely to be effective.

SUPPLY-SIDE MIRAGES

Most people's perceptions of the reasons for poor job prospects for low-income earners are that large numbers of people appear to be marginal candidates in the job market for the 'supply-side' reasons set out in the previous section. It is therefore hardly surprising that the government's response, in almost all countries with apparently inadequate job opportunities, is to tackle supposed supply-side deficiencies. The objective is to make the economy more efficient, and thus better able to secure enough of the world's purchasing power to keep a higher proportion of the labour force employed. This activity is frequently devoted to efforts to improve productivity in the hope that this will make the economy more competitive.

The scale of much of this activity is enormous. In the US, this is reflected in major current initiatives on education and training, though these are dwarfed by actions in some other countries. France, afflicted by unemployment rates of more than 12% of its labour force, has recently been spending almost 0.75% of its entire gross national product on training schemes. Sweden and Denmark spend even more – over 1% of their GNPs. Nor do efforts to improve competitiveness cover only training. Higher levels of investment are also perceived to be a key factor, especially if the investment can be orientated to producing products with high value added. This often shades into claims that high technology is the key to improving productivity and competitiveness, generating initiatives to move advanced economies away from relatively 'low-tech' activity to the 'higher-tech' end of the spectrum, where it is thought that it would be easier to compete with producers in less developed parts of the world.

Because this approach generally requires substantial capital expenditure, another plank in the policy platform is then to encourage more savings to finance increased investment, particularly in manufacturing industry. Fast-growing economies reinvest a much higher proportion of their national incomes than the relatively slow-growing economies of the West. It is therefore assumed that if investment were increased, this would tend to lead to high rates of growth. It is also argued, although again more in Europe than in America, that the state has a major role to play in enhancing the infrastructure to make the economy more competitive. Improving the road and rail system and developing more advanced telecommunications, proponents of this type of investment claim, will improve the capacity of any country to export and to compete in the world.

Unfortunately, evidence for the overall efficacy of any of these policies is almost totally lacking. Of course, more training gets some people into jobs which they might not otherwise have been able to secure, and it is certainly the case that wilting levels of investment weaken any economy's capacity to compete in the future. This is a different matter, however, from being able to show that all these state-driven supply-side efforts to cope with poor employment prospects have been successful. On the contrary, the evidence strongly suggests that they have failed to provide the sought for solutions in all the advanced Western countries which have spent large sums of money on them.

These policies have failed to work because none of them begins to cope effectively with the real reason why there are so many people across the developed world in the West with poor job prospects. This has little to do with supply-side problems, and everything to do with lack of sufficient demand for the goods and services which Western economies are capable of producing. When looked at in this light, it becomes comparatively easy to see why all the huge efforts currently being put into employment measures are not going to work in the absence of changes in the overall economic environment.

The fundamental problem with trying to use education and training programmes and increased investment to make any slow-growing country more competitive, is that it is much easier to run such programmes successfully in economies which are already growing rapidly. Advanced Western economies are not the only ones with education and training programmes. Every developed country has them, and so, too, do developing countries. Furthermore, in countries which are growing quickly, with buoyant tax revenues and rapidly expanding and profitable enterprises, high-quality education and training can be afforded relatively easily, both in academic and on-the-job environments. The incentive for everyone to improve his or her skills is also clearly evident. With a tight labour market, everyone can find a job, so time spent on training courses is seldom wasted. As a result, the effort and money spent on education and training has an immediate pay-off for almost everyone concerned.

In countries with sluggish growth, the cards are stacked the opposite way. First, it is impossibly difficult to increase the skills of the labour force as quickly in a slow-growing economy as in one which is growing fast, because the opportunities for using increased training are so much less. Slow-growing economies thus progressively slip further behind, and become even less competitive. Second, because there is still not enough work to go round, much of the education and training that takes place is wasted since those on the courses cannot obtain work where they can use their new-found skills once their training is completed. Even if they can, all too often they do no more than displace someone else, who then finds his or her way either on to the dole queue or back to another training course. This is much too close to being an expensive and dispiriting zero-sum game.

Nor is the encouragement of investment any more of a panacea in the absence of overall economic changes. As with education and training, it is far easier to implement successful investment projects in economies that are already growing fast than in ones which are static or growing slowly. Profitability is much greater, making them easier to finance. Wages and salaries in the enterprises making them are relatively high, attracting able entrepreneurs and managers, who are likely to make good decisions. When mistakes are made, which inevitably they will be, it is easier to pay for them. As wave after wave of investment takes place, so the experience in managing the highly skilled process of organising a successful investment strategy becomes honed. It is extremely hard to succeed against competitors who have accumulated this kind of expertise. Far from it being easier in high-tech industries, furthermore, it is likely to be more difficult. Running high-tech operations successfully usually involves accumulating years of experience in managing rapid technical change. The chances of companies anywhere being able to move into these fields from scratch and to compete successfully are not good. Logic and experience strongly suggest that it is generally easier to compete in industries where the technology is well established, and where the risks and skill requirements are lower, provided that the overall cost base is favourable.

The reality is that it is not high levels of savings and investment which produce high growth rates. It is high growth rates which produce high levels of savings and investment. The key to better economic performance is not to subsidise and cajole reluctant investors into putting more money into new projects than they would if left to themselves. It is to create a macro-economic environment where high rates of growth are strongly encouraged by rising effective demand. Investment will then follow as profitable opportunities open up. The reason for relatively low levels of capital expenditure in US – or European – manufacturing, compared to the fast-developing areas of the world, is that the prospects for making money out of new plant, machinery and factories in fast-growing economies tend to be much better than in those in North America and Europe which have a much lower average growth rate.

There is, nevertheless, a broad issue as to what strategies are the right ones to pursue when there are millions more people available for work than the economy really needs to achieve its current output. Does it really make no sense to try to improve productivity in conditions where there are very large numbers of people with no jobs, as is the case in Europe? Is it really better to adopt the American solution, which is to arrange the welfare system so that it drives productivity down to a point where output per head is low enough for nearly all the potential labour force to be employed? Simply posing questions in this form, however, exposes how far many government policies in the Western world may have drifted from providing effective solutions to pressing problems. They also point the way to some important and widely believed fallacies about productivity and supply-side remedies, and the link between competitiveness, improved economic performance and better job prospects. If asked what needs to be done to improve the US growth rate, the stock answer from most quarters is that the only solution is for American corporations to raise investment, productivity, quality, innovation and value added. Is any of this true?

As we have already seen, productivity is not at all the same as competitiveness. If it were, the richest countries would always successfully out-strip the poorer ones. This is clearly, however, not the experience of much of the world today. Nor has it ever been in the past. The reason is that output per head has everything to do with the standard of living, but almost nothing to do with competitiveness. It is the exchange rate – or more accurately the prices each country charges the rest of the world for the combined cost of all its factors of production – which determines whether the economy grows fast, or slowly, or remains static. Increasing productivity to make the economy more competitive will only work if it can be done quickly enough to reduce prices more rapidly than the world average, without reducing profit margins. Achieving this objective from a position where economies are growing more slowly than the rest of the world is an impossibly difficult task, and attempts to achieve it are virtually bound to fail.

Of course, quality and innovation are important. No doubt the better the quality the higher the price which can be charged. What can be done, however, if an economy starts from a position where quality is poor, and the products sold are old-fashioned? Making them better is expensive, and everyone else in the world is trying to improve their products at the same time. The companies which are likely to succeed are those which are already profitable and expanding – in fast-growing countries. Those in economies which are expanding slowly are likely to be growing less rapidly, to be less profitable and with lower levels of investment, and therefore not in a position to afford to implement improvements nearly so easily. This is why fast growth is the easiest and fastest route to product enhancement. Trying to use increasing quality and innovation as ways of raising competitiveness and growth, rather than seeing them as byproducts of an expanding economy, is again to set an impossibly difficult target which will almost certainly not be achieved.

Value added has similar characteristics to productivity. The total value added in any economy is more or less equivalent to total output. If the economy does not expand, total value added will stay the same. If productivity then increases in some parts of the economy, it will have to go down in others. This is the root problem with trying to raise value added and productivity without tackling the macro-economic environment. Even if successful in those parts of the economy where the policies are effective, if there is no overall output increase, the result has to be a corresponding reduction in performance in other parts of the economy which the policies have not touched. Increasing average productivity in some areas, while the economy stays the same size, does no more than guarantee worsening job opportunities somewhere else. In particular, if productivity increases among those with already high output but the level of demand on the economy remains the same, then those already worse off are bound to see their employment prospects deteriorating.

The truth is that the connections between productivity, quality, innovation and value added and improved economic performance are indeed significant, but different from those normally perceived. It is not improved productivity or any of the other quality measures of output which produces more growth. The sequence is the other way round. This does not, of course, mean that productivity and related measures of economic performance are unimportant. On the contrary, they determine the standard of living, and are thus of vital significance. It is the output per employee which multiplies up to the gross domestic product. Whether an economy has a high or low standard of living, however, tells us nothing about the ability of its producers to compete in the world and whether, therefore, its total output, and with it productivity, quality, innovation and value added will increase or not. The economy's growth is determined by an altogether different factor, which is whether its output is competitively priced in the home and export markets. This is an exchange rate issue, and not one where any realistic policies on improving productivity, quality, innovation and value added, in isolation from macro-economic policy changes, have a chance of being successful on their own.

As with so many other economic matters, feedback makes it difficult to distinguish between cause and effect. In this case, as elsewhere, it is all too easy to confuse symptoms and root causes. Determining the direction of causation is, however, critical to formulating proposals which are going to work. Many billions of dollars can be spent on supply-side policies designed to improve competitiveness and growth by increasing investment, productivity, quality, innovation and value added. Little or nothing will be attained. No money needs to be spent, however, on implementing the policy which will actually achieve the results which otherwise appear so elusive. Bringing down interest rates, raising the money supply, and positioning the exchange rate correctly so that effective demand is increased, all cost nothing. Much more rapid growth will then follow, bringing enhanced investment, higher productivity, improved quality, innovation and greater value added effortlessly in train, as market forces drive the economy to expand. Job opportunities, especially for those on relatively low incomes, will then progressively cease to be a major problem. As happened to the US labour force during the world wars, and as, at least until very recently, was the experience in the Tiger economies, once the labour market gets tight enough it becomes worth training almost everyone. This is the only secure and certain route to the increases in productivity and wages among the less well-off, which are otherwise so easy to advocate and so difficult to achieve.

GROWTH AND THE TRADE BALANCE

The most important reason why the US economy suffers from low productivity among a high proportion of its labour force has nothing to do with any supposed deficiencies which supply-side policies might be able to cure. The real reason so many people earn such low wages is that there is insufficient demand for what they could produce if their output per head was significantly higher. Until this deficiency is remedied, low productivity will remain an intractable and insuperable problem. The only solution to low US productivity and stagnant real wages is to raise the level of demand for the output which the US economy is capable of producing to a sufficient extent to make it worth while employers increasing the training, job prospects and earnings of all the lower paid. How much demand is missing? The calculations are not particularly difficult to follow, and they are set out below.

It is easiest to start from a hypothetical country to illustrate the principles, and then to apply them to individual countries. It is also simpler to exemplify the position in a country where the impact of insufficient demand has led to unemployment, which is easily measurable, and then to extend the conclusions to the US where the effect has been primarily on productivity and wage levels – that is, on under-employment – instead of on joblessness. The simplest method is therefore to consider the problems faced by countries such as those in Europe, and then to relate their policy change requirements back to those of the US.

The starting point is to consider a country whose level of unemployment is at a higher level than is regarded as acceptable. If the reason for lack of jobs to keep everyone in work is insufficient demand, total demand within the economy will have to be increased until unemployment has been reduced to a level which is regarded as reasonable. How much extra is needed? If the potential output per head from those out of work was the same as those in work, the answer would be easy to work out. The increase in effective demand would have to be proportional to the increase in employment that was needed. For example, to reduce 10% unemployment – close to the EU average in recent years – to 3% would require an increase in demand to lift the proportion of those in work from 90% to 97% of the potential labour force, an increase of 7 divided by 90, or about 8%.

It is clear, however, that this is much too simple, even if we are only looking for broad approximations rather than exact figures. There are three significant adjustments which need to be taken into account to produce acceptably reliable results.

First, there is substantial evidence that to reduce the registered unemployment rate by, say, 100 000 people, much more than 100 000 new jobs need to be created. The reason for this is that increased employment opportunities attract back into the labour force many people who would not otherwise register as out of work. The ratio varies, depending on a variety of circumstances, but the average across a number of European countries where lack of work has been a major problem shows that during the major changes in unemployment rates which took place in the late 1980s, for every 100 000 people taken off the unemployment register, roughly 150 000 new jobs had to be created. As about the same proportions of the total population are in work in the US as in the EU – just over 40% in both cases – approximately the same ratio is likely to apply in the American case too.

Second, increasing demand is bound to lead to higher remuneration for existing employees, as the labour market tightens, even without hourly wage rises. More shift work will be needed, increasing overtime and payments for operating during unsocial hours. People now counted as employed, but involuntarily working part time, may take on full-time jobs. As a result, the average remuneration for all the existing labour force is likely to go up. Clearly, the larger the rise in demand, the more pronounced this tendency will be.

Third, it is unlikely that the output per head of those currently unemployed will be as high as the average if they are reabsorbed into the active labour force. It will almost certainly be lower by a significant margin. Furthermore, the higher the level of unemployment from which we start, the larger this discrepancy is likely to be. We are not dealing with exact figures here, but within reasonably narrow limits it seems probable that this and the previous adjustment are likely to cancel each other out.

Making this assumption then provides a relatively simple formula for calculating the rise in effective demand needed to increase employment by any given percentage. If registered unemployment is 10% and the target is to reduce it to 3%, effective demand has to be increased by the 8% already calculated, multiplied by an additional 50% to take account of the extra people drawn into the labour force. The total rise needed, therefore, will be approximately 8% times 1.5, which comes to about 12%.

How can demand be stimulated to achieve much lower levels of unemployment? It has to be done both by increasing the money supply and by expanding import-saving and export-led demand. The credit base needs to be increased sufficiently both to stimulate greater activity and to accommodate the new and higher volume of transactions which will need to be financed as the economy expands. The ratio between the money in circulation and the volume of transactions tends to fall as money becomes cheaper and more plentiful, and more idle balances materialise. As a result, the increase in the money supply is likely to have to be significantly greater in percentage terms than the proportionate rise in domestic demand which will be needed.

It is not possible for any economy to increase demand by a significant percentage without regard to the impact this change would have on its balance of payments position. The next stage is therefore to calculate the balance of payments and exchange rate implications of a large increase in domestic demand. Again, it is easier to consider a hypothetical economy first, and then to apply the conclusions to the real world.

Suppose that the economy we are considering had a trade balance within acceptable limits before domestic demand was increased, and by way of illustration, suppose that the increase needed was 12% – the same figure considered above. Again, as an approximate estimate, the result is likely to be that exports of goods and services would stay the same as they were before but imports would rise by the same proportion as the increase in domestic demand. A balance of payments deficit would therefore be created. To correct this, there would have to be a devaluation. How much depreciation would be needed? Again, it is not difficult to calculate the broad magnitude required.

Large numbers of studies have been done into the sensitivity of the imports and exports of developed countries to price changes. All these studies show results that cluster round the same values. These are referred to as the price elasticities of demand, and the studies show that both imports and exports have elasticity values (ignoring their signs) of about one.

This means that if any economy with these elasticities devalues its currency, the volume of exports will rise by 1%, while the volume of imports will fall by 1%. If, again as an approximation, but not far from experience, import prices are set by world prices, and export prices are set in the domestic economy, a devaluation of 1% will have the following effects:

The value of imports, measured in the domestic currency, will stay the same as they were before. This will happen because they will rise in price by 1%, but fall in volume by 1%, these two changes cancelling each other out.

The value of exports, measured in the domestic currency, however, will increase by 1%. This happens because their price, measured in domestic currency stays the same, but their volume increases by 1%.

The overall effect of these impacts on imports and exports taken together is that a 1% depreciation will improve the trade balance of the devaluing economy by 1%. This ratio then feeds straight back to the change in the trade balance required from the increase in domestic demand. If a 12% increase in demand is needed to reduce unemployment to acceptable levels, as a first approximation, this will need to be accompanied by a devaluation of the same size. This will both provide the stimulus needed to trigger off more growth and investment to sustain it, while also ensuring that there is no balance of payments constraint to check progress. Although this is not obvious, in fact these relationships remain the same whether the economy concerned has a large or a small proportion of its output involved in foreign trade. The sums of money involved in financing a trade deficit, compared with total GDP, however, would obviously be smaller if the economy had less of its GDP concerned with the import and export of goods and services.

Turning now to the US, we have seen from a previous series of calculations (see p. 99) that the shortfall in demand on the US economy for the decades following 1973 was approximately twice as high as it was for all the EU economies taken together – about 2% per annum compared to 1%. By far the largest reason was the US exchange rate policies pursued during the last quarter of a century, particularly but not exclusively during the Reagan presidency, which led to the international value of the dollar being much higher than it should have been over this period. Again, some fairly easy calculations provide a quantitative picture of the scale of the problem. For all the years between 1973 and 1992 the arithmetical average trade weight for the dollar was 98, with the base year, 1972, being 100. The dollar's trade-weighted value in 1997 was 96. This indicates that as a first sighting shot, the dollar needs to fall by roughly twice the 12% calculation for the EU for the same period – that is, by approximately 25% from its 1997 value against all currencies. When President Clinton was elected in 1992 the trade-weighted value of the dollar stood at 83. It needed to fall to about 73. The fact that it has risen 15% instead of falling the 12% which was really required will have the same profound effects on the future of American living standards for all except the already rich, as did the over-valuation between 1973 and 1992.

One more set of calculations shows how much difference would have been made to the living standards of the average American if the value of the dollar had been 25% lower than it actually was for the decades following 1973. Using the same import and export demand elasticities as previously, with the dollar 25% lower, the initial effect would have been to increase the value of exports in relation to imports by about 25%. Most would have been manufactures, safeguarding the US industrial base. Thereafter, the economy would have been able to continue to grow much faster than it did, freed from balance of payments constraints and oiled by the relatively relaxed monetary stance and low interest rates which would have been necessary to achieve the lower dollar parity.

The result would have been that the economy would have grown at a cumulative rate matching the increase in productivity per head which is relatively easy to achieve in advanced economies. This is about 2.5% per annum, to which has to be added, in the US's case, a significant percentage to allow for the growth in the US labour force over this period, which increased at a compound 1.7% per annum. This would have provided a cumulative growth rate for the US economy over the period of about 4.2%. This growth rate would have been roughly in line with what the world average for the period would have been, allowing for much better US performance than actually occurred, but assuming that this had no knock-on effects elsewhere in the world. If this scenario had materialised, the average US citizen would now be just over 60% better off than he or she actually is. The productivity problem would have been solved. The distribution of income and wealth would be much more even. The huge fiscal and foreign exchange deficits which have dogged the US would never have occurred. Of course, new problems would have crept into view as old ones were solved. This is always the way. America's history for the last quarter of a century, however, could have been very different.

It is important to stress again that the calculations set out above are approximate and that they involve assumptions and simplifications which mean that the conclusions drawn are rough and ready rather than exact. These qualifications do not mean, however, that the orders of magnitude have been wrongly assessed or that, allowing for margins of error, it is unsafe to rely on these results within broad limits. On the contrary, they point clearly to the direction in which policy needs to be moved, and they provide a reasonably reliable quantified indication as to the size of the changes required. It is significant that they are by no means out of line with the scale of the exchange rate adjustments which have occurred frequently in the past, or indeed, the change in the trade-weighted value of the dollar – albeit in the wrong direction – over the last five years. This is a further indication that the orders of magnitude have been correctly calculated.

If a continuous compound growth rate for the US of 4.2% or so is possible in present conditions, is this the limit, or could Americans choose to have their economy growing even faster? If it is possible to increase the growth rate from 2.2% to 4.2% per annum, what about 6.2%? We turn to this possibility in the next section.

WIDER PERSPECTIVES

It is now possible to see the twin problems of slow economic growth and high levels of unemployment or low productivity growth in the same context. The solution to them both has a substantial overlap. The policies for all economies suffering from slow growth and under-employment of the labour forces have to be changed in two vital respects. Their internal level of demand has to be expanded to a point where their labour forces are fully stretched. Their exchange rates have to be positioned at a level which enables them to shift to a much higher rate of growth. We need now to explore in more detail the conditions required not only to achieve an increase in output while the labour force is used more effectively and under-used resources are brought back into commission, but also to maintain an optimum growth rate for the foreseeable future.

The only way to do this is for a high and rising level of demand to be sustainable at whatever growth rate is considered desirable, without the economy running into either capacity constraints, or – the other side of the same coin – unacceptable inflationary problems. These conditions can be achieved, but to understand how to attain them we need to revert to some of the issues discussed in Chapter 4. Bringing the dollar exchange rate down to a level which gets productivity to rise at around 2.5% per head each year is certainly a very important first step. Accomplishing this objective is not, however, a sufficient condition for ensuring that the US economy grows with the vigour currently exhibited in many countries in the Far East, or by Japan and most of Europe in the 1950s and 1960s. Other steps will have to be taken to ensure that these conditions are achieved.

A major move in the right direction would have been taken if the US economy could be made to grow at a little over 4% on average each year, though even this would require very substantial changes to current macro-economic policies. At least the US would then hold its own with the world average growth rate. American living standards would then cease falling compared to the world average, as they have done over recent decades. To do this, the US economy would have to obtain and keep a sufficient share of the investment and production which has the falling cost curves and large returns characteristic of international trade. This means that the costs of output in the US, allowing for American productivity levels, would have to be as low as the world average. If this does not happen in future, footloose investment and production of both goods and services – primarily in light industrial manufacturing – will continue to migrate to other parts of the world where overall costs, measured internationally, are lower.

It is, however, possible to predict with a high degree of certainty what will happen to the competitiveness of the US economy if it continues to grow much more slowly than the world average. If its growth rate is less than that of the rest of the world, it is inevitable that this will be reflected in rates of gross investment below those of the economies which are expanding more quickly. It is then equally inescapable that the proportion of the investment which takes place in the US of the highly productive internationally tradable kind will be lower than in rapidly growing economies. The unavoidable consequence is that the US will become progressively less able to compete in the world, unless, eventually, exchange rate adjustments take place.

Indeed, a general rule can be promulgated which applies to the US as much as to anywhere else. Any economy which is growing at less than the world average rate, which is currently close to 4% per annum, will find its ability to compete falling away, while any growing faster than the world average will find its competitiveness increasing. This is a direct consequence of the self-reinforcing tendency for economies with exceptionally low-cost international tradable sectors to grow more rapidly than the average, as they attract more and more investment, and their competitiveness increases. Exactly the reverse happens to the weaker economies whose ability to compete steadily diminishes, a reflection of rising costs, making them progressively less attractive sites for more investment.

There is thus a universal tendency for fast-growing economies to develop currencies which become stronger and stronger, while those of slow-growing economies weaken. They are then faced with the all too familiar choice in the West – to deflate or to devalue. If devaluation is ruled out, the deflation which follows will progressively worsen their condition, as their investment ratios and competitiveness fall further and further away.

Even a consistent growth rate of about 4% per annum, close to the world average, is still quite low by the standards of the Pacific rim countries, or in comparison with the achievements of many European economies in the 1950s or 1960s. Would it be possible for the US to move up to growth rates of 6% or even 8% or more, if it wanted to, as are regularly achieved in the Far East? It probably would be, but still greater downward movements in the exchange rate would be required, to enable the US to achieve the super-competitive status that would be needed to promote it to the same growth league as Taiwan, South Korea and China. If only to show how 8% or more rates of growth could be achieved, however, it is worth exploring the structural changes which would be required to bring the American economy up to the Pacific rim level of performance, to see how such high growth in output could be obtained. Table 4.1 in Chapter 4 suggests that the dollar exchange rates might have to drop perhaps another 20% *vis à vis* those in the Far East to do it. How would the returns on investment then produce the very high growth rates which the Far East economies achieve?

Consider again the total returns achieved by different types of investment projects, encompassing all the increases in income received by everyone in the economy as a result of investment. These include higher wages, better products, greater tax receipts and higher profits, as well as the returns to those who put up the money. Recall the important point that returns on investment projects vary enormously. In some of the private sector, and much of the public sector, they are little more than the rate of interest, and sometimes lower. This is typically the total rate of return obtained on investments, for example, in housing, and many roads and public buildings. At the other end of the spectrum, in some light manufacturing and parts of the service sector, the total rate of return is often far larger. It can be as great as 100% per annum in favourable cases. In the middle are investments in heavy industry, which typically produce total rates of return of around 20% or 25%.

Investment projects with exceptionally high total returns are characteristically those involved in international trade in goods and services. They therefore tend to be heavily concentrated in countries with low exchange rates, and are strongly discouraged by high currency values. Furthermore, the high total returns on these investments both produce large resources for reinvestment and ample opportunities for new profitable projects. The result is that a much greater proportion of the national income goes into investment than in slow-growing economies. Now consider two examples:

Country A has total gross investment of 15% of GDP; two thirds of this – 10% of GDP – produces an average total return of 10%, and one third – 5% of GDP – produces an average total return of 20%. This economy will have a growth rate of $(10\% \times 10\%) + (5\% \times 20\%)$ – a total of 2% per annum.

Country B has a total gross investment of 35% of GDP. In terms of GDP share, 15% produces an average 10% total return, 10% produces a 20% total return, and 10%, in the highly competitive internationally traded sector, produces a 50% total return. This economy will have a growth rate of $(15\% \times 10\%) + (10\% \times 20\%) + (10\% \times 50\%)$ – a total of 8.5% per annum.

Of course this is an oversimplified model, but this does not prevent it from demonstrating an important insight into how economies produce different growth rates, and how their structures adapt to and reinforce the opportunities which their foreign trade relations open up for them. With an 8.5% growth rate, and gross investment running at 35% of GDP, productivity rises rapidly. The competitiveness of the internationally tradable sectors grows fast. Education and skill levels increase exponentially. The problem which these economies have is to avoid the growth of export surpluses, and the appreciation of their currencies, eroding away the competitiveness which makes such high increases in output possible.

Should the US aim for as high a growth rate as this? Difficult decisions would be required. The sheer size of the US economy may make it hard for the US to secure a sufficient proportion of the world's high return investment for a growth rate as ambitious as 8% or more to be sustainable. The social and environmental strains entailed by very rapid economic expansion are substantial. On the other hand, the increase in living standards and the extra ability to cope with novel developments which exceptionally rapid growth opens up are potentially exceptionally rewarding. Also, with a fast-growing economy would go a corresponding ability for the US at least to retain, and probably to enhance, its international power and influence rather than seeing it slowly whittled away as other parts of the world grow much faster. The point to grasp is that it is possible for these kinds of choices to be made. It is not inevitable that the US should be left to languish near the bottom of the growth league while other countries take advantage of opportunities which the US could seize. If the US wanted to see its economy growing at 6% per annum or more, it could almost certainly do so. US citizens should be allowed to choose the future they desire. Americans do not need to have static or declining real incomes, as too many of them have at present.

6 Inflation and Living Standards

'Some people would believe anything, especially if it eliminates awkward social and political problems.'

Lord Balogh

There is a widespread fear that exchange rate changes automatically generate inflationary pressures in devaluing economies. It has always been a major tenet of the monetarist position that any benefits secured from depreciation will at best be temporary. They will soon be lost, it is argued, as a result of increasing inflation in the devaluing country, leaving the economy concerned in no more competitive a position than it was before, after a short adjustment process, but also with the legacy of an enhanced level of inflation.

It is also widely believed that a devaluation necessarily produces a reduction in the living standards of any economy where the external value of its currency is falling. There are two reasons usually advanced to support this proposition. The first is that if a country devalues, there will inevitably be an adverse movement in its terms of trade. This means that, after the fall in the parity, the amount of imports which can be purchased for each unit of exports is bound to fall, depressing the national income. The second, which overlaps with the first, is that to make up for the reduction in the terms of trade, more room will have to be found for goods and services to be sold abroad. The only way of achieving this objective is to shift resources out of current living standards into exports, thus lowering average real incomes and depressing the real wage.

Even if these arguments were correct – and we shall see that there are good reasons for believing they are false – they would not apply with any great force in the US, where the proportion of GDP involved in foreign trade is relatively low. Much of the case in this book is that over the medium term, the exchange rate is of critical importance in determining the growth rate and increases in productivity and the standard of living, even if the economy's foreign trade exposure is comparatively small. In the short term, however, the immediate effect of a dollar depreciation on the US price level and living standards is not large. In particular, changes in the terms of trade – the ratio between the prices for US imports and exports – have never had more than a small impact on US living standards.

There can be little doubt, however, that the almost axiomatic strength of monetarist arguments has persuaded large numbers of people that devaluations are inflationary, reduce living standards, upset business plans, discourage investment, and ought to be avoided if at all possible. This is the standard case for fixed parities. Even a brief look at economic history, however, shows that these views are almost entirely unfounded. There have been large numbers of exchange rate changes in recent decades which can be used to test the validity of the widely believed monetarist case, and several of the most prominent are set out in Table 6.1 Without exception, they show that even large exchange rate changes generally make little or no difference to the rate of inflation, unless the economy concerned was already operating at full stretch – as was the case in France, for example, at the end of the 1950s. Even then, however, the sharp increase in prices, to which the double devaluations under Charles de Gaulle undoubtedly contributed, quickly abated.

Table 6.1: The Effects of Exchange Rate Changes on Consumer Prices, the Real Wage, GDP, Industrial Output and Employment[*]

	Year	Cons-umer Prices	Wage Rates	Real Wage	GDP Change	Industrial Output Change	Unem-ployment (%)
Britain – 31%	1930	–6.0	–0.7	5.3	–0.7	–1.4	11.2
Devaluation	1931	–5.7	–2.1	3.6	–5.1	–3.6	15.1
against the US	1932	–3.3	–1.7	1.6	0.8	0.3	15.6
dollar in 1931	1933	0.0	–0.1	–0.1	2.9	4.0	14.1
	1934	0.0	1.5	1.5	6.6	5.5	11.9
France – 27%	1956	2.0	9.7	7.7	5.1	9.4	1.1
Devaluation	1957	3.5	8.2	4.7	6.0	8.3	0.8
against all	1958	15.1	12.3	–2.8	2.5	4.5	0.9
currencies in	1959	6.2	6.8	0.6	2.9	3.3	1.3
1957/58	1960	3.5	6.3	2.8	7.0	10.1	1.2
	1961	3.3	9.6	6.3	5.5	4.8	1.1
USA – 28%	1984	4.3	4.0	–0.3	6.2	11.3	7.4
Devaluation	1985	3.6	3.9	0.3	3.2	2.0	7.1
against all	1986	1.9	2.0	0.1	2.9	1.0	6.9
currencies over	1987	3.7	1.8	–1.9	3.1	3.7	6.1
1985/87	1988	4.0	2.8	–1.2	3.9	5.3	5.4
	1989	5.0	2.9	–2.1	2.5	2.6	5.2
Japan – 47%	1989	2.3	3.1	0.8	4.8	5.8	2.3
Revaluation	1990	3.1	3.8	0.7	4.8	4.1	2.1
against all	1991	3.3	3.4	0.1	4.3	1.8	2.1
currencies over	1992	1.7	2.1	0.4	1.4	–6.1	2.2
1990/94	1993	1.3	2.1	0.8	0.1	–4.6	2.5
	1994	0.7	2.3	1.6	0.6	0.7	2.9

continued

Table 6.1: *continued*

	Year	Cons- umer Prices	Wage Rates	Real Wage	GDP Change	Industrial Output Change	Unem- ployment (%)
Italy – 20%	1990	6.4	7.3	–0.9	2.1	–0.6	9.1
Devaluation	1991	6.3	9.8	3.5	1.3	–2.2	8.6
against all	1992	5.2	5.4	0.2	0.9	–0.6	9.0
currencies over	1993	4.5	3.8	–0.7	–1.2	–2.9	10.3
1990/93	1994	4.0	3.5	–0.5	2.2	5.6	11.4
	1995	5.4	3.1	–2.3	2.9	5.4	11.9
Finland – 24%	1990	6.1	9.4	3.3	0.0	–0.1	3.5
Devaluation	1991	4.1	6.4	2.3	–7.1	–9.7	7.6
against all	1992	2.6	3.8	1.2	–3.6	2.2	13.0
currencies over	1993	2.1	3.7	1.6	–1.6	5.5	17.5
1991/93	1994	1.1	7.4	6.3	3.9	10.5	17.9
Spain – 18%	1991	5.9	8.2	2.3	2.2	–0.7	16.3
Devaluation	1992	5.9	7.7	1.8	0.7	–3.2	18.5
against all	1993	4.6	6.8	2.2	–1.1	–4.4	22.8
currencies over	1994	4.7	4.5	–0.2	2.0	7.5	24.1
1992/94	1995	4.7	4.8	0.1	2.8	4.7	22.9

[*] All figures are year-on-year percentage changes

Source: OECD, *Economic Outlook 1997*, IMF, *International Financial Statistics*, July 1997, supplemented by a variety of earlier OECD, IMF, and British official statistics.

Furthermore, far from the average standard of living falling after a devaluation, it almost invariably rises, because the GDP of all devaluing countries tends to increase significantly shortly after the currency has depreciated. There is also a marked tendency for industrial output to rise sharply soon after a devaluation, triggering increased investment, while the experience of Japan, after the yen's strong revaluation in the early 1990s, shows the opposite outcome equally strongly. In most cases, the real wage tends to rise as well, shortly after the exchange rate falls. This is calculated in Table 6.1 as being the difference between the change in average wage rates and the change in the consumer price level. The increase in the real wage is not so pronounced as the rise in GDP, because devaluations tend to increase employment, thus reducing the numbers out of work, but also diluting average earnings. This bias can be seen in the US experience after the dollar fell in the second half of the 1980s as the GDP rose, but the number of people in work increased very rapidly. The table also shows the opposite results occurring in the major case of Japan's revaluation of the yen during the early 1990s. There the growth rate went down, the real wage stayed static, and unemployment began to creep up.

These may well be unexpected results to many people who have been led to expect a very different outcome. In particular, the figures in Table 6.1 provide no justification at all for the widely believed monetarist view that it is impossible to secure a permanent advantage in terms of competitiveness and growth by exchange rate adjustments. Perhaps the widespread conviction that devaluation will have the damaging results so frequently anticipated stems from the fact that many people might like these predictions to be true. Everyone who has a stake in seeing interest rates kept high and money tight might be inclined to share such a view. This tends inevitably to include a large proportion of the banking and financial community. Those doing well out of importing goods into economies with over-valued exchange rates, because the costs of production are so much cheaper elsewhere than in the home market, may also tend to find the same opinions particularly acceptable. Undoubtedly the monetarists have helped support the case, with appropriately impressive theorising, which neatly underpinned what many people, from simple motives of self-interest, were only too pleased to hear. All the same, it is extraordinary that so many believe these propositions to be true when there is so much simple and incontrovertible evidence easily to hand to show that the assumed relationships between depreciation, inflation and the standard of living are incorrect.

On the contrary, if, as Table 6.1 shows, it is possible for any industrial economy to devalue, especially when the economy concerned has substantial unused resources, without any significant inflationary penalty being paid, this is a very important policy matter. It means that long-lasting adjustments, which are highly beneficial in terms of growth, productivity and employment prospects, are in fact entirely feasible, even although their possibility may be denied by monetarist theory. It can then no longer be claimed that any economy stuck in the doldrums has no practical way out of its predicament. On the contrary, the way is open for any country which is having difficulty competing and keeping all its resources employed, especially its labour force, to remedy the position by making appropriate exchange rate adjustments. Far from the benefits of devaluations being only temporary, shortly to be eroded away by extra inflation, they tend to be self-reinforcing, as arguments in previous chapters have shown.

This is not to say that inflationary problems can be ignored if parity changes continue to take place. Good management of the economy is required in all circumstances. The evidence in Table 6.1 makes it clear, however, that many of the widely held opinions about the relationship between devaluation, price rises and the real wage are at variance with the facts, and therefore cannot be well founded in theory. There is much evidence that the problems with inflation are more diverse and more manageable than is often recognised. We turn now to see what these may be.

DEVALUATION AND THE PRICE LEVEL

Those who believe that exchange rate changes will affect prices are right in at least one sense. Any parity reduction is bound to exert upward pressure on the costs of all imported goods and services in the devaluing country. While the prices of both imports and exports will almost certainly rise measured in the domestic currency, there may also be a tendency for import costs to increase faster than export prices, worsening the terms of trade. In this sense, too, there is a direct cost to the economy. Furthermore, there is no value in a policy of depreciation unless it makes imports more expensive relative to home market production. A major objective has to be to price some imports out of the home market by making it relatively cheaper than it was previously to produce locally rather than in other countries. It follows that there will have to be price increases for imported goods and services, otherwise there will be no new bias towards production from domestic output.

The evidence presented in Table 6.1, however, clearly indicates that other factors have to be taken into account. If, as is commonly supposed, it is only import prices which are significant, the figures in the table would show increasing inflation and declining living standards after a depreciation, and not, generally speaking, the opposite. How are the figures in the table to be explained? The answer is that the impact of a devaluation on the price level is more complicated than is often recognised. Many of the effects are disinflationary rather than the reverse, and tend to increase the national income rather than reduce it. Obviously, the more exposed any economy is to foreign trade, the larger the immediate impact of exchange rate changes will be on living standards and the price level. Although the US economy's exposure is relatively small, it is still easily large enough to make the consequences significant.

First, one of the immediate impacts of a devaluation is to make all domestic production more competitive in both home and export markets than it was before. Within a short period of time, this leads to increased output. Of course there are time lags and not all the potential increases in sales will be realised immediately, but almost any rise in production will help to reduce average costs. Increased capacity working spreads overhead charges across more output. We have seen that production and service industries involved in international trade typically have falling cost curves, a reflection of the fact that the marginal cost of production is well below the average cost. Enterprises of these sorts cannot fail to benefit from a depreciating currency. Obviously some of their input expenses, if they include either imported goods and services, or a switch to a domestic producer who has now become competitive, will rise. This is part of the price that has to be paid for devaluing. The increased volume of output which can now be obtained, however, is clearly a substantial factor weighing in the balance on the other side.

Second, some of the policies which have to be associated with bringing the parity of the currency down also directly affect both production costs and the cost of living generally. One of the most important of these is the rate of interest, which almost invariably comes down with the exchange rate. Borrowing costs at high real rates of interest are a heavy and expensive burden on most firms which produce goods and services. A lower rate reduces production costs. Interest rates are also an important component of the retail price index, particularly in countries where a large proportion of personal outgoings are on variable rate loans, such as mortgage payments. A substantial reduction, designed to bring down the exchange rate to a more competitive level, itself makes an important contribution to holding down the rate of inflation.

Third, rising productivity, which flows from increased output, not only has the immediate effect of reducing costs. It also makes it possible to meet wage claims of any given size with less impact on selling costs. Whatever the going rate for wage increases may be, the less the inflationary impact as output rises. Nor is this just a factor which applies for a short period until those responsible for formulating wage claims adjust to a new situation and then increase their claims. The international evidence strongly suggests that economies with rapidly expanding output have a better wage negotiation climate generally, and thus achieve wage rises more realistically attuned to whatever productivity increases are actually being secured.

Fourth, one of the major objectives of reducing the parity is to switch demand from overseas sources to home production. While the price of imports is bound to rise to some extent, there is strong evidence that the increase in costs from exchange rate changes are seldom passed on in full. Foreign suppliers are inclined to absorb some of the costs themselves, calculating that what they lose on margin they may make up by holding on to market share. Furthermore, if demand is switched from imported goods and services to home production, this purchasing power will not be affected – at least not directly and in full – by the increase in import prices. It will benefit in cost terms from the fact that domestic output is now relatively cheaper than imports.

Fifth, it is possible to employ the much improved fiscal position which higher growth produces to have a directly disinflationary impact, using the tax system. It is often argued that if there is a depreciation, the government of the devaluing country necessarily has to deflate the economy to make more room for exports. This argument cannot hold water, however, if there are large numbers of unemployed or under-employed people, and considerable slack in the economy. In these circumstances, it is not difficult to combine increasing output, stimulated by a lower exchange rate, with an expansionary monetary and fiscal policy. It is then possible to structure tax changes so that they have a positive disinflationary impact. Reducing taxes on labour, where this is possible, is particularly effective, because it both directly cuts production costs and encourages more employment.

Taxation policy may help to secure a further crucially important objective to avoid price increases if there is a devaluation not only immediately after the parity has come down, but subsequently as well. If the first round effects of higher import prices can be neutralised by greater output, rising productivity and tax changes, then there will be no second and subsequent rounds of price rises flowing from the change in parity. This is clearly an extremely desirable state of affairs to achieve, making it much easier to manage the economy in a way which protects the increased competitiveness flowing from devaluation from erosion.

When each of these disinflationary factors is taken into account, all of which apply in varying degrees whenever the parity comes down, the figures in Table 6.1 become very much easier to understand. It is evidently not true that devaluation necessarily increases the rate of inflation. Still less is it true that it must always do so to such a degree that any extra competitive advantage is automatically eroded away.

At the cost of a few more again fairly simple calculations, it is possible to set out in quantified form why this should be the case. Suppose that the currency is depreciated by 25%, and that on average import prices rise by two thirds of this amount, while foreign suppliers absorb the rest. Assume that imports of goods and services make up around 30% of gross domestic product – a fairly typical ratio among developed countries – so the impact on the price level from increased import prices in these circumstances is likely to be about two thirds of 25% × 30%, which comes to 5%.

On the other side, consider all the factors which work to reduce the price level when the external value of the currency falls by 25%. First, the output of all enterprises in the domestic economy is likely to rise substantially on average. Suppose that the growth rate rises by 3% per annum. If two thirds of this increase in output could be achieved in the period immediately following the devaluation by using the existing capital stock and labour force more intensively and efficiently, the benefits from economies of scale of this type would amount to around a 2% contribution to reduced prices in year one.

Second, the total money supply currently represents about 85% of GNP across the developed world, including the US. All of the money supply is essentially debt of one kind or another, and nearly all of it is interest bearing. If base rate interest charges were reduced from, say, 5% to 2%, not all interest charges would be affected, but a significant proportion would be. If half were reduced on average by 3%, the interest charged on the whole of the money supply would fall by about 1.7%. This would produce a reduction of around another 1.5% in the retail price index.

Third, one of the most important reasons for a depreciation is to switch demand from imports to home production. Suppose this happens to 10% of all demand. Allowing for an import content of one third, the remaining two thirds of this new output would, broadly speaking, not be affected by increased costs as a result of the exchange rate changes. Perhaps half of it, however, would only become economical to produce at rather higher world prices than applied previously. These ratios multiply up as $10\% \times 25\% \times \frac{2}{3} \times \frac{2}{3} \times \frac{1}{2}$. This factor reduces the inflationary impact by a little more than another 0.5%.

Fourth, another major impact on the economy from reducing the parity would be vastly to improve the public sector's finances, as tax receipts rose and calls on public expenditure for welfare benefits fell away. If some of this improvement were used to reduce taxation on items sensitive to the consumer price index it should not be difficult for the government to bring down inflation by a further 1%, by reducing taxes by this amount.

These calculations are again broad-brush and subject to margins of error. They nevertheless show that the disinflationary impacts that can be garnered from a well-managed devaluation are likely to counteract, quite possibly in full, the impact of higher import costs, even if the devaluation is substantial. This is why a devaluation is not necessarily inflationary at all, as ample empirical evidence shows is the case, except perhaps when resources were already fully employed – as in the French example at the end of the 1950s. This is clearly an extremely important conclusion, and one, again, with major policy implications.

Nor does depreciation lower the standard of living; in fact, it quickly does exactly the opposite in almost all circumstances. It is easy to see why this should be the case. If the domestic economy expands after the exchange rate has gone down, as the figures in Table 6.1 show that it almost invariably does, the standard of living, on average, is bound to go up. So, sometimes after a time lag, does the real wage. The proposition that lowering the exchange rate necessarily impoverishes the devaluing country is the reverse of the truth. Again, this is an outcome of great policy significance, making it politically much easier to implement a reflationary and expansionary policy than is generally supposed.

These conclusions do not mean, of course, that inflation is no longer a problem. A well-managed devaluation may not cause inflation to increase, but there are other reasons why the price level may move up. They all need careful management, but with reasonable judgement they are all containable. They are leading sector inflation, external shocks, 'demand-pull' price rises caused by bottlenecks and overheating, excessive growth in the money supply which may in particular lead to asset price inflation, and 'cost-push' wage and salary increases outstripping productivity gains. Many of these are closely related to other elements of the policies confronting all developed economies, and the following pages consider them in turn.

LEADING SECTOR INFLATION

While almost everyone agrees that in general lower rates of inflation are desirable, there is considerable evidence that very low, and especially zero, rates of price increase are impossible to combine with any significant rate of economic growth. At some stage a trade-off between inflation and growth has to be faced. The higher the priority given to stabilising prices, the less likely it is that the economy will grow rapidly. Certainly the notion that squeezing inflation out of the economy altogether is the way to economic prosperity flies in the face of universal experience. On the contrary, although there may be some inflationary price to pay for considerably higher growth, it is not likely to be a large or a dangerous one. Furthermore, recent developments, particularly the gains in efficiency from computers and increasing world competition, suggest that the risk that faster growth will produce price rises at unacceptable rates is even less than it was previously.

Table 6.2 shows the rates of inflation and economic growth in ten OECD countries, and the OECD as a whole, during the sixteen years from 1953 to 1969, a long period of almost continuous growth in world output. This table indicates that over this sixteen-year period not one of these countries managed to avoid a steady increase in the price level, albeit a relatively moderate one. It also shows a tendency for those economies growing most rapidly to have rather higher inflation rates than those growing more slowly. Obviously other factors were at work than those solely concerned with the differing growth rates, but the correlation between high inflation and higher growth is clearly there.

Table 6.2: Growth and Inflation Rates in Ten OECD Countries
between 1953 and 1969

Country	Cumulative Growth Rate (%)	Cumulative Inflation Rate (%)
Japan	10.0	4.0
Spain	6.0	6.3
Germany	5.8	2.7
Italy	5.5	3.4
France	5.4	4.5
Netherlands	4.9	4.3
Switzerland	4.5	3.3
Belgium	4.0	2.5
United States	3.6	2.4
United Kingdom	2.8	3.4
OECD Average	4.4	3.0

Source: OECD: *National Accounts* of OECD countries 1953–69.

At first sight this seems the reverse of what one would expect. How did Japan manage to achieve a cumulative compound growth rate of 10% if the Japanese rate of inflation was above the average for the whole of the OECD, and well above the rate at which consumer prices rose in a number of countries, including the United States and Britain? Why were British exports not becoming more and more competitive with those of Japan? Clearly this cannot have been the case, judging by the slow British growth rates over the period, contrasted with the high performance of the Japanese economy.

This paradox is easily resolved. In all the major countries of the developed world, increases in productivity were enabling sustained economic growth to take place, while growth in turn generated rising output per head. These increases, however, were neither spread evenly throughout any of the individual economies concerned, nor between them. In all countries there were some parts of the economy where productivity growth was slow, non-existent or even negative. If the number of children taught by each teacher goes down, each child may be better taught, but the output of teachers measured in economic terms tends to fall. If legal aid is extended to people who could not otherwise afford to obtain justice, society may be fairer, but there is no increase in GDP which corresponds fully to the extra skilled manpower required to make the legal system work more fairly. The really high rates of productivity growth were to be found in those parts of manufacturing and the service sectors, especially in fast-growing economies, where mechanisation, falling unit costs with longer production runs, and much more efficient use of labour were possible. The results were costs which dropped rapidly in real terms, and often in money terms too, even though average prices in the economy were rising. These are the sectors of the economy which are the familiar generators of fast rates of economic growth.

This phenomenon was seen markedly in Japan, with one of the fastest growth rates, but also an above average rate of increase in the consumer price level. It was caused by leading sector inflation. Those employed in parts of the economy with rapidly rising productivity secured large wage increases, which were offset by increased output. Those working in jobs where such improvement in economic performance were unobtainable also pressed for and received wage rises. The prices of the goods and services produced by those where no significant increase in output could be achieved therefore had to go up. The faster the economy grew, the more marked these price increases were. The overall inflation rate was a result of the averaging process which took place between the high- and low-productivity growth parts of the economy. In Japan the results were truly astonishing. Despite the relatively large Japanese overall domestic inflation rate, for many years their export prices barely rose at all. Indeed over the whole of the period 1952–79, while the general price level in Japan rose by 364%, the average price of Japanese exports rose by only 33%. In Britain, over the same period, the general price level rose by 442% and export prices by 380%. No wonder Britain kept losing more and more markets to Japanese competition.

The initial competitiveness of Japanese exports, and those of most of the economies of Western Europe after their recovery from World War II, enabled all of them to break into the virtuous circle of rapid growth. Once established, all these countries maintained high growth for years on end, concentrating economic activity in those areas where productivity increases were at their greatest. We have seen the same process at work today in the Far East, not only in countries such as Taiwan, Malaysia and Korea, but also, perhaps most conspicuously of all, in China. The American and British experience has been exactly the opposite. Starting from uncompetitive positions after World War II, both the US and Britain have allowed the costs of their exports compared to the world average to rise and rise.

Despite all the indications to the contrary, it is still said that price stability is the condition needed to maximise economic growth on a sustainable basis. There is no evidence from round the world that this is true. Nor does economic history provide any support for such a view. During the period when the Gold Standard operated, just as much as subsequently, prices were constantly changing. Only the price of gold remained fixed. It is argued that low inflation allows interest rates to be low too, and in nominal terms this may be correct. Unfortunately, however, it is not only the nominal rate that counts. It is the real rate, when inflation is subtracted from the nominal rate, which is the true cost of borrowing. Squeezing inflation down with monetarist policies has a dismal record of producing much higher real rates of interest than more accommodating strategies, thus pushing up the exchange rate and discouraging investment and growth by making the real cost of borrowing greater than it would otherwise be.

The lessons from international comparisons and economic history indicate that rapid growth is associated with price changes in all directions, some upward, particularly where productivity increases are hard to achieve, and some downward, especially where there are falling cost curves. Nor has experience shown that nominal interest rates have been particularly low in fast-growing economies, although real rates have often been negative, at least after tax. In rapidly growing economies – 8–10% per annum – rates of inflation tend to be above the world average, mainly because of leading sector inflation, but in most cases the rate at which prices increase is still relatively stable. In the 1950s and 1960s, the Japanese economy grew at 10% per annum with average inflation running at 4%. In economies growing at 5–6% per annum, the optimum combination of rapid productivity growth without too much leading sector inflation seems to be achieved. This was the experience of most countries in Western Europe during the 1950s and 1960s where, over a long period, inflation rates averaged just under 4%, with similar nominal base interest rates. If the objective is to get the US economy to grow faster, perhaps at 4% or even 6% per annum, it is likely that we will have to expect a similar experience with price rises and interest rates as prevailed in other economies achieving growth results of this order.

SHOCKS TO THE SYSTEM

Seen from the vantage point of the late 1990s, the 1950s and 1960s look like a period of remarkable stability and growing prosperity in the Western world. At least until 1968, low and quite stable levels of inflation were combined with rapidly increasing standards of living almost everywhere. After the adjustments of 1949 there were few exchange rate changes, the most significant being the double French devaluations in 1958, the British devaluation in 1967 and the German revaluation in 1968, followed by some consequential parity changes in other countries. By the standards of what was to follow, price increases were low, although they attracted a good deal of concern at the time. All the advanced economies were helped by the falling cost of raw materials, many of which came from the Third World. The biggest shock to the system, albeit a temporary one, was the Korean War at the beginning of the period, which led to a sharp increase in commodity prices. These quickly collapsed, however, as the war ended. Inflation then fell away as the long boom in the 1950s and 1960s got under way. No period of economic history of any length is devoid of inflationary shocks, however, and at the end of the 1960s a much more turbulent period began.

The rate at which prices increased in the US during the thirty years from the late 1960s to the late 1990s, following the calmer period which preceded it, exhibited upsurges when major inflationary shocks materialised, followed by declines back to more usual levels within two or three years. The end of the 1960s saw the year-on-year increase in consumer prices peaking in 1969 as a result of the inflationary pressures generated by the Vietnam War and the implementation of the Great Society programme, but the index was back to a 3.3% increase by 1971. The next peak, at 12.3% year on year, came in 1974 as a result of the early 1970s boom and the quadrupling of oil prices, but the index had fallen back to a 4.9% increase by 1976. The third major shock came at the end of the 1970s with the next oil price increase, causing a further year-on-year peak of 13.3% in 1979, but by 1982, the index was back to 3.8%. Other countries had similar experiences, although there was a wide variation between the overall rises in the domestic price level over two or three decades between low inflation countries and others which had many more difficulties containing price increases. Between 1975 and 1995 consumer prices rose 183% in the US, but 84% in Germany, 322% in Britain and 640% in Spain.

Looking back over the whole period since World War II, the ups and downs which have taken place in inflation both in the US and in the world as a whole have clearly been caused by a wide variety of different factors. From a global point of view, only one of all the major events pushing up inflation – during the early 1970s – appears to have been the direct result of excessive credit creation, in this case initially in the US during the late 1960s. With appropriate policies, the rest of the world could have avoided much of the inflation which followed, as indeed happened in some countries. Germany's year-on-year price rises in the mid-1970s never rose above about 7%, compared to a 24% peak in Britain. In most of the developed world the real money supply – that is, net of inflation – remained remarkably stable, although it fluctuated much more than the average in Britain and the Netherlands. In the US, it has also been much less constant than elsewhere. The widest money supply measure, 'L', as a percentage of GDP, rose from 80% in 1971 to a peak of 93% in 1986, and then back to 76% in 1994. By 1996 it was back to 80%.

Other causes of rises in prices had little or nothing to do with changes in the credit base. All of them, however, because they caused higher inflation and thus pushed up the requirement for money, had to be accommodated by increasing the money supply if more deflation was to be avoided. When the supply of money fell in real terms – as, for example, it did during the period of the 1974–79 Labour government in Britain, when it was reduced by 27% – the deflationary effect was very powerful. Interestingly, during the Reagan era, although interest rates were raised to exceptionally high levels, the restrictions on the money supply were modest. Much the heaviest squeeze has been recently, particularly in the late 1980s and early 1990s. Both the M3 and L measures of the money supply fell in real terms every year from 1987 to 1994, pushing the US money supply down well below the international average. There is little doubt that this is one of the major reasons why the dollar is currently so strong.

The history of the last fifty years therefore shows a remarkable ability by all the countries in the developed world to absorb inflationary shocks, from wherever they have come, despite the variety of different events which, over the years, have been responsible for initiating rapid increases in the price level. Once the initial cause of the surge in inflation disappeared, however, the rate of price increases soon fell back, given an absence of further shocks and reasonably competent management of the macro economy. This ought not to cause surprise. Reasonably rapid rates of economic growth are powerfully effective at absorbing inflation.

If this is so, however, it removes the underpinning for a major component of economic policy employed in varying degrees by almost all major Western governments since the 1970s. They have all tended to assume that the best way to counteract inflationary shocks has been to deflate their economies, rather than to absorb the disturbances by increasing output. The monetarist argument that all increases in inflation are caused by antecedent rises in the money supply, and that only monetary discipline will stop prices rising more and more rapidly, is only a more precise formulation of a view which has underlain conservative economic policy making for a long time before monetarism became fashionable. On the contrary, the international evidence shows that the resulting deflation has been both damaging and destructive, and not particularly effective at keeping inflation rates down. If most of the events which have generated upsurges in inflation are not caused by anything to do with the money supply, and the international experience is that inflation nearly always recedes once the immediate causes have been removed irrespective of the monetary stance in the economies concerned, what indeed is left of the argument that the money supply is both the cause and the cure for all inflationary ills?

Moreover, the picture is even worse than this if the prospect for the coming period is one of continuing slow growth. The historical evidence suggests that economies which have used growth to dampen down inflation have done at least as well at restraining price increases as those which have used deflation, and perhaps better. Table 6.3 shows the record for the major Western economies for the period 1973–78, when all of them were suffering in various degrees from the upsets of the 1970s, and for the following five years, 1978–83. Japan, with much the highest growth rate, was far the most successful in bringing down inflation. All the remaining countries, whose growth rates fell between the first and second periods, had similar or higher rates of inflation in the later period compared to the earlier one. This evidence reinforces the view that economies which have reasonably strong growth rates are better at absorbing external shocks than those which are growing more slowly.

Table 6.3: Economic Growth and Inflation Rates in Selected Countries between 1973 and 1978, and 1978 and 1983

Country	1973–78		1978–83	
	Average Growth Rate (%)	*Average Inflation Rate (%)*	*Average Growth Rate (%)*	*Average Inflation Rate (%)*
Japan	3.7	12.8	4.1	4.2
France	3.1	10.8	1.4	11.8
United States	2.8	8.0	1.3	8.8
Italy	2.1	16.6	1.5	17.3
Germany	2.1	4.7	1.2	4.7
United Kingdom	1.7	12.4	0.7	11.2

Source: *The Economist: Economic Statistics 1900–1983*.

Without doubt, there will be more random shocks and policy changes in the future which will cause upsurges in inflation. The issue is whether, when they come, the best policy to pursue is one of cautious deflation, or whether the safest solution is to keep economies growing to absorb pressures for rising prices with increased output. The evidence from international experience shows that in both the short and the longer term a reasonable measure of boldness pays. Restricting the money supply and deflating the economy is not the most efficient way to contain inflation. Rising output is the most efficacious agent for slowing down increases in the price level. If this is so, the poor job prospects for many people, the lost output and the social strains caused by the deflation and slow growth which so many Western economies have been through during past decades, primarily to fight inflation, have been unnecessary, and could have been avoided.

EXCESSIVE DEMAND

If a much more expansionist policy was adopted in the US it would necessitate a significant devaluation of the dollar. It is not likely that the exchange rate adjustment required, of itself, would necessarily lead to any great inflationary problems during the early or later stages. The causes of inflation, however, are not only those already discussed. There is a further potentially substantial generator of price increases of a different sort. This is to over-expand demand, so that the economy becomes overheated. Once demand on any economy outstrips its capacity to supply, prices will start to rise. This is a prospect which must be taken seriously, and avoided.

'Too much money chasing too few goods' is the classic definition of inflation. While one of the central propositions in this book is that the solution to this problem should, wherever possible, be found by expanding the supply of goods rather than restricting demand, there must inevitably be a point where too many local shortages and bottlenecks have an increasingly serious effect on the price level. This problem has not been a significant one among Western economies for almost all the period since the Korean War, but it could become one in the future.

There are, however, good reasons for believing that these difficulties are likely to be relatively easy to contain. There is a vast reservoir of under-utilised labour in the US. Years of low demand have taken their toll on American manufacturing capacity, but plant utilisation of what remains leaves room for significant increases in output before capacity constraints start to bite hard. Some labour will have rusty skills. Much of the plant and machinery may not be as modern or efficient as it should be, as a result of relatively low levels of investment over recent decades. All these resources, however, are much better than nothing, and there is no doubt that substantial extra output could be obtained from them.

While there is a significant reserve of unused or under-used resources to draw on, these will not last for ever, and the problems of sustaining economic growth without overstretching the economy will then become more acute. One of the major disadvantages which decades of unmanageable competition have inflicted on US manufacturing is not just the closed plants and the fall in manufacturing employment, but also the break-up of teams of people with design and production experience. The US has still managed to retain a lead in a number of the newer industries, such as the advanced use of electronics and biotechnology, but there is still a wide swathe of production where foreign imports dominate the market – in toys, giftware, household and hardware products, for example – many of which could and would be made in the US, given a suitable exchange rate. Although most of these products are comparatively straightforward to manufacture, which is why the US could easily produce them competitively if it had the appropriate international cost base, it still takes time and skill to achieve high-quality standards, and to market them efficiently. Building up successful industrial operations is not achieved in a day. The damage done by the weakening of the US's manufacturing base is not going to be put right in a few months. These problems can, however, be solved over a reasonably short period of years; meanwhile they can be contained or minimised.

First, we have seen that the more the resources of the economy are deployed into those sectors concerned with falling cost curves and foreign trade, the easier it is for self-sustaining growth to be achieved. The faster the US economy is to grow, the more vital it is that wages and salaries in the import-saving and exporting sectors of the economy should rise relative to those everywhere else. There will be a pressing need to attract the most talented people, capable of making good quickly the management deficiencies that are bound to exist after years of slow growth. The large returns on investment which are obtainable in these sectors should be able in turn to provide enough new output to finance all the additional investment required, without calling on the resources of the rest of the economy. There is thus an extremely strong case for fostering this kind of self-sustaining growth and avoiding unnecessary obstructions to its taking place. There will also inevitably be pressure to expand expenditure in other directions. To avoid overheating, however, it is important not to siphon too many resources away from those parts of the economy which are achieving large increases in output towards those which cannot do so, by poorly judged taxation or public investment policies. The ways to fast growth are to let wealth be created before it is taxed too heavily, and to allow as much investment as possible to be concentrated in projects which have short pay-off periods and high returns.

Second, for at least some shortages, there is considerable scope for importing inputs not available from home production. One of the strongest arguments against the strategy of reflating the economy behind the shield of import tariffs or quotas, and protectionist policies generally, is that they would reduce or preclude the availability of alternative sources of supply at competitive prices to cope with domestic shortages. This is not an advantage which the US should throw away. Not all materials, however, can be imported in practice. Nor, in particular, is there an inexhaustible supply of skilled labour, much of which has been drained away from manufacturing industry by relatively poor wages, bad working conditions and uncertain prospects. Too many skilled engineers have now turned their hands to other ways of earning a living outside the industrial sector. They need to be attracted back with improved wages and conditions.

Third, any serious attempt to reflate the US economy, designed to bring the labour force back to full stretch, again faces a major training, retraining and educational task, particularly for all forms of engineering and technical work. One of the consequences of the decline of manufacturing in the US has been that a far smaller proportion of the university-level students take engineering courses than is the case in other countries. In America, in 1994, 78 000 students gained batchelor's degrees in engineering; 6.7% of the total degrees awarded, down nearly 20% from the number ten years previously. In Germany, with a population less than one third of that of the US, around 50 000 students begin university-level engineering courses every year, representing over 20% of all students. This is a similar ratio to Japan where around 100 000 engineering graduates are produced per annum, forming more than 20% of all graduates. Typically, in other countries with a longer history of manufacturing decline, the position is much worse. In Britain only a little over 20 000 students graduate in engineering annually. Training courses may nevertheless have little value if there is insufficient demand available to provide work for those who have been through them. They are, however, a vitally important component of success once new opportunities for employment come on stream. Undoubtedly, they will be supplemented by large amounts of 'on the job' training as employers need to upgrade the skills of their workforces.

The unemployment figures in the US would clearly be much higher if they were to include those not registered as unemployed, such as housewives and those who have been involuntarily retired early, who would like to work but have given up the prospect of finding a job as hopeless. There is also a major problem with lack of skills among those in menial, low-output positions. The problem with the type of jobs which are needed to lift the US growth rate substantially is that a much lower proportion than at present would be completely unskilled. Nearly all would require at least basic skills such as the ability to drive a motor vehicle or to use a keyboard, and the scope for employment for those who cannot read or write properly would inevitably be limited. Long years of poor job prospects may have sapped the motivation of a generation of children, especially in deprived areas, and in many cases the educational attainments are poor, and considerably worse than they were a few years ago. Similar problems of outdated or rusty skills apply to those who are older. The US cannot afford either for social or economic reasons to fail to get a high proportion of its unemployed labour force back into much more productive jobs. It owes it to them to provide them with the training to enable them to hold down the better-paying jobs which could be created in the future. The experience of the years during World War I but particularly World War II shows that it is possible to find worthwhile employment for almost everyone, if the will and the determination is there.

Fourth, the US authorities should be wary of trying to contain problems of shortages of either raw materials or labour, especially skilled labour, by government action to implement wages and price freezes. The fact that prices and labour costs rise when shortages occur are signals that more resources in these areas are particularly needed. The changes in the economy which are required would involve considerable shifts in relative wage and salary levels, to attract high quality labour into the those parts of the economy concerned with international trading, and away from other sectors. In particular, there would have to be substantial increases in remuneration for those involved in manufacturing industry. Suppressing the necessary price and wage rate signals will only aggravate shortages, leading quickly to even more pressure on prices and wages to rise.

There are better ways of dealing with profiteering and excessive wage increases than centrally imposed freezes. They have never worked for any length of time in the past in any country, and are unlikely to do so in future. Far the best alternative is not to expose the economy to strains which cause excessive bottlenecks and shortages in the first place by a two pronged approach. The first is to create conditions where output can expand quickly in those sectors of the economy which are capable of achieving fast self-sustaining growth. The second is to refuse to allow overall demand to increase more rapidly than the rate at which even rejuvenated economies are capable of responding. Achieving this balance is not an impossible task.

LABOUR COSTS

In the end the most important determinant of inflation trends is the rate of increase in wages and salaries. Payments to labour represent an average of some 70% of total costs in the US economy – well above the international average of about 60%, mainly because the US savings and investment ratio is so much lower than in most other economies. If the wage and salary bill rises faster than output, the extra costs are bound to be reflected in higher prices. If economies are run with a much greater level of demand which is intended, among other things, to produce a very substantial reduction in the level of unemployment, is it inevitable that high levels of wage inflation will be the consequence?

Before attempting to answer this question, it is worth looking again at the historical record and current experience in comparable countries to the US throughout the developed world. A glance at the unemployment percentages in other parts of the world and at other periods, as an indication of the tightness of the labour market, and the rates of inflation which go with them, must surely cause some concern even to those who are most convinced that wage inflation is inevitable. Table 6.4 provides some of the relevant figures. Those for the earlier period, before the general increase in inflation in the mid-1970s, show a wide range of countries combining low rates of unemployment with moderate rates of inflation. At the beginning of the 1990s, countries as varied as Japan, Austria, Norway and Switzerland all managed to combine nearly full utilisation of their labour forces with low increases in the price level.

Table 6.4: Unemployment and Inflation Rates in Ten OECD Countries at Selected Periods between 1963 and 1993

	1963–73		1974–79		1980–89		1990–93	
Country	Unem-ploy-ment Rate %	In-fla-tion Rate %	Unem-ploy-ment Rate %	In-fla-tion Rate %	Unem-ploy-ment Rate %	In-fla-tion Rate %	Unem-ploy-ment Rate %	In-fla-tion Rate %
United States	4.8	3.2	6.7	8.5	7.2	5.5	6.5	3.9
Japan	1.3	6.2	1.9	9.9	2.5	2.5	2.2	2.5
Austria	1.7	4.2	1.7	6.3	3.3	3.8	3.6	3.6
Norway	1.3	5.1	1.8	8.7	2.8	8.3	5.6	3.0
Switzerland	0.5	4.2	0.5	4.0	0.6	3.3	2.2	4.6
France	2.0	4.6	4.5	10.7	9.0	7.3	10.0	2.8
Germany	0.8	3.4	3.4	4.7	6.8	2.9	7.3	3.6
Italy	5.3	3.9	6.6	16.7	9.9	11.2	11.0	5.5
Spain	2.5	4.7	5.3	18.3	17.5	10.2	18.1	5.8
United Kingdom	1.9	5.1	4.2	15.6	9.5	7.4	8.3	5.1
OECD Average	3.2	4.1	5.0	10.8	7.2	8.9	7.2	5.5

Source: OECD *Historical Statistics* 1995 Edition.

Much of the argument about the level of unemployment in developed countries has centred round the concept of the non-accelerating inflation rate of unemployment, or its acronym, the NAIRU. It is argued that, unless there are sufficiently large numbers of unemployed people, the pressure for wage increases will tend to outstrip the growth in output which the economy can provide, necessarily leading to increased inflation. The NAIRU, it is said, is higher in countries which have more inflexible labour markets, with more rigidities in the form of restrictive practices both in the way labour is deployed and in wage bargaining. While training and improved economic performance clearly have a role to play, the only fundamental solutions to the problem of unemployment, it is argued, are to reduce supply-side rigidities by making wage rates and the labour market more flexible, to reduce job security, and to weaken the power of trade unions to fix wages which are unrelated to productivity gains.

A major benefit enjoyed in this respect by the US is that its labour market is much less rigid than those of almost all its competitors. There is no doubt, however, that at some point there is a trade-off between fuller and fuller employment and rising inflation. To argue, however, that the NAIRU requires a level of registered unemployment as high as that presently seen in the US, even before any allowance is made for under-employment, appears to be completely incompatible with all the international and historical evidence. Evidently, it was possible to combine relatively high rates of growth and low levels of unemployment with moderate inflation for twenty-five years after World War II in most of Europe, but more particularly in Japan, when supply-side restrictions of all kinds were at least as prevalent as they are now, and in many cases much more so. Why should it therefore not be possible to achieve low levels of unemployment now, particularly in the US, where the labour market is exceptionally flexible. It might take some time to get there, but arguments about the NAIRU provide no convincing reason nowadays to believe that it would not be possible to achieve an unemployment rate in the US of perhaps 3%. This should be achievable within perhaps four to five years, if appropriate policies are implemented, with almost all the labour force in jobs which stretch their holders' talents, and in most cases pay much better than they do now.

To start with, there is no evidence that the US's present use of its labour force has any clear relationship at all with the NAIRU. The NAIRU relates not to the total number of people who are out of work, but to the total who are actively seeking employment, or better employment, and who are therefore competing at least to this extent with those who are in work. The US clearly has very large numbers of people in these categories. The US welfare system, combined with all the competitive pressures now operating on the job market, means that the likelihood of wage inflation taking off, even if there was much fuller demand for labour than there is now, seems comparatively remote. Supposing, however, that wages did show signs of being likely to rise significantly more rapidly than productivity was increasing, what could then be done to bring the NAIRU down to 2% or 3%, as it used to be for decades in many countries, and which it has sometimes been in the US? There is a great deal that can be done to achieve this objective.

First, wage determination is in the end as much a political as an economic process. The wage increases for which people are prepared to settle are not decided by a totally mechanistic process. Persuasion also counts. Even more difference may be made by the prospect of a rational economic policy which is capable of delivering results, and which is therefore seen to be one where some sacrifice of current wage and salary increases is worth while to obtain more in the future. Certainly a major objective must be to create a climate for wage negotiation which is conducive to average money wage increases at as low a level as possible, hopefully with the support of trade union leaders, to secure larger real wage rises as soon as practical in the future.

A complicating factor in wage determination, if the American economy is going to make a transition towards much faster rates of economic growth, is that it will not be possible to have the same wage or salary increases for everyone. There needs to be a substantial relative adjustment. If talent at every level is going to have to be switched to those parts of the economy capable of producing high productivity increases, and rapid investment pay-off periods, rises in pay will have to be considerably higher in these areas of economic activity than elsewhere. This suggests that aiming for relatively low general wage increases, but with substantial wage drift at the level of individual enterprises, is the most realistic policy.

Another problem is that there are going to be shortages of certain types of skilled labour, and also a pressing need for a considerable amount of retraining to enable the labour force across the US to be adequately prepared for the new types of jobs which will become available. Government programmes have a major role in providing training and retraining to enable there to be a sufficient response to this challenge, supplementing training carried out on the job. If bottlenecks in the form of skilled labour shortages are to be avoided, the places where these are likely to occur need to be identified as far in advance as possible, and training put in hand as early as it can be to provide the manpower needed at adequate skill levels. The type of training required is likely to be fairly precisely orientated towards specific job opportunities. Improving general standards of education and motivation in schools is another vital component, but takes much longer to pay off. Preparing those already of working age will almost certainly have to be given even higher immediate priority.

There clearly is potential for wage pressure if these changes are taking place, and all the dampening effect of increasing output in absorbing whatever wage increases there are will be needed. There is no reason, however, why the major disinflationary influence of increasing production should not be supplemented where possible by government actions on the price level. There is much to be said against prices and incomes policies if they can be avoided, but there are other steps which the state can take apart from freezing or limiting increases in prices, wages and incomes. Lowering interest rates, which has many other advantages, reduces the cost of living. If the economy needs reflating, there are several ways which have already been mentioned in which this can be done which actually reduce costs, such as lowering taxes to keep down the price level. All this should help to produce a more helpful wage climate in addition to acting directly on both the cost of living and of producing output of all kinds in the US.

When all these factors are put together, it becomes clear how other countries manage with a NAIRU which allows much fuller use to be made of their labour forces than has been achieved for many years in the US. Faster growth makes larger money wage claims possible without inflationary consequences. Rising output in an economy run in a way which appears rational and sustainable makes a degree of wage restraint seem a sensible policy. Flowing from this comes something closer to a consensus. This should make economically unjustified wage claims look irrational and greedy, instead of being the only way available to buck trends which never seem to end, as has been the experience too often in the past in countries with a long record of slow growth such as the US. If other countries can operate with 3% or 4% rates of unemployment, with all the rest of their labour forces in jobs which stretch its members' talents, there is no reason why America cannot do so too.

SUMMARY

There is little doubt that a major reason why many people who might otherwise be willing to contemplate using exchange rate changes to improve economic performance oppose such a policy is because they believe it would both push up the price level and reduce the standard of living, at least in the short term. They treat it as axiomatic that inflation must rise in any economy where the currency is devalued, and that in consequence the real wage would fall. It therefore seems worth summarising at the end of this chapter the reasons for believing that these fears are misplaced. On the contrary, the case put forward is that the evidence shows that even major devaluations do not lead to any significant rise in inflation, while almost invariably quickly increasing the standard of living in economies whose currencies have depreciated. If this is true, it then becomes far more feasible and attractive than is generally assumed to use exchange rate changes to provide both the stimulus and the flexibility to allow the economy to grow faster, and vastly to improve employment and compensation prospects for the labour force without taking undue risks with inflation.

The proposition that increasing the money supply within reasonable bounds, lowering interest rates, and encouraging the exchange rate to fall will necessarily lead to an immediate increase in inflation may be widely believed. There is, however, very little empirical evidence from the history of the developed world to support it. On the contrary, the record of all the devaluations over the nearly seventy years since the break-up of the Gold Standard system in 1931 shows the opposite tendencies manifesting themselves to a greater or lesser extent on almost every occasion. The expected impact of a depreciation on the price level does not materialise because lowering the exchange rate involves disinflationary factors which are as powerful, and sometimes even more so, than those tending to push prices up. Furthermore, if policies are implemented which assist these tendencies, such as reducing taxes where this is not only possible but desirable on other grounds, then the influences working against inflation become even more pronounced. In the medium term, with a much higher growth rate, the prospects are for fairly low but sustainable levels of inflation, the main generator of price increases being leading sector inflation if the rate of growth is very high. There should be no reductions in living standards at any stage.

The evidence from across the world shows that many of the causes of prices rises have had little directly to do with the money supply, though some inflationary upsurges have been caused by monetary mismanagement and excessive credit creation. Most of the increase in the money supply in all countries has been the result of the need to accommodate economic growth. Inflation has then occurred for non-monetary reasons. Recent developments, particularly deregulation and the growth of new forms of money, have tended to increase the requirement for credit. This makes monetary ratios even more unreliable than they were before. Especially in conditions like the present, therefore, where inflationary pressures requiring any kind of deflationary solution are not a serious threat, the risk of price rises from excessive money supply is low. The problem in the US at present is not too much credit creation, but too little.

There are bound to be more random inflationary shocks both to the world and to the US economy, and governments everywhere have to be prepared to deal with them. They ought, however, not to cause undue difficulty. The international evidence strongly indicates that there is a universal tendency for inflation to die back in advanced economies which are reasonably competently run, once the causes of individual upsurges have been removed. This is best achieved by using increasing productivity and output as a sponge to soak up inflationary pressures, and, in particular, as the way to accommodate wage and salary increases which might otherwise push up the price level.

There is no evidence for the view that all increases in prices are ultimately due to one sole cause, and therefore only amenable to one solution. On the contrary, the causes of inflation are varied. The way to deal with any particular inflationary problem depends on careful diagnosis of the specifics rather than the application of general monetary theories which may not be relevant, and which may indeed be counterproductive. Different causes of inflation require different policies to deal with them.

Overall, however, the problems associated with ensuring that price rises stay at relatively low levels, at least for most of the time, even if the economy is growing very quickly, do not look particularly daunting. With a sustained growth rate of around 4% – or even 6% – it ought to be possible to keep inflation at no more than around 4% per annum, as it was for years on end in the fast-growing economies of Europe in the 1950s and 1960s. Between 1954 and 1969 the French economy grew cumulatively at 5.4% per annum, with an average annual inflation rate of 4.5%. Over the same period, the German economy grew at 5.8% per annum, with average per annum inflation of 2.7%. Even Japan, which grew at 10.0% per annum over this period, had an annual inflation rate of only 4.0%.

If mistakes are made, or external shocks are experienced, either of which push up the rate of increase in the price level, it is not usually difficult to get it down again without plunging the economy into deflation. In advanced economies, the main causes of inflation which are subject to policy control appear to be far from unmanageable, though all require self-discipline and good government. Allowing the economy to become overheated, tolerating the creation of an excessive money supply, mishandling the wage bargaining process and using the tax system to pay for wasteful public expenditure are all avoidable provided that relevant policies are implemented reasonably efficiently. Whatever the institutional background, whether nationally or internationally, if mistakes or misjudgements are made in these areas, rising inflation and falling living standards will be the consequences. There are no short-cuts to responsible behaviour and political maturity. The cushion of increased output and productivity provided by a fast rate of economic growth, however, ought to make all these policy issues easier and not more difficult to handle.

Even if events were to prove this thesis wrong, however, which the evidence does not suggest they would, and there was some significant extra inflation in the US if the dollar were substantially devalued and the economy grew much more quickly, there is still a strong case for believing that it would be worth it. The standard of living is, in the end, far more important than the cost of living. It would be worth paying a modest inflationary price to raise the US economy's growth rate from its current level to the world average or beyond, and vastly to improve the job prospects and productivity of the American labour force. In any event, such an inflationary surge would almost certainly be temporary, and quickly absorbed. This does not, however appear to be the real choice. It is not necessary to choose between more growth with significantly more inflation or less growth and much lower price rises. In the short term, as well as the medium and long term, high rates of growth and manageably low rates of inflation can and should be made to go hand in hand.

7 America's Soluble Problems

'The urgent question of our time is whether we can make change our friend and not our enemy.'

Bill Clinton

The previous chapters provide a vantage point from which we can now move on to assess whether there are realistic and practical policy changes which could be made to deal with many of America's most pressing problems. The issue is whether there is a common cause for most of them which could be rectified by nothing more complicated than altering macro-economic policies in entirely manageable ways. The changes to be made would need to achieve a sufficiently positive response from all the relevant sectors of the US economy to provide the resources and the incentives to lead the US in a new and much more purposeful direction.

The thesis is that although the US economy, by world standards, has performed in many respects exceptionally well over the half-century since the end of World War II, it has nevertheless substantially under-achieved in relation to its potential. The standard of living in the US has been higher than in any other major country in the world since 1945, mostly by a wide margin, but this does not mean that it could not have been greater still. Indeed, the prosperity which is so evident in much of the US is likely to be the main reason why it may be hard to persuade most people of the scale of the opportunity which has been missed. This may be particularly so as the richest and most influential sections of the US population have generally suffered least in relation to the extra increases in output and living standards which could have been achieved. The major losers, relatively speaking, have been all other US citizens. Their losses in many cases have been substantial, and over a wide swathe of those on lower incomes, they have been huge.

The case put forward is that the root problem of the US's current under-achievement lies in the macro-economic policies which the US has pursued since the end of World War II. Without ever seriously considering what the alternatives might be, perhaps because nearly all the time the requirement to do so never seemed to be there, the US authorities have pursued policies whose effect has been to keep the international value of the dollar at a much higher level than it should have been. For some of the time, particularly during the 1980s under the Reagan presidency, the dollar rose to heights which, in retrospect, most people would regard as far too great, and there is now a broad consensus that this was an extremely damaging episode. The Reagan years, however, were only a peak. During all the years since 1945 the extent of the dollar over-valuation varied – greater at some periods and less at others. It appears, from the calculations provided earlier in this book, to have been on average about 25% stronger than it should have been during the decades since 1973. The trends during the earlier period, with the US economy growing more slowly than the world average and losing share of world trade, strongly indicate that problems of roughly the same order of magnitude applied then too.

The results of the dollar over-valuation were to make exporting more difficult and importing more profitable than in other countries, hugely to the disadvantage of the US. In the breakdown of the US balance of trade, as with all advanced economies, manufactured goods are by value much the largest component. Nowadays, just over three quarters of all US merchandise exports are manufactured goods, as are just under 85% of all its imports. Advantages of climate, soil, and the availability of mineral and other natural resources are largely irrelevant to where manufacturing output is located. Overwhelmingly the most important determinant is the overall costs of all the factors of production, with labour charges adjusted for productivity being the largest component. As between different countries, by far the biggest influence on overall competitiveness is the exchange rate.

Because the cost of manufacturing a vast range of products was, through the exchange rate, made artificially higher than it needed to have been in the US compared to elsewhere, investment in manufacturing plant was much greater in other countries than it was in America. Because it was much easier to make money out of making and selling products in these other countries than it was in the US, more talented people elsewhere went into producing and marketing goods rather than services. A combination of high investment levels, talent and profitability then set these economies into the upward, self-reinforcing spiral of export-led growth, unconstrained by balance of payments problems which were easily held in check because domestic production was highly competitive with imports. By their very nature, because they all tend to share falling unit costs as production volume increases, the goods and services which are internationally traded are exactly those where productivity gains are easiest to achieve. Any country which manages to corner more than its fair share of this kind of economic activity will therefore tend to grow faster than the average.

Because the demand for labour was high in economies like these, it paid everyone to make sure the labour force was educated and trained to a high standard, and then used to the full. Skill levels and productivity rose exponentially. Unemployment barely existed. The societies created by this kind of experience – recently mostly in the Far East, although much of Europe had two decades of very high growth in the 1950s and 1960s – then exhibited far more equal distributions of income, educational attainment and life chances than in the much slower-growing economies now typical of the West. It is hardly surprising then to find that social bonds are stronger, crime rates are lower and expectations for the future are higher. Because real incomes are rising fast, the domestic as well as the corporate savings ratio tends to be much greater, so financing rapid expansion and a high reinvestment level is simply not a problem.

In the US, all the opposite tendencies have manifested themselves. Because, for large volumes of tradable goods and services, but particularly for manufactures, it has been cheaper to produce elsewhere, the US's share of this kind of production has fallen precipitately, and with it the US share of world trade. The US has, as a result, forgone a large proportion of both the scope for productivity increases from this source, and its ability to pay its way in the world, which it might otherwise have had. In consequence, for a generation at least, there has been no pressure on US employers to get the best out of scarce labour. So much has been available that it has paid corporations and individuals to use it extensively rather than intensively, to skimp on investment and training, and to pay relatively little for the low volumes of output which much of it created.

Rising productivity does not, however, occur only in the internationally tradable sector of the economy, although, given favourable conditions, rapidly rising output per head is much more likely to be found here than elsewhere. It also tends to increase in other parts of the economy, but not so fast. During the last few decades, world trade has become freer, competition has increased, the pressure for better management has grown, job training has become more focused and the computer revolution has overtaken activities of all kinds. As a result, output per head has gone up, particularly in the more favoured areas of the economy, allowing the same or an increasing volume of goods and services to be produced by fewer people. If overall demand had been rising fast enough, this might have generated large increases in incomes for everyone. In the US, however, this never proved possible. The constraints of the balance of payments, combined with relatively tight monetary policies, kept increases in demand well below the true output potential of the economy. The result was that the productivity gains achieved among those capable of taking advantage of them led to millions of people losing good jobs and being pushed out into the labour market where only much lower-quality employment was available. Alternatively, they retired or dropped out of the job market altogether.

The US labour force has thus been caught in a pincer movement. On the one hand, the US economy failed to take sufficient advantage of the productivity increases typically found in internationally traded goods and services, which could easily have been shared throughout the nation's labour force. On the other hand, the generally available benefits from computers, training and better management were used to improve the prospects of those already most advantaged at the expense of thinning out the job opportunities for everyone else. The results are then clear to see. They have materialised as stagnant real incomes for twenty-five years for the vast mass of blue-collar workers in the US, static or falling levels of productivity for huge swathes of the US labour force, and a far more divided society than the US ever needed to be.

Nor is this the end of the damage which the over-valued dollar has done. The US has for many years had an exceptionally low savings ratio. This is attributable to several separable factors. First, US domestic savings as a percentage of personal incomes are only a fraction of those in most other countries. Second, the corporate sector does not save and reinvest as much as its competitors elsewhere in the world. Third, for many years the US government has run a large fiscal deficit, which has soaked up a good part of the savings which the US has managed to achieve in the personal and corporate sectors.

Low levels of savings are often blamed for the balance of payments deficit from which the US suffers. The argument goes that because any deficit on the balance of payments on current account has to be matched, as an accounting identity, by an equal and opposite flow of capital funds, it is lack of savings, and thus the need to borrow from elsewhere in the world, which is responsible for the US current account deficit. If only, therefore, the US savings ratio could be improved, the need to borrow from abroad would be reduced, and the balance of payments on current would then move to being less in the red than it is now.

If the root cause of the US's problems is an over-valued dollar, however, a much simpler and more plausible explanation for both the foreign payments and the fiscal deficits immediately becomes apparent. It is not the low US savings ratio which has caused the deficits to occur. It is the over-strong dollar which has caused the trade deficit and depressed the savings ratio. The direction of causation is then reversed, and the relationships between the various components of the problems faced by the US become clearer and much more amenable to control by appropriate policy changes than is generally appreciated.

The US balance of payments deficit on current account is not caused by the US borrowing abroad. The borrowing has to happen because the gap between imports and exports of goods and services has to be financed, but the current deficit is the primary cause and the borrowing is the secondary consequence. The reason for the current account gap is that the strong dollar makes exporting too difficult and importing too easy. Balance of payments problems then add an extra constraint to economic policy, slowing the rate at which the economy can be expanded. This in turn explains the low savings ratio. The domestic sector saves less because its incomes are increasing only slowly or not at all. The corporate sector distributes more in dividends and spends less on capital equipment, because slow growth diminishes investment prospects. For the government, poor economic performance reduces tax income and increases the demand for expenditures, particularly on welfare.

There is a series of links in a chain of causation, therefore, which, when taken together, explain the major problems from which the US suffers. All of them stem from the same source, which is the extent to which the operation of the American economy has been skewed by an over-strong dollar not just during the Reagan period, but for all the half-century since the end of World War II. This is the single most important policy issue which the US needs to address.

AGENDA FOR THE FUTURE

If the US wants dramatically to improve its economic performance, it would be relatively easy for it to do so. The solutions to all the major problems holding it back lie in the same area of macro-economic policy. The US would have to increase the money supply, lower interest rates and reduce the value of the dollar against all the rest of the world's currencies by about 25%. Is this a feasible objective, and, if so, how could it be accomplished?

It is first well worth recalling that even as recently as 1992 the trade-weighted value of the dollar was 83, 13% below its average index value for 1997, which was 96. The notion that the dollar's foreign exchange value cannot be moved has therefore to be wide of the mark. Indeed, had the change in value over the last five years been of the same magnitude, but in the opposite direction to that which actually occurred, the necessary adjustment would have already been made. Why has the dollar strengthened over the last five years? There are three major explanations, all highly revealing of the changes in perception about macro-economic policy that the US authorities need to achieve.

First, by end of 1997, the dollar was at a considerably higher level against the main European Union currencies than it had been five years previously. In 1992, the average exchange rate between the dollar and the Deutsche Mark was $1.00 = DM1.56. By 1997 it was $1.00 = DM1.73, an increase of nearly

11%. The reason why the Deutsche Mark, and with it all the other EU currencies in the European Exchange Rate Mechanism, had weakened was because the authorities in Germany in particular had increased the money supply and kept interest rates down. These steps had been taken to promote a recovery in the EU from the very low growth rates achieved there in the early 1990s. The prospect of Monetary Union, which constrained borrowing by EU governments to no more than 3% of GDP, had made stimulating the EU economies by fiscal means an imprudent course. This left monetary relaxation as an attractive alternative which both increased growth and improved the fiscal balance in Member States. Between January 1993 and December 1997 the German economy grew by 8.7%, but the broad money supply (M3), net of inflation, went up by just under 20% and the narrow money supply (M1) by almost 30%. Over the same period, day to day money rates fell from 5.3% to 3.1%. Other EU economies followed the German lead.

Second, the Japanese economy, which had gone into the doldrums in 1991, and where growth since then had been very slow, also reversed its exchange rate policy. The major mistake made by the Japanese over the decades since World War II had been to protect their domestic market, partly as a direct result of the highly competitive yen exchange rate but partly in other more subtle ways. The result was that the Japanese produced huge balance of payments surpluses on current account, mirroring deficits elsewhere, particularly in the US. In the end, these surpluses drove up the value of the yen from 1985 onwards to a point where by the early 1990s the Japanese economy had stalled. Between 1985 and 1993, the exchange rate between the dollar and the yen fell from $1.00 = ¥238 to $1.00 = ¥111. By 1995 it was $1.00 = ¥94. By 1997, however, the yen was weakening again, and the exchange rate was $1.00 = ¥121. This happened because Japanese interest rates fell to almost zero, while, as with Germany and other EU economies, there was a large increase in the money supply.

Third, in many of the fastest-growing countries in the Far East in 1997, a rash of financial problems and bankruptcies heavily depressed the value of their currencies. Although taken individually none of these countries were major trading partners for the US, the combined impact of the collapse in value of the Korean won, the Malaysian ringgit, the Thai baht and the Taiwanese new dollar, and others, was sufficient to give the trade-weighted value of the dollar a further fillip.

No doubt part of the reason for the strength of the dollar in 1997 was the stability which the US economy appeared to exhibit compared to other parts of the world, although the increasing balance of payments deficit might have been a warning sign that some, at least, of the US's stable appearance might be an illusion. Much more significant, however, were the monetary policies pursued by the US authorities over this period. They were those classically required to push the exchange rate up, and the reverse of those applied by the US's main trading partners. Interest rates fell by 60% between the first five years of the 1980s and the 1990s, from a federal funds average of 12.3% to 4.9%, which helped to bring the dollar exchange rate down from its Reagan heights, but a major offsetting factor since then was a significant tightening of every measure of the money supply. As Table 7.1 indicates, between 1986 and 1996, all showed a real reduction of around 15%. At a time when all the US's major competitors were providing their economies with easier money, the US relentlessly tightened the screw. Nor were US interest rates low by international standards even in the 1990s. On the contrary, they have been significantly higher. Between 1994 and 1997 they averaged 5.2% in the US, only just over 4% in Germany and barely 1% in Japan.

These are the reasons why by 1997 the dollar was so strong. It is macro-economic policies which produced this result which urgently need to be reversed if the US economy is to prosper as it could and should do in future. The money supply has to be increased and not reduced. Interest rates have to be lower. The US administration needs to state that it wants to see a substantial fall in the value of the dollar. Unquestionably, if all these actions were taken, the value of the dollar would fall.

To achieve a sustained growth rate of 4% plus – the minimum needed to stretch the US economy to its current potential – the dollar needs to go down to a trade-weighted value of about 75, based on current US statistics where 1972 is 100. To achieve this fall, the most generally used measure of the money supply, M3, would probably have to rise in the US to around the international average of 85% GDP. In 1997 it was 60%. It would then have to be further increased each year, maintaining about the same ratio to GDP, to accommodate the much more rapid growth in US output that a much lower exchange rate would induce. Interest rates would need to come down to a base rate of perhaps 2%, and maybe even less, partly to provide a better investment climate within the US and partly to discourage the inflow of capital which has been a significant factor in holding up the value of the dollar in recent years. Without the US being able to borrow hundreds of billions of dollars a year, the dollar would have depreciated from its present level long ago.

The classic response to policy suggestions of the kind set out above is that they would drive the US economy into an upward inflationary spiral. Where is the evidence, however, to indicate that this would happen? The recent economic history of the world is littered with cases of exchange rate changes which have not produced the predicted inflation. The US's own experience in the mid-1980s is only a most recent example. On the contrary, as always

Table 7.1: US GDP and Money Supply Figures and Ratios

Year	US GDP	US GDP % Change	M1	M1 % Change	M1:GDP Ratio	M1 Real % Change	M3	M3 % Change	M3:GDP Ratio	M3 Real % Change	L	L % Change	L:GDP Ratio	L Real % Change
1970	1035.6		214.4		0.21		677.1		0.65		814.8		0.79	
1971	1125.4	8.7	228.3	6.5	0.20	-2.2	776.0	14.6	0.69	5.9	902.6	10.8	0.80	2.1
1972	1237.3	9.9	249.2	9.2	0.20	-0.8	886.0	14.2	0.72	4.2	1022.8	13.3	0.83	3.4
1973	1382.6	11.7	262.8	5.5	0.19	-6.3	985.0	11.2	0.71	-0.6	1141.5	11.6	0.83	-0.1
1974	1496.9	8.3	274.2	4.3	0.18	-3.9	1070.0	8.6	0.71	0.4	1248.5	9.4	0.83	1.1
1975	1630.6	8.9	287.4	4.8	0.18	-4.1	1172.0	9.5	0.72	0.6	1366.5	9.5	0.84	0.5
1976	1819.0	11.6	306.3	6.6	0.17	-5.0	1312.0	11.9	0.72	0.4	1516.6	11.0	0.83	-0.6
1977	2026.9	11.4	331.2	8.1	0.16	-3.3	1472.5	12.2	0.73	0.8	1705.3	12.4	0.84	1.0
1978	2291.4	13.0	358.4	8.2	0.16	-4.8	1648.8	12.0	0.72	-1.1	1911.3	12.1	0.83	-1.0
1979	2557.5	11.6	382.9	6.8	0.15	-4.8	1806.6	9.6	0.71	-2.0	2121.2	11.0	0.83	-0.6
1980	2784.2	8.9	408.9	6.8	0.15	-2.1	1992.2	10.3	0.72	1.4	2330.0	9.8	0.84	1.0
1981	3115.9	11.9	436.8	6.8	0.14	-5.1	2240.9	12.5	0.72	0.6	2601.8	11.7	0.84	-0.2
1982	3242.1	4.1	474.6	8.7	0.15	4.6	2442.3	9.0	0.75	4.9	2845.9	9.4	0.88	5.3
1983	3514.5	8.4	521.2	9.8	0.15	1.4	2648.8	8.5	0.75	0.1	3150.6	10.7	0.90	2.3
1984	3902.4	11.0	552.2	5.9	0.14	-5.1	2979.8	12.5	0.76	1.5	3518.6	11.7	0.90	0.6
1985	4180.7	7.1	619.9	12.3	0.15	5.1	3198.3	7.3	0.77	0.2	3827.0	8.8	0.92	1.6
1986	4422.2	5.8	724.4	16.9	0.16	11.1	3486.4	9.0	0.79	3.2	4122.3	7.7	0.93	1.9
1987	4692.3	6.1	749.7	3.5	0.16	-2.6	3672.5	5.3	0.78	-0.8	4339.9	5.3	0.92	-0.8
1988	5049.6	7.6	787.0	5.0	0.16	-2.6	3912.9	6.5	0.77	-1.1	4663.5	7.5	0.92	-0.2
1989	5438.7	7.7	794.2	0.9	0.15	-6.8	4065.9	3.9	0.75	-3.8	4892.8	4.9	0.90	-2.8
1990	5743.8	5.6	825.8	4.0	0.14	-1.6	4125.9	1.5	0.72	-4.1	4976.6	1.7	0.87	-3.9
1991	5916.7	3.0	897.3	8.7	0.15	5.6	4180.4	1.3	0.71	-1.7	5006.2	0.6	0.85	-2.4
1992	6244.4	5.5	1025.0	14.2	0.16	8.7	4190.4	0.2	0.67	-5.3	5078.0	1.4	0.81	-4.1
1993	6558.1	5.0	1129.8	10.2	0.17	5.2	4254.4	1.5	0.65	-3.5	5167.8	1.8	0.79	-3.3
1994	6947.0	5.9	1150.7	1.8	0.17	-4.1	4327.3	1.7	0.62	-4.2	5308.4	2.7	0.76	-3.2
1995	7265.4	4.6	1129.0	-1.9	0.16	-6.5	4592.5	6.1	0.63	1.5	5697.6	7.3	0.78	2.7
1996	7636.0	5.1	1081.1	-4.2	0.14	-9.3	4920.5	7.1	0.64	2.0	6071.7	6.6	0.80	1.5
1997	8034.4	5.2	1068.7	-1.1	0.13	-6.4	5333.0	8.4	0.66	3.2				

Source: *Economic Report of the President*, 1998, Tables B-68 and B-1.

happens with reasonably competent government, although import prices may rise, all the other disinflationary factors would come into play. Particularly in view of the huge measure of under-utilised resources in the US, especially in the labour market, combined with all the other counter-inflationary pressures which exist, a well-founded bet would be that the US inflation rate would barely flicker if the trade-weighted dollar fell to an index of 75. Other changes to the US economy's prospects, however, would be dramatic.

First, a large volume of business activity, which at present it is not economic for US corporations and individuals to undertake, would become viable again. Primarily, these would be in parts of the economy which are particularly liable to international competition; many would be in manufacturing. A primary component of the strategy proposed is that the US should regain an appropriate share of the world's manufacturing capacity. Of course, it is true that as economies become mature, the proportion of their output derived from services increases in relation to manufactures. Part of the reason for this tendency is that because productivity increases are so much easier to achieve in manufacturing than in services, the price of manufactured goods has shown a marked tendency to fall compared to those of services – by about 20% in the US over the last two decades alone. This is no argument, however, for the US or any other developed country not maintaining as large a share of world manufacturing as it reasonably can. Still less does it provide a case for allowing the situation which has occurred in the US, where the economy now imports vastly more manufactured goods than it sells abroad every year. In 1996 the gap between the two was $175bn, up from $115bn as recently as 1993. In 1998, it will inevitably be much higher, perhaps over $200bn, and on a remorseless upward trend unless policies are changed.

Second, a prime objective would be to produce a tighter market for labour in the US, driving up the need to use human resources more carefully, to educate and train people better, to make it worth providing them with more and superior capital equipment, and to ensure that their productivity and earnings rose dramatically but in tandem with each other. Higher incomes are a problem if output per head is static. This is indeed the way to wage-induced inflation. If output per head is rising, on the other hand, the economy needs the additional purchasing power that higher incomes can provide. As long as productivity rises in line with wages, there is no reason why new price rise pressures should materialise. This is the way to cure the problem of middle America's stagnant living standards.

Third, as the growth rate of the economy picked up, the problem of low savings ratios would also right itself. There is every chance, from international experience, that the domestic sector would save a larger proportion of its rising incomes. Profits would increase in the corporate sector, as would opportunities for profitable investment, particularly in light manufacturing where the turnaround in opportunities is likely to be greatest. Rising tax receipts and falling needs for expenditure would provide the US government with a much easier task of balancing the fiscal budget. As exports rose, and US manufacturers recaptured large swathes of the import market currently lost to foreign suppliers, the balance of payments on current account would no longer be in deficit. America could then forgo the need to borrow vast sums of money from abroad each year, in an important sense, mortgaging its future. It could pay its way instead.

The calculations done earlier in this book indicated that if the US were to reduce the value of the dollar compared to all other currencies by about 25%, the growth rate in the US GDP would be shifted from the current trend rate of about 2.6% per annum to well in excess of 4%. Allowing for about 1% growth in the population per annum, GDP per head would rise from about 1.6% to over 3% per annum, while labour force productivity, and hence hourly real wage rates, would increase by the same amount. Over a decade or two this would make a huge difference to the standard of living prospects of the average American. It would also transform the US's international prospects, securing the US's relative position in the world. By growing as fast as the world average the US could maintain its relative position compared to other nations. Its future would not be eroded by more successful parts of the world, as some of their unreasonable current advantages in competitiveness would be clawed back. There are surely here some prizes worth seeking.

Perhaps it would be worth pushing the dollar down still further and aiming for an even higher growth rate. The more competitive the US exchange rate, the faster the American economy would expand. Of course, sooner or later constraints would start to bite, and even if a very much greater rate of expansion was achievable, it should not necessarily be chosen. The important perception to grasp, however, is that options along these lines exist. It is not inevitable that the US economy should grow at its current trend rate or indeed at any other speed. On the contrary, Americans could choose how fast they want their economy to grow within wide limits. If they want it to grow much more rapidly than at present, this choice would be one which any clear-sighted and determined administration could implement.

PITFALLS AND REALISM

While the policy set out in the previous section may be seen to have major attractions for the US, would the rest of the world allow such changes as are suggested to be made? Even if they did, or if they could not stop them occurring if they opposed them, would countries outside the US be damaged if the dollar had a much lower value, and in consequence the American economy grew much more quickly? These are important questions, and the answers to them need careful consideration.

Could other countries stop the value of the dollar falling against their currencies if the US authorities were determined to see this occurring? The answer is no. The process to be used to bring the value down is entirely within the purview of the American government, in association with the Federal Reserve Bank. No external government could stop the US from lowering its interest rates and increasing its money supply, if that is what the US authorities decided to do. Nor could other countries stop the Fed selling US dollars to help push down the exchange rate. There is also almost nothing effective that they could do to retaliate against the US, supposing they were minded to do so. The ability of most of the major trading countries in the world in present conditions to ease their money supplies and to lower their interest rates still further, in competition with the US, is heavily constrained by the extent to which they have already pursued such policies. In most cases they already have low real interest rates and much looser macro-economic policies than the US, and there is little further that realistically they can go. It is possible to lower interest rates to almost zero, but making them negative is a different matter. Beyond a certain point, further expansion of the money supply does not increase output or competitiveness. It produces excess demand and inflation.

Nor would a more competitive US dollar necessarily be disadvantageous to the rest of the world. On the contrary, provided that the US avoided behaving in the predatory way unfortunately exhibited for many years by countries such as Japan, Germany and Taiwan, with their massive trade surpluses, there is no reason why any harm should be done. Obviously, there would have to be adjustments as the US trade deficit was vastly reduced, or even eliminated, but this is hardly an unreasonable requirement to put forward. It would not be in the US's interest to export more than it imported, and a significant trade surplus would not be to America's advantage. A much better and, in world terms, more responsible aim would be to keep the trade account in balance taking one year with another, without surpluses or deficits accumulating. This can hardly be described as a beggar my neighbour policy. On the contrary, the rest of the world would then benefit from being able to buy American exports at cheaper prices. At the same time, as the US market grew more quickly, rising American imports would provide better prospects for the rest of the world's exporters. This is a game at which, with reasonably sensitive management, everyone can be a winner.

Some countries might have more difficulty than others in adjusting to the new trading environment which would be produced, particularly those which have become accustomed to running large bilateral trade surpluses with the US, such as Japan. Here again, however, the changes which would need to be made are by no means necessarily to the disadvantage of America's trading partners. In many ways, the Japanese economy is the mirror image of that of the US. It combines extremely competitive, high-productivity export industries, based largely on manufacturing, with an often surprisingly wasteful and inefficient domestic economy. If the US trade deficit disappeared, of course not all the adjustment would be with Japan. The US has multilateral trading relations with the whole world. There is little doubt, however, that the general impact of a much more competitive dollar would be to present the Japanese with the economic and political necessity of accepting a substantial reduction, if not elimination, of their trade surplus. No doubt this would present the Japanese government with some difficult political choices. Faced with the necessity to respond, however, the thrust of the decisions which would need to be taken are obvious. The solution would be a combination of domestic reflation and liberalisation of imports, both of which would benefit the Japanese while also helping the rest of the world away from being hobbled by the Japanese trade surplus. If the Japanese refused to adjust their policies along these lines, the alternative would be for the yen to become even more over-valued as the US dollar fell. It is true that there would then be a danger of Japan plunging into a major recession. The fact that the Japanese authorities would then be faced with this prospect may, however, be the way the rest of the world has to force Japan to make long overdue changes which everyone else urgently needs to see being carried out as much as the Japanese themselves.

Would a substantial downward change in the value of the dollar upset world trade, removing the convenience and readiness with which the American currency is used to finance the buying and selling of goods and services of all kinds all over the world? Again, the answer is no. No such disruption occurred when the value of the dollar fell by over 30% on a trade-weighted basis between 1984 and 1988. Nor were there any significant problems as the index rose 15% between 1992 and 1997. All business people would prefer prices not to change, because dealing with alterations in costs involves extra work and produces less certainty. There is no evidence, however, that changing prices and exchange rates deter business activity, as study after study by international organisations has shown. Manufacturers and traders simply have to tolerate the instability which surrounds them all the time.

Another objection which might be put to the US economy growing much faster is that the world ecology might be put under increasingly unacceptable strain if this happened, since the US still represents so substantial a share of total world output. A different concern might be that the standard of living in the US is already so high that it might be difficult for it to go on rising rapidly before some kind of ceiling was reached. Both of these fears, however, seem wholly misplaced. All the available evidence suggests that greater wealth and disposable incomes increase humanity's capacity to deal with environmental problems rather than reducing it. Most environmental programmes are expensive, and much more easily afforded out of incomes which are high and rising rather than low and stagnant. The consumption of raw materials and the generation of waste tends to fall rather than rise as a percentage of rising incomes, while the money available to deal with their ecological impact increases. As to the notion that the desire for additional goods and services in the US has reached the point where satiation is in prospect, surely few people can be convinced that anything approaching this situation has been reached. The rich show no problems at all in spending their hugely increased incomes, while the poorer sections of society work longer and longer hours to try to keep their living standards from falling. At some point all economic wants may be satisfied, but we seem to be a safely long way off this state of affairs at the moment.

Perhaps the most telling question of all, however, is that if there is a comparatively simple answer to most of America's most serious problems, as this book suggests there is, why has it not been canvassed before? This is a fair question deserving a full response, which I will now put forward.

REASSESSING THE PAST

This book has argued that the macro-economic policies which the US has pursued at least since World War II have led to the dollar being consistently over-valued. It has also suggested that the consequence of the US currency being too strong has been that the US economy has under-performed in relation to its potential to a much greater extent than is commonly realised. This shortfall, in turn, provides a comprehensive explanation for many of the US's most pressing problems. The conclusion is that there is a relatively simple way of overcoming these difficulties – bringing down the value of the dollar – which any administration, given the will and understanding, could carry out. The evidence strongly suggests that success on the economy is the biggest single determinant of approbation on the political front, with major electoral implications. It therefore seems unlikely that either Democrats or Republicans would refuse to contemplate a change in policy which is comparatively easy to implement, assuming that they were convinced that it would work.

If the argument in this book is essentially correct, however, it clearly is at variance with almost all of what Professor Kenneth Galbraith has aptly described as the conventional wisdom. A major reduction in the value of the dollar is not the policy prescription found in any US newspaper, in any of the many books which have been published about America's problems, in any of the major political parties' manifestos, or anywhere in the academic literature. Those reading the proposals set out in this book may therefore be tempted to presume that devaluing the dollar cannot be an effective remedy, otherwise many people would have thought of it before. Before reaching this conclusion, however, the reader is invited to consider the following very powerful reasons for believing that the remedy on offer, though effective, might be surprisingly difficult to detect.

First, it needs to be said yet again that the US economy, whatever its deficiencies may be, has done extremely well for a long time. It has provided its citizens, on average, with a higher standard of living than any other country. It is by far the biggest economy in the world. It has pioneered new industries. It has exhibited technical prowess in every field from the space programme to computers, from biotechnology to the Boeing 747, which has left people everywhere in awe. Visitors to America are amazed at how efficiently so many services are provided in the US compared to most other parts of the world. America invented supermarkets and the Internet. Its culture and management techniques permeate the world. With this record of efficiency behind it, it has been hard to comprehend how vulnerable in some important ways the US economy has been.

Nor have the countries which have challenged the US hegemony over the past decades been successful in denting America's apparent invincibility. In the 1950s and 1960s, there were real concerns that the Soviet bloc might overtake the US in economic power and living standards, but this threat was steadily reduced during the stagnation of the Brezhnev years, and disappeared when the Soviet Union broke up following the Gorbachev era. Later, there were fears that Japan might overtake the US, at least in terms of GDP per head, and perhaps in terms of the total size of its economy. These have become a good deal less pressing during the 1990s as Japan's fabled growth has melted away. There may be a threat from China, and perhaps from some of the other Tiger economies, either in terms of their absolute size or their living standards, but it is hard to envisage this risk materialising in the course of the next few years, even though, unless there are changes, it may become more visible within decades. In the meantime, however, America's hegemony looks as secure as it ever has done.

Second, it may well be that the sheer efficiency with which so much of the US economy runs has blinded people to its competitive weaknesses. Perhaps understandably, there is a vast amount of confusion between productivity, efficiency and competitiveness. It is very easy to assume that because American plants are much more productive than those almost everywhere else in the world – which they are – that therefore they must be competitive internationally. This is, however, certainly not necessarily a correct conclusion. Even if output per head is much higher in the US than in China, the average Chinese product may still be more competitive – and indeed generally nowadays it is if it involves reasonably straightforward and widely available production techniques. This has nothing to do with productivity, because Chinese output per head is far below that of the US in almost every branch of economic activity. It has everything to do with the exchange rate.

This is not to belie the importance of productivity. It is of critical significance. The level of output per head in every economy determines the real wage rate and hence the standard of living. Unfortunately, however, this tells us nothing about competitiveness. There is simply no necessary correlation between the average level of productivity, on the one hand, and ability to compete successfully in the world, on the other. This is easily seen from the fact that some poor countries have highly competitive output and grow very quickly, while other advanced countries have much more trouble selling their exports abroad. Advanced economies can grow quickly too, however, if their exchange rates are correctly positioned. Both Taiwan and Norway nowadays are impressive examples of this phenomenon.

Third, there have been serious misunderstandings about the role and importance of manufacturing. It is true that as economies become more advanced, and the standard of living rises, there is a tendency for the proportion of the GDP involved in the production of services to rise in relation to the ratio involved in manufacturing. This happens partly because of a price effect. Because productivity increases are so much more difficult to achieve in services, the relative cost of manufactured goods tend to fall, making them look less significant than in volume terms they really are. No doubt, however, there is also an important inclination for those with rising incomes to spend more of their money on services. The result is that it is easy to assume that as any economy becomes increasingly advanced, the proportion of its GDP devoted to manufacturing will fall away exponentially, and that this is inevitable and does not really matter.

A vital theme running through this book is that this perception is misplaced. This does not imply that services are of no significance and that industrial output should always be given priority. A sense of balance is obviously required. It does entail, however, recognising that manufacturing – and, indeed, all those activities whose output particularly lends itself to international trading – have a peculiarly important role to play in two critical regards. First, they comprise the parts of the economy where productivity increases are most easily achieved, and hence they are critical to the growth rate. Second, they provide the production to be sold abroad to pay for imports, and it is therefore critically important that there should be enough available at competitive prices. If not, balance of payments problems and constraints on economic expansion will be the inevitable outcome. The implication is that America, if it is to grow at the same rate as the rest of the world, needs to have an appropriate proportion of the world's manufacturing capacity functioning within its own borders.

Fourth, America may have been mesmerised by its unemployment statistics. These show the US apparently doing much better than other comparable areas of the world, particularly Europe. The US has created far more jobs. Many more new businesses have been established. As a result, compared with around 11% in the European Union, unemployment as a percentage of the US labour force at the end of 1997 was less than 5%. If the US has done as well as this in creating jobs for its people, the argument goes, then there cannot be that much wrong with the way the economy has been run.

Previous chapters in this book, however, have argued that this is a serious delusion. The US may not suffer from unemployment, which is manifestly a major issue in the EU. Instead it has a different but, when quantified, substantially more serious problem of under-employment. Far from using its labour force efficiently, the US has used it profligately and wastefully. This is why most middle-income Americans have seen their real wages stagnate for a generation, as their productivity has barely increased and their output per head has remained almost static. Worse than this, in swathes of the American economy, productivity has not just stayed still. On the contrary, it has fallen dramatically – by almost 14% between 1980 and 1996 over the whole of that part of US GDP described in American statistics as 'services', employing almost a quarter of the US's labour force not categorised as working elsewhere in the economy. Perhaps if more people in the US were aware of just how bad these figures are, they might be correspondingly more willing to look at radical proposals to put things right.

Fifth, although there has been a large number of books published about the problems which America is perceived to have – some of them bestsellers – and a vast profusion of academic articles and publications on these and related topics, their recommendations have been remarkably confusing and muted. The bestselling books are – or were – full of spine-chilling statistics about the advance of Japanese manufacturing techniques and anecdotes about relatively poor US performance in response, but their recommendations as to how to overcome these problems are generally very unconvincing, if not plain wrong. Some have advocated various forms of fairly straightforward protection, apparently without seeming to recognise that this is just a backdoor and relatively inefficient way of changing the exchange rate. Others favour a variety of confrontational 'get tough' policies, mainly with the Japanese, which are really protection in another guise. A different school has seen the solution in industrial strategies, concentrating resources on 'high-tech' industries; mostly, it appears, without bothering to look up the statistics to see whether the recommendations had any foundation in economic reality. The notion that high-tech industries produce higher value added per employee is simply incorrect. For example, in 1995, as Professor Paul Krugman has pointed out, the average annual earnings of those in the long-established and relatively low-tech cigarette producing industry (SIC 211) were 56% higher than those manufacturing electronic components and accessories (SIC 367), and 30% higher than those producing aircraft and parts (SIC 372).

Nor has the academic economic world been much help, despite the vast amount of publications produced. Perhaps the most serious attempt to find a solution to the inability of US companies to compete successfully in the world has comprised the extensive studies carried out on Strategic Trade Policy. They have involved investigations as to whether a temporary period of protection for specific industries would provide them with permanent long-term advantages. The conclusion reached is that in certain circumstances such a policy might work, but in the real world convincing examples have been hard to find. Even if specific cases could be located, fitting the criteria required, the difference which would be made to the US's overall economic performance would be so small as to be virtually imperceptible. Apart from Strategic Trade Policy, the American economic establishment has had remarkably little of substance to say about how to improve US economic performance. Most of its members apparently believing that there is little in practice that can be done. Despite the talent it has attracted, US economists have been no better than their equivalents elsewhere in the Western world at producing convincing explanations of the causes of economic growth, the conditions needed to ensure it occurs, and prescriptions on related issues where there are obvious trade-offs, such as full employment and inflation.

Sixth, and perhaps most fundamentally of all, there are the many social and cultural forces which bear so heavily on the framework of ideas which shape both public opinion and the menu of policy options viewed in Washington and elsewhere as being practical and acceptable. Ideology permeates economics, and establishment views heavily influence opinions on what choices are within and without the pale. The US is a conservative and, despite its problems, broadly contented and proud country. Its social structure is stable. The rich and established have done exceptionally well, and generally do not want to see policies which have served them so satisfactorily being changed. While liberals might be happy to see the distribution of income in the US becoming more equal, provided their own pockets were not hit, this is not necessarily the case with those of a more conservative turn of mind. Those on the right of the political spectrum may therefore not be inclined to favour a change in policy which would make the poor richer, even if it did not make the rich poorer. There is also the fear of inflation to be taken into account. The monetarist creed, which appeals so strongly to those in established positions because it produces such a wonderfully persuasive justification for the circumstances which suit them best, states as a catechism that devaluation will produce inflation. All the evidence suggests that this canon of the monetarist faith is false, but many millions of people believe that it is true all the same. As a result, depreciating the value of the dollar, with its supposed although illusory risks of inflation, is regarded as a policy to be strongly avoided if possible, rather than encouraged.

All of these sentiments are wrapped up in the rhetoric about the exchange rate which is so widely used. When the value of the dollar is high it is strong. When it is low it is weak. When it depreciates its value falls. When it appreciates it rises. All these loaded terms colour everyone's perceptions. The reality, however, is different. If the dollar is too strong, US exports wither, manufacturing declines, investment and the savings to pay for them fall, living standards for most people stagnate, life chances deteriorate, the fiscal balance goes into deficit, and America's power and position in the world declines. This is a terrible price to pay for misconceptions which need to be exposed, and which ought not to prevail.

CHOICES FOR THE FUTURE

The twentieth century has certainly been the American century. The US overtook Britain in terms of standard of living per head in the early 1900s. Thereafter, its pre-eminence lasted through two world wars and the long, more peaceful period from 1945 onwards. Looking backwards in history, however, perhaps Americans should not be too sure of the future. As we have seen, Spain was probably the richest country in the world in the sixteenth century per head of the population, France in the seventeenth, the Netherlands in the eighteenth, and Britain in the nineteenth. There has been no security of tenure for those at the top. There is no guarantee that leadership in the past will persist in the future.

No government of any of the countries which allowed their leads to slip away permitted this to happen deliberately. In all cases, no doubt, they tried their best, judged by the knowledge and information available to them, to provide conditions which would allow growing prosperity to continue, maintaining their relative position. History shows, however, that in each case they failed to do so, allowing some often previously disdained rival to overtake them.

The fact that there is no immediate threat to the US's position in the world should not, therefore, be a cause for complacency. As we have seen, a difference in growth rates of quite a small percentage makes a huge difference over two or three decades. If one economy grows at 2% per annum and another at 6% cumulatively for twenty-five years, the first will grow by 64% over this period and the second by 329%. If living standards were 50% lower in the second economy at the beginning of this quarter-century than the first, by the end they would be over 30% higher. If the US were to allow its growth rate to sink to a cumulative 2% per annum, which is not an impossible outcome by any means on present trends, its leadership position would almost certainly be under threat before very far into the twenty-first century.

It might be argued that this is unlikely to happen because other countries would not be able to sustain an expansion in output of 6% a year cumulatively for long enough to enable this to occur. Perhaps this will turn out to be correct. Certainly the Japanese, long held up as models, have allowed their economy to perform exceptionally badly in the 1990s as their growth rate has slumped. If the argument in this book is correct, however, this need not have happened. The Japanese lost their way in the growth stakes not because of any historical inevitability, but because they made avoidable mistakes. During the years when their growth rate was high, they allowed export surpluses to pile up instead of letting their domestic market have the benefit of import competition. When the size of these surpluses became intolerable, and the value of the yen was driven up, the Japanese government failed to take the action it could have done to stimulate domestic demand. Instead, the export surpluses continued, driving up the yen still further. When, eventually, interest rates were brought down to very low levels, the yen fell, but not sufficiently to take up the slack. As a result, the value of Japanese assets remained in the doldrums and many banks and other financial institutions were on the edge of insolvency, and some failed. Neither consumption nor exports nor domestic investment rose significantly, and the cumulative Japanese growth rate between 1993 and 1997 was 1.7% per annum.

It may turn out to be correct that all rapidly growing economies will eventually make the same sort of mistakes so that their growth rates slow. This book has explored some of the social and political pressures which have tended to make this happen. It is not the case, however, that policies necessarily have to be adopted which slow down the growth rate. The success which some countries have achieved in continuing to grow for long periods attests to the truth of this.

The message in this book is that the conditions which create and sustain growth, which achieve the full use of the potential of the labour force, and which can be combined with tolerable levels of inflation, are not determined by blind history. On the contrary, they are the subject of policy choices which any government, democratic or otherwise, is free to take. The risk to America can then be simply stated. If other countries make the right decisions and the US makes the wrong ones, then the US will lose its lead and its long-lasting hegemony will be eclipsed.

Of course, this is not the only reason why the US should get its growth rate up. There are other reasons too, of greater importance to the millions of Americans who may have enjoyed a high standard of living compared to the rest of the world during past decades, but who could have done better. There is a huge amount of potential waiting to be unleashed in the US. There is no reason why the living standards of middle America should not rise at least as fast as the world average, and perhaps faster, if that is the democratic choice. This should not only make the average person much better off, but it should also relieve other strains which currently scar American society, particular the condition of the worse-off. Hopefully, a richer America would also be a more contented country across all the income bands – and therefore less divided, less prone to violence and more at ease with itself.

If this is to happen, however, more than alterations in policy will be needed. Some significant changes in the way American society perceives itself – its sense of values, its role models and its appreciation of the contribution made by different parts of the economy – will be required. Some of these changes will involve a shift in perceptions back to those more prevalent two or three generations ago. A career in industry will need to have the same cachet in the future as it had fifty years ago. America will need to recover the esteem with which making and selling the products the world wants ought to be regarded. Respect for occupations of this kind – never as far below the surface in the US as it has been in some other advanced countries – needs to be re-established. These are not ways of earning a living of secondary importance. They are the ones on which the future prosperity of America, relative to all the rest of the world, directly depends.

Correspondingly, there will have to be some diminution in the regard with which some other professions and ways of making a living are currently viewed. Whatever the importance of the rule of law, it is not lawyers who generate increased wealth. Nor, except to a surprisingly limited extent, is it bankers, government officials, politicians, the military, church leaders, academics or those in the media. However much the services provided by all these groups are valued, and however much many of them get paid, their contribution towards increasing prosperity in American is inevitably going to be remarkably small. Worse than this, it may be negative. The service sector's record on increasing productivity and output is, as we have seen, on average, abysmal.

The US therefore needs to shift perceptions of its role models, and if it grew much faster this would happen naturally. Social status and political power depend hugely on who has the high incomes, and where wealth is generated. Struggling areas of the economy are not those which generally have much clout. American society, perhaps more than most, holds in higher esteem those who are not having a problem earning or making a reasonable amount of money. If US policies were changed in the ways suggested in this book, using macro-economic weapons to increase the profitability of those parts of the American economy pre-eminently involved in international trading, the status of those doing well there would soon increase. This would then reinforce their ability, through the political process, to stop policies drifting back to favouring other sections of the economy of much less importance to America's future prosperity.

Recognising the significance of these tradable activities is not intended to downgrade, except relatively, the importance of the large part of the US economy which will never be involved to any great extent with foreign transactions. Of course it is important that the US has a well-run banking system, that it has lawyers and politicians of ability and integrity, that its wholesale and retail trades and distribution systems are efficiently run, and that the multitude of other services a modern economy needs are well provided. The critical issue is that the prestige and functions of these parts of the American economy do not become dominant, because they are not the major generators of economic growth. It is for this reason that America also needs to devote as high a proportion of its most talented people as it can to running world-class businesses in every sector of the US economy where international trading is involved. Success is vital in all categories of commercial activity, but pre-eminently in those involving international competition. This includes not only corporations producing and selling glamorous products like computers and aeroplanes, but also those manufacturing run-of-the-mill toys and household products, which are just as important as high-tech products in world trade. This is where most of the wealth and exponentially increasing productivity are created – not by investment bankers, lawyers and chat show stars.

Finally, it is not just the US which needs to see its economic affairs being run better. It is also the whole world. Although easy to criticise, everyone outside the US owes America an enormous debt of gratitude for most of the things it has done since World War II. From Marshall Aid, to the huge contribution the US has made to NATO, to its major funding of other aid programmes, and to the initiatives it has provided on trade negotiations, American world leadership has mostly been a remarkable success story. The US has also shaped much of the world's culture, provided a continuing technological lead, and combined all of this, most of the time, with a steadiness of adherence to the best of liberal and democratic values which puts much of the rest of the world to shame. The US economy is so powerful and resilient that even if it is not run as well as it might be, it will probably still retain its lead for a while. Our planet might be a better place to live, however, looking further ahead, if the US were to retain its hegemony for a rather longer period.

Bibliography

Aldcroft, Derek H. *The European Economy 1914–90*, London: Routledge, 1993.

Aldcroft, Derek H. and Ville, Simon P. *The European Economy 1750–1914*, Manchester: Manchester University Press, 1994.

Ayres, Robert U. *Technological Forecasting and Long Range Planning*, New York: McGraw Hill Book Company, 1969.

Beckerman, Wilfrid *In Defence of Economic Growth*, London: Jonathan Cape, 1974.

Beckerman, Wilfrid *Small is Stupid: Blowing the Whistle on the Greens*, London: Duckworth, 1995.

Blaug, Mark *Economic History and the History of Economics*, New York: Harvester Wheatsheaf, 1986.

Blinder, Alan S. *Hard Hearts Soft Heads*, Reading, Mass: Addison-Wesley, 1987.

Block, Fred L. *The Origins of International Economic Disorder*, Berkeley, Los Angeles and London: University of California Press, 1977.

Bootle, Roger *The Death of Inflation*, London: Nicholas Brealey, 1996.

Brandt Commission *North–South Co-operation for World Recovery*, London and Sydney: Pan Books, 1983.

Brittan, Samuel *The Price of Economic Freedom*, London: Macmillan, 1970.

Brittan, Samuel *Is there an Economic Consensus?*, London: Macmillan, 1973.

Brittan, Samuel *A Restatement of Economic Liberalism*, London: Macmillan, 1988.

Caves, Richard E. *Britain's Economic Prospects*, Washington DC: The Brookings Institution, 1968.

Chafe, William H. *The Unfinished Journey: America Since World War II*, New York and Oxford: Oxford University Press, 1995.

Chowdhury, Anis and Islam, Iyanatul *The Newly Industrialising Economies of East Asia*, London and New York: Routledge, 1995.

Connolly, Bernard *The Rotten Heart of Europe*, London: Faber and Faber, 1995.

Denison, Edward E. *Why Growth Rates Differ*, Washington DC: The Brookings Institution, 1969.

Denison, Edward E. *Accounting for United States Growth 1929–1969*, Washington DC: The Brookings Institution, 1974.

Eltis, Walter *Growth and Distribution*, London: Macmillan, 1973.

Feldstein, Martin *The Risk of Economic Crisis*, Chicago and London: The University of Chicago Press, 1991.

Ferris, Paul *Men and Money: Financial Europe Today*, London: Hutchinson, 1968.

Foreman-Peck, James *A History of the World Economy since 1850*, New York: Harvester Wheatsheaf, 1995.

Friedman, Irving S. *Inflation: A World-wide Disaster*, London: Hamish Hamilton, 1973.

Friedman, Milton and Schwartz, Anna Jacobson *A Monetary History of the United States 1867–1960*, Princeton and London: Princeton University Press, 1963.

Galbraith, J.K. *The Affluent Society*, London: Hamish Hamilton, 1960.

Galbraith, J.K. *American Capitalism*, London: Hamish Hamilton, 1961.

Galbraith, J.K. *The New Industrial State*, London: Hamish Hamilton, 1968.

169

Galbraith, J.K. *Economics and the Public Purpose*, London: Andre Deutsche, 1974.

Galbraith, J.K. *A History of Economics*, London: Penguin Books, 1987.

Galbraith, J.K. *The Culture of Contentment*, London: Sinclair-Stevenson Ltd, 1992.

Galbraith, J.K. *The Good Society: The Humane Agenda*, London: Sinclair-Stevenson Ltd, 1996.

Goldsmith, James *The Trap*, London: Macmillan, 1994.

Guttmann, William and Meehan, Patricia *The Great Inflation*, Farnborough: Saxon House, 1975.

Hayek, F.A. *The Road to Serfdom*, London and Henley: Routledge & Kegan Paul, 1944.

Hicks, John *Capital and Growth*, Oxford: Clarendon Press, 1965.

Hirsch, Fred *Money International*, London: Allen Lane, 1967.

Hirsch, Fred *Social Limits to Growth*, Cambridge, Mass: Harvard University Press, 1976.

Isard, Peter *Exchange Rate Economics*, Cambridge: Cambridge University Press, 1995.

Ito, Takatoshi *The Japanese Economy*, Cambridge, Mass and London: The MIT Press, 1996.

Jones, E.L. *The European Miracle*, Cambridge: Cambridge University Press, 1993.

Kindleberger, Charles P. *World Economic Primacy 1500 to 1990*, New York and Oxford: Oxford University Press, 1996.

Krugman, Paul R. *The Age of Diminished Expectations*, Cambridge, Mass and London: The MIT Press, 1990.

Krugman, Paul R. *Peddling Prosperity*, New York and London: Norton, 1994.

Krugman, Paul R. *Rethinking International Trade*, Cambridge, Mass and London: The MIT Press, 1994.

Krugman, Paul R. *Strategic Trade Policy and the New International Economics*, Cambridge, Mass and London: The MIT Press, 1995.

Krugman, Paul R. *The Self-Organizing Economy*, Malden, Mass and Oxford: Blackwell, 1996.

Krugman, Paul R. *Pop Internationalism*, Cambridge, Mass and London: The MIT Press, 1997.

Kuznets, Simon *Modern Economic Growth* London: Yale University Press, 1965.

Lang, Tim and Hines, Colin *The New Protectionism*, London: Earthscan, 1993.

Layard, Richard *How to Beat Unemployment*, Oxford: Oxford University Press, 1986.

Lipton, Michael *Assessing Economic Performance*, London: Staples Press, 1968.

Maddison, Angus *Economic Growth in the West*, London: George Allen & Unwin, 1964.

Maddison, Angus *Economic Growth in Japan and the USSR*, London: George Allen & Unwin Ltd, 1969.

Maddison, Angus *Dynamic Forces in Capitalist Development*, Oxford: Oxford University Press, 1991.

Maddison, Angus *Monitoring the World Economy 1820–1992*, Paris: OECD, 1995.

Maynard, Geoffrey and van Ryckeghem, W. *A World of Inflation*, London: Batsford, 1976.

Mayne, Richard *The Recovery of Europe*, London: Weidenfeld & Nicolson, 1970.

Meade, James E. *The Intelligent Radical's Guide to Economic Policy*, London: George Allen & Unwin Ltd, 1975.

Mishan, E.J. *21 Popular Economic Fallacies*, London: Allen Lane, 1969.

North, Douglass C. *The Economic Growth of the United States 1790–1860*, New York and London: W.W. Norton & Co., 1966.

Okita, Saburo *The Developing Economies and Japan*, Tokyo: University of Tokyo Press, 1980.

O'Leary, James J. *Stagnation or Healthy Growth? The Economic Challenge to the United States in the Nineties*, Lanham, New York and London: University Press of America, 1992.

Olson, Mancur *The Rise and Decline of Nations*, New Haven and London: Yale University Press, 1982.

Ormerod, Paul *The Death of Economics*, London: Faber and Faber, 1995.

O'Sullivan, John and Keuchel, Edward F. *American Economic History: From Abundance to Constraint*, Princeton, NJ: Markus Wiener Publishing Inc., 1989.

P.E.P. *Economic Planning and Policies in Britain, France and Germany*, London: George Allen & Unwin, 1968.

Pilbeam, Keith *International Finance*, London: Macmillan, 1994.

Robbins, Lord *Money, Trade and International Relations*, London: Macmillan, 1971.

Rohwer, Jim *Asia Arising*, London: Nicholas Brealey Publishing, 1996.

Rome, Club of *The Limits to Growth*, London: Potomac Associates, 1972.

Rostow, W.W. *The Stages of Economic Growth*, Cambridge: Cambridge University Press, 1960.

Salter, W.E.G. *Productivity and Technical Change*, Cambridge: Cambridge University Press, 1969

Schonfield, Andrew *In Defence of the Mixed Economy*, Oxford: Oxford University Press, 1984.

Singh, Jyoti Shankar *A New International Economic Order*, New York and London: Praeger Publishers, 1935.

Slichter, Sumner H. *Economic Growth in the United States*, Westport, Conn: Greenwood Press, 1961.

Stein, Herbert *The Fiscal Revolution in America*, Chicago and London: University of Chicago Press, 1969.

Stewart, Michael *Keynes in the 1990s: A Return to Economic Sanity*, London: Penguin, 1993.

Thurow, Lester C. *The Zero-Sum Society*, New York: Basic Books, 1980.

Tsoukalis, Loukas *The New European Economy*, Oxford: Oxford University Press, 1993.

Index

The subjects listed in the index do not include references to the USA, World War I and II, nor to concepts such as unemployment, growth and inflation, because references to them occur so frequently in the text.

Agricultural Adjustment Administration, 34
American Civil War, 25, 27
Atlanta, Georgia, vii
Australia, 25, 26
Austria, 25, 140

Balogh, Lord, 121
Bank of the United States, 28
Belgium, 25
Bimetallism, 29
'Black Friday', 32
Bork, Robert H., 23
Bretton Woods, 5, 17, 40, 42
Brezhnev, Leonid Illyich, 160
Britain, viii, 6, 10, 11, 16, 18, 24, 25 , 26, 27, 30 , 31, 33, 35, 38, 44, 46, 51, 57, 69, 88, 130, 131, 132, 133, 138, 164,
Brokers' loans, 32
Brookings Institution, ix
Bruning, Chancellor, 33
Burkitt, Brian, ix
Bush, George H.W., 56, 58, 63, 64, 67
Business failure rate, 63

Chicago, 48
China, ix, 6, 11, 71, 85, 118, 131, 160, 161
Clinton, William (Bill) J., 12, 56, 60, 63, 64, 67, 115, 147
Club of Rome, 7
Cold War, 36
Common Market, 89
Conservative Party, 88
Coolidge, Calvin, 95

De Gaulle, General Charles, 89, 122
Declaration of Independence, 25
Democrat Party, 34, 41, 56, 63, 64, 159,
Denmark, 25, 26, 27, 106
Desegregation, 40
Distribution of Income, 61
Dollar Gap, 37
Dow Jones Index, 32, 63, 68

Economic Report of the President, ix, 11
Economist, The, ix

Essinger, Eric, ix
Euro-Dollars, 43
European Commission, xi
European Exchange Rate Mechanism, 152
European Monetary Union, 152
European Union, 2, 9, 44, 72, 95, 96, 97, 98, 99, 102, 162
European Union Common External Tariff, 77

Family Assistance, 60
Federal Debt, 62
Federal Emergency Relief Act, 34
Federal Reserve Bank, 12, 15, 157
Franc Fort, 89
France, 16, 20, 25, 30, 31, 35, 44, 69, 71, 88, 91, 106, 122, 145, 164
Franco, General Francisco, 76
Free Trade, 76, 105
French, 132
Friedman, Milton, 48, 50

Galbraith, John Kenneth, 44, 160
Gardiner, Geoffrey, ix
General Motors, 32
Germany, 6, 14, 16, 20, 26, 30, 31, 33, 35, 42, 44, 69, 71, 89, 132, 133, 138, 145, 153, 157
Gold Bloc, 33, 35
Gold Standard, 29, 30, 131
Gorbachev, Mikhail Sergeyevich, 160
Gould, Bryan, ix
Great Society, 4, 41, 133
Greece, 51
Greenspan, Alan, 12

Hayek, Friedrich Auguste von, 48
High Technology, 15, 107, 108, 163
Hitler, Adolf, 33
Hong Kong, 104
Hoover, Herbert C., 69, 34,
Hudson, Michael, ix

India, 23
Indonesia, 15

Industrial Revolution, 7, 23, 24, 70, 102, 103
Institute for the Study of Long Term Economic Trends, ix
International Labour Organisation, 97
International Monetarism, 87
International Monetary Fund, ix
Israel, 43
Italy, 71

J Curve, 90, 91
Jackson, Andrew, 28
Japan, 1, 2, 6, 11, 13, 14, 15, 16, 20, 26, 35, 37, 38, 39, 42, 44, 46, 76, 77, 78, 85, 90, 93, 117, 123, 124, 130, 131, 132, 135, 138, 140, 145, 152, 153, 157, 158, 160, 165
Jay, Douglas, 28
Jeffersonians, 4
Johnson, Lyndon B., 40, 41

Kennedy, John (Jack) F., 40
Keynes, John Maynard, 37, 43
Korea, 15, 71, 73, 84, 85, 86, 87, 131, 152
Korean War, 36, 132
Krugman, Paul, 163

Labour Party, 88, 134
'Laffer Curve', 61
Lend-Lease, 35
Liesner, Thelma, ix
Lump of Labour Fallacy, 103

Maastricht Treaty, 44
MacArthur, General Douglas, 37
Maddison, Angus, ix
Malaysia, 15, 85, 131, 152
Marshall Aid, 36, 37
Mayflower, 18
Medical Insurance, 5
Mill, John Stuart, 1
Minneapolis, Minnesota, vii
Mitchell, Austin, ix, x
Monetarism, 43, 44, 45, 48, 52, 54, 124, 134, 164
Money Supply, 50, 51, 52, 133, 134
Montgomery Ward, 32
Morrill Tariff, 29
Multi-Fibre Agreement, 75

Napoleonic Wars, 6, 25
National Income and Product Accounts, ix
National Recovery Administration, 34
Nazi Party, 33

Netherlands, 6, 11, 24, 25, 51, 69, 133, 164
New Deal, 5, 34, 35
New York, 1
New Zealand, 26
Nixon, Richard M., 42
Non-Accelerating Inflation Rate of Unemployment, 140, 141
North American Free Trade Area, 77
Norway, 44, 140, 161

Olson, Mancur, 18
Organisation for Economic Co-operation and Development, ix
Organisation of Petroleum Exporting Countries, 5

Pearl Habour, 35
Popular Front, 33
Price Elasticities of Demand, 114
Protectionism, 75

Reagan, Ronald W., 56, 57, 58, 62, 63, 88, 115, 134, 147, 148, 151, 153
Reconstruction, 18, 28
Reichsmark, 31
Renaissance, 24
Republican Party, 56, 57, 64, 65, 159
Roman Empire, 23
Roosevelt, Franklin D, 5
Rousseau, Jean-Jacques, 7

Sayers, Professor, 49, 52
Schwartz, Anna Jacobson, 48, 50
Second Bank of the United States, 28
Shore, Peter, ix
Smithsonian Institution, 1, 42
Smoot-Hawley Tariff, 34
South Korea, 118
Soviet Union, 39
Spain, 6, 11, 76, 133, 164,
Starkey, Charles, x
Statistical Abstract of the United States, ix
Stewart, Shaun, ix
Supply Side Economics, 61
Sweden, 25, 26, 27, 106
Switzerland, 140

Taiwan, 71, 73, 84, 85, 118, 131, 152, 157, 161
Taj Mahal, 23
Tennessee Valley Authority, 34
Thailand, 152,
Thatcher, Margaret, 57
Total Factor Productivity, 70

United Nations, ix
United States Steel, 32
US Government Printing Office, ix
US Treasury Bonds, 13

Velocity of Circulation, 50, 51
Versailles Treaty, 31
Vietnam War, 4, 40, 41, 42, 61, 133

Washington DC, 163
Westmoreland, General, 41
Wichita, Kansas, ix
Wilson, Woodrow, 29
World Trade Organisation, ix

Yellowstone National Park, 1
Yom Kippur War, 5, 43